This ethnography examines the ways in which native and new citizens of Kodaira, a Tokyo suburb, have both remade the past and imagined the future of their city in a quest for an "authentic" Japanese community. Jennifer Robertson analyzes the repetition in various contexts of the term *furusato*—literally, "old village"—which has been evoked on the national and local levels as the dominant representation of the Japanese past and future. In contemporary Japan, with its urban and industrial economy, *furusato* is infused with nostalgia for a remembered or imagined past. *Furusato-zukuri,* or "old village-making," is one of the main vehicles for reproducing a sense of the past.

In the case of Kodaira, contradictions between native and newcomer—expressed partly as competing appropriations of *furusato*—provide the dialectic that energizes *furusato-zukuri* in that city. Some of the contexts within which these contradictions emerge include shrine and citizens' festivals and ritual practices, land reclamation and settlement patterns, religious consociations, and neighborhood associations. The focus on the dialectic of native and newcomer highlights forces and relations that sustain the difference between the two sectors and at the same time shows how each appropriates the other.

At its best, *furusato-zukuri*, as an expression of the politics of nostalgia, can encourage among Kodaira residents in particular and Japanese citizens in general an appreciation for natural resources and local or regional differences. At its worst, however, it can foster an ahistorical attitude to culture that glosses over problems, such as sex and race discrimination, industrial pollution, rural depopulation, urban sprawl, and bureaucratic centralization.

Native and Newcomer

Native and Newcomer

Making and Remaking a Japanese City

Jennifer Robertson

UNIVERSITY OF CALIFORNIA PRESS

Berkeley / Los Angeles / Oxford

The costs of publishing this book have been defrayed in part by an award from the Books on Japan Fund in respect of *Native and Newcomer: Making and Remaking a Japanese City*, published by the University of California Press. The Fund is financed by The Japan Foundation from donations contributed generously by Japanese companies.

University of California Press
Berkeley and Los Angeles, California

University of California Press, Ltd.
Oxford, England

Library of Congress Cataloging-in-Publication Data
Robertson, Jennifer Ellen.
    Native and newcomer : making and remaking a Japanese city /
Jennifer Robertson.
        p.   cm.
    Includes bibliographical references (p.   ) and index.
    ISBN 0-520-07296-0 (cloth)
    1. Kodaira-shi (Japan)—Social life and customs.   I. Title.
DS897.K623R63   1991
952'.135—dc20   90-27918
                                                                          CIP

Printed in the United States of America
1   2   3   4   5   6   7   8   9

For beloved Serena

Your funeral pyre is getting cold
but we will keep your words
to chase the serpents coiled around our histories
to dream new mythologies
to light our common fire.

Contents

Illustrations

Tables

Preface

The following is a brief sketch of the historical periods and institutions referred to in this book. The Edo (or Tokugawa) period, 1603–1868, was distinguished by an agrarian-based social and political order unified under a hereditary succession of generals (shogun) from the Tokugawa clan based in the capital city of Edo, whose ruling power was valorized by a hereditary succession of reigning emperors based in Kyoto. *Bakufu* was the term for the military government. A Confucian social hierarchy adapted from China divided the population into four unequal classes of people: samurai, farmers, artisans, and merchants, in that order. Each class was further bifurcated by a patriarchal sex/gender hierarchy. There were several categories of "nonpeople" as well, including outcastes and itinerants. Out of the vigorous urban commoner culture that developed in the late seventeenth century emerged several fine-art and performing-art genres regarded today as "traditional," such as the puppet theatre, kabuki, woodblock printing, and haiku. A policy of seclusion kept the country more or less closed to foreign contact and exchange for 250 years.

Victorious antishogun forces restored the emperor to a ruling position in 1868, marking the beginning of the Meiji period (1868–1912) and social changes summed up by the slogans "civilization and enlightenment" and "rich country, strong army." Agrarianism gave way to industrialization, and the seclusion policy to one of imperialism. Japan's first constitution and elected assembly were informed by European (especially Prussian) government systems. The occupational hierarchy of the Edo social system was replaced by a class system premised on economic stratification and noble lineage. Strict distinctions between female and male divisions of labor and deportment were codified in the Meiji Civil Code, operative until 1947. Generally speaking, the industrialization, militarization, and imperialism of the Meiji period escalated during the succeeding Taishō (1912–1926) and Showa (1926–1989) periods. Although universal male suffrage was inaugurated in 1925, women did not vote until 1947, when sociopolitical reforms were initiated during the American Occupation (1945–1952) following World War II. The late 1930s and 1940s in particular were marked by the military mobilization of the population and the state's appropriation of the Shinto religion as a national creed. The present constitution, which renounces war and (theoretically) the right to possess military potential, became effective in 1947. The emperor is recognized as a symbol of state; sovereignty rests with the people, and the Diet is the highest organ of the state.

Throughout the book, Japanese names are presented family name first unless the person publishes in English, in which case the given name appears first. All translations from Japanese to English are mine unless otherwise indicated.

Acknowledgments

This book is dedicated to the late N. Serena Tennekoon (28 March 1957–2 January 1989), whose love, mind, elegance, and courage are now and forever a sacred memory. The last stanza of a poem written by Serena in 1987 in memory of a Sri Lankan woman, a feminist activist, appears on the dedication page.

The first incarnation of this ethnography was in the form of a doctoral dissertation (1985), and my first readers were the members of my dissertation committee at Cornell University. Robert J. Smith (Chair) was especially helpful at that time. There are many persons who may not read this book but whose assistance, expertise, and goodwill greatly facilitated its production at various stages. I must thank Hishinuma M., Miura S., Miyazaki H., Oda T., Ogawa S., and Ōto S., all of Kodaira; the staff of the Civic Life and Social Education Departments, Kodaira City Hall; the staff of the Kodaira welfare center; the staff of the Kodaira central and branch libraries; the director, staff, and steering committee of the Research Institute for Oriental Cultures, Gakushuin University, Tokyo; and D. Chenail, P. Bryant, S. Bushika, and L. Tolle, faculty secretarial office, Williams College. I am grateful to Keith Brown, Larry Carney, Michael Cooper, Ezoe Midori, Stephanie Jed, Vivien Ng, Otobe Junko, Helen Robertson, Sugiura Noriyuki, and Sunada Toshiko for their assistance and support at various stages of this project. Many thanks to Sheila Levine, Amy Klatzkin, and Dorothy Conway for their editorial expertise, and special thanks to Maria Teresa Koreck for critical feedback.

The fieldwork and archival research making possible this book were facilitated by the following awards: the U.S. Department of Education, Fulbright-Hays Research Abroad award (no. G008300855); the International Doctoral Research Fellowship Program for Japan of the Social Science Research Council and the American Council of Learned Societies with funds provided by the Ford Foundation and the National Endowment for the Humanities; the Wenner-Gren Foundation for Anthropological Research award (no. 4492); the Japanese Ministry of Education, Monbusho Scholarship; and Sigma Xi, the Scientific Research Society.

Abbreviations

HKSS	*Higashikurume-shi shi* (A history of Higashikurume City)
HMSS	*Higashimurayama-shi shi* (A history of Higashimurayama City)
KBH	*Kodaira bōhan nyūzu* (Kodaira crime report)
KC	*Kodaira chōshi* (Local history of Kodaira)
KCH	*Kodaira chōhō* (town newspaper)
KGR	*Kodaira-shi gikai kaigiroku* (Proceedings of the Kodaira City Assembly)
KK	*Kyōdo Kodaira* (Local Kodaira)
KSH	*Kodaira shihō* (city newspaper)
TKSS	*Tachikawa-shi shi* (A history of Tachikawa City)
TSK	*Kurashi to tōkei* (Livelihood and statistics)
YC	*Kodaira shisei ni tsuite yoron chōsa* (Public opinion survey on the administration of Kodaira City)

Introduction

Ethnography and Making History

The original title of my book was *The Making of Kodaira; Being an Ethnography of a Japanese City's Progress*. Its source was Gertrude Stein's ethnographic *The Making of Americans; Being a History of a Family's Progress* (1925). Stein was a consummate ethnographer; she succeeded in illuminating the "bottom nature" of her subjects and their worlds through the process of "condensation." That is, she scrutinized her subjects until, over time, there emerged for her a repeating pattern to their words and actions. Her literary portraits (e.g., Stein 1959) were condensations of her subjects' repeatings, an ethnographic technique quite the opposite of the "social scientific" process of ideal typing.

Nisbet has likened ideal typing to sculpting. Like sculptors, social scientists, figuratively speaking, chip away at a block of marble in order to expose the Michelangelesque sculpture within. This method involves a priori knowledge of both the presence and the exact form of the ideal-type figure trapped inside: "the object, whether structure or personage, [is] stripped, so to speak, of all that is merely superficial and ephemeral, with only what is central and unifying left" (Nisbet 1977, 71). Contrarily, the wholeness of Stein's subjects bespeaks the acquisitive—as opposed to reductive—nature of her mode of portraiture. She did not presume to know beforehand what was superficial and what was central. These are arbitrary criteria not isolable in any one individual or group. Those features labeled either "superficial" or "central" exist in a flux of words and actions differently repeated over time and space by individuals or groups. As Stein recounts in "The Gradual Making of *The Making of Americans*":

When I was up against the difficulty of putting down the complete conception that I had of an individual, the complete rhythm of a personality that I had gradually acquired by listening seeing feeling and experience, I was faced by the trouble that I had acquired all this knowledge gradually but when I had it I had it completely at one time. . . . And a great deal of The Making of Americans [*sic*] was a struggle . . . to make a whole present of something that it had taken a great deal of time to find out, but it was a whole there then within me and as such it had to be said. (Stein, in Dubrick 1984, 13)

Stein in this passage identifies what I perceive as the salient features of the ethnographic process: it is personal; it requires time and patience, for knowledge and understanding are acquired gradually; and it involves a struggle to convey critically that knowledge and understanding about a pluralistic world in flux through the relatively static medium of (English) words (Dubrick 1984, 93). In a similar vein, Agar has noted that

the dominant rhetoric for the discussion of social research as a general process fits poorly with ethnographic work. The traditional linear model of hypothesis–operationalization–sampling design–data collection–analysis is a powerful one, relevant to many questions that might be asked by one human group of another, but at most it plays only a partial role in ethnographic work. Yet the norm is to translate ethnographic work into this rhetoric when discussions move to a general level. The results are a bit like talking about a computer in cubic yards—you can do it, but somehow it misses the point. (1986, x)

Knowledge of the sociohistorical constructedness of cultural practices does not preclude either understanding and appreciating them or working within their parameters (cf. Bourdieu 1986, 2, 4; Dubrick 1984, 26). This practical knowledge,[1] moreover, is crucial if an ethnographer is to avoid the reifications and spurious homogeneity that ideal typologizing, as a form of objectivism, can promote. Bourdieu, for example, has cautioned that

failing to construct practice other than negatively, objectivism is condemned either to ignore the whole question of the principle underlying the production of the regularities which it then contents itself with recording; or to reify abstractions, by the fallacy of treating the objects constructed by science, whether "culture", "structures", or "modes of production", as realities endowed with a social efficacy, capable of acting as agents responsible for historical actions or as a power capable of constraining practices; or to save appearances by means of concepts as ambiguous as the notions of the rule or the unconscious, which make it possible to avoid choosing between incompatible theories of practice. (1986, 26–27)

Thus, anthropologists of Japan must recognize that the arbitrary model of "the Japanese" as "homogeneous," "middle class," and, since the mid-1980s, "affluent" is a schema of Japanese and non-Japanese manufacture alike. Many of us try to minimize or avoid the fallacious tendency of forcing Japanese cultural practices into Western analytical categories. But we must also strive to distinguish those practices from the dominant ideology—the "ruling definitions of the 'natural'" (Comaroff 1985, 6)—operating in Japan at different historical moments.

My subject is not City Japan but, rather, Kodaira, a city whose texture is a distinctive composition of particular sociohistorical events, practices, and personages. At the same time, because Kodaira is a Japanese city, its composition is not exceptional or anomalous; elements of its texture derive from larger historical, political, and economic conditions affecting the country as a whole. Nevertheless, as I explain below, I did not select to work in Kodaira because it was representative of the majority of Japanese cities (in the way that, say, the Embrees selected Suye-*mura* as the ideal village for their "community study" [Smith and Wiswell 1982, xxiv]).

One of the ironies of determining the ideal-typeness (such as the Village Japan-ness) of a place is that a city, town, or village often may be selected as a fieldsite because certain features fit the contours of a stereotype or the requirements of a prevailing theory or research proposal. In other words, the particularity of the stereotype, theory, or research proposal is emphasized over that of a place (the fieldsite) and the experiences of its inhabitants. Although my point is made polemically, the situation described is not untypical and, to some extent, is to be expected. Obviously, anthropologists are influenced in their assumptions and choice of a research project or theoretical approach by the disputatious environment of academia and by larger sociohistorical exigencies.[2] However, because of the (increasingly questioned) convention of objectivity in fieldwork, the influential controversies that animate and color inhabited places sometimes remain unheeded or unacknowledged. Moreover, an ethnography framed in the "ethnographic present" effectively brackets the sociohistorical agency and agents of those same controversies.[3]

The initial research for this book was informed and shaped by various social forces and discourses intersecting in Kodaira during the two-year period 1983–1985, when I conducted the bulk of my fieldwork.[4] In other words, the reflexivity of my text lies in my acknowledged sensitivity to those forces and discourses, and not in a narrative of my trials and tribulations in the field. What I basically want to show in the following chapters is how a problem was created and dealt with (as opposed to solved) during my period of fieldwork.

This ethnography is, to a large extent, a literary portrait of Kodaira condensed from the various repeatings of a particularly cogent word, or trope, in just as many contexts. That trope is *furusato*, literally "old village," whose resonances and ramifications on the national and local levels are explored critically in chapter 1. The "making and remaking" of my title refers to ongoing discourses about the place of Kodaira past and present, discourses in which the trope of *furusato* has figured prominently, in recent times, in mediating the past-present relationship. Verbalized as *furusato-zukuri*, or "old village"–making, this trope has been activated as one of the main ways in which a sense and popular memory of the past are (re)produced outside of professional history writing. Each chapter of this book elaborates on some aspect of *furusato*, which, as I argue, has been evoked in the Japanese media and elsewhere—increasingly since the "oil shocks" of the early 1970s and consistently during the 1980s—as the dominant representation of "the Japanese" past and future. This representation is collective without being unitary in its meaning (cf. Corrigan and Sayer 1985, 197). Readers should not assume that *furusato-zukuri* is some sort of central-government conspiracy to force a return to a totalitarian past. Since I explore the sociohistorical conditions under which *furusato* acquired its representative power and pervasiveness both in Japan and Kodaira in the following chapters, I will limit my discussion here to my understanding and use of the interrelated terms *history*, *past*, and *future*.

History is both a spatiotemporal process and a social production constituting ways in which the past is continuously organized, represented, reclaimed, reworked, and reproduced as memory, which may be private or public and popular. A crucial focus in this book is on "popular memory," which "exists *in* its relations to the dominant discourses and not apart from them or by itself" (Bommes and Wright 1982, 255). The study of popular memory is a necessarily *relational* study. It has to take in the dominant historical representations in the public field as well as attempts to amplify or generalize subordinated or private experiences. .... The study of "popular memory" is concerned with *two* sets of relations. It is concerned with the relation between dominant memory and oppositional forms across the whole public (including academic) field. It is also concerned with the relation between these public discourses in their contemporary state of play and the more privatized sense of the past which is generated within a lived culture. (Popular Memory Group 1982, 211)

The past is constructed and remade in more ways than the written or literary, and by more people than professional historians. Despite a field of competing and contested representations of the past, certain constructions achieve dominance and centrality while others are marginalized (ibid., 206, 207). In this connection, as I show, not only did *furusato* emerge in the 1970s as the dominant national representation of "the Japanese" past and future, but a particular representation of *furusato*, one infused with nostalgia, achieved dominance.

The making of Kodaira today largely is a process of remaking the past and imagining the future—a process of reifying a Kodaira of yesterday to serve as a stable referent of and model for an "authentic" community today and tomorrow. In short, as "images, places, and spaces turn from mnemotechnic aids into topoi they become that which a discourse is about" (Fabian 1983, 111). This business of remaking the past, or making history, is a political, practical project in and for the present, for "the proper object of history is not the past but the past-present relationship" (Popular Memory Group 1982, 240), or rather, I would amend, the past-present-future relationship.

"Making history" also describes (in a Steinian sense) the process of ethnography, just as the past-present-future relationship also characterizes it. Ethnography not only "constantly turns us toward the past," but "our past is present in us as a *project*, hence as our future. In fact, we would not have a present to look back from at our past if it was not for that constant passage of our experience from past to future. Past ethnography is the present of anthropological discourse inasmuch as it is on the way to become its future" (Fabian 1983, 93; italics in the original). It should become apparent that there are many ethnographers of Kodaira, many makers of history, although this book represents my particular contribution.

Furusato-zukuri is a political project not just because of its recent appropriation by the Liberal Democratic Party (LDP) as the dynamic of its domestic platform but, more important, in the sense that it is the means by which a consensual version of the past vis-à-vis the present, and the future vis-à-vis the past, is established. Not all of the current agencies and agents through which the image of *furusato* is stereotyped are linked to the LDP; some are relatively autonomous, such as the "localist" study groups noted in the following chapters. Finally, the vividness, naturalness, and apparent concreteness of the remade past camouflage the rhetorical strategies used in its construction. One of my aims is to make visible both those strategies and the agencies and agents through which they are deployed.

Kodaira City, Ethnographically

Like Stein in *The Making of Americans*, I am up against the difficulty of "putting down" the various textures of a city that I have experienced both during my childhood and as an adult and a professional anthropologist. I spent my childhood and early teens in Kodaira, and while reminiscing about those eight years (and another two in nearby Musashino City) facilitated many an interview, my personal past did not directly influence my selection of Kodaira as a fieldsite and home from June 1983 through August 1985. A colleague, Matsumura Mitsuo of the Institute for Areal Studies in Tokyo, suggested that the Musashino region in central Tokyo metropolitan prefecture would be an ideal locus for a historical anthropological study of village-making (*mura-zukuri*), the substance of my initial research proposal. That I wound up living in my old neighborhood in Kodaira was determined more by the availability of a suitable apartment than by a nostalgic curiosity about my childhood haunts. As it turned out, I could not have landed in a better place at a better time.

Kodaira City is located approximately in the center of Tokyo metropolitan prefecture. Covering about twenty-one square kilometers and shaped like an arrowhead, the city lies about twenty-six kilometers west of central Tokyo (map 1). In 1940 Kodaira was a chiefly agricultural village of about 8,600 persons; its population increased by over five times that number within twenty-five years because of a tremendous influx of newcomers during the late 1950s and early 1960s. The population has remained stable at roughly 153,000 persons since the late 1970s.

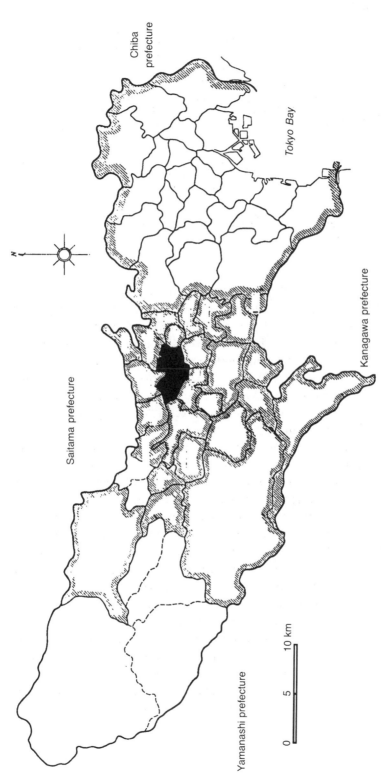

Map 1. Tokyo metropolitan prefecture. Kodaira City is blackened in for identification. (Adapted from the map in *Zenkoku shichōson yōran* 1989)

Chiba prefecture

Tokyo Bay

Saitama prefecture

Kanagawa prefecture

Yamanashi prefecture

N

0   5   10 km

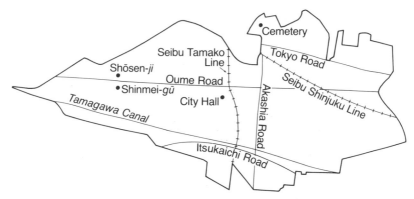

Map 2. Kodaira City. (Based on the version in *KK* 1983; see map 6 for further details)

Kodaira is bisected into northern and southern halves by Oume Road, which, from a sociohistorical perspective, is the most important road in the city (map 2). It was along Oume Road that the area's initial homesteads were founded in the mid-seventeenth century as part of a massive *shinden* (land reclamation) program engineered by the Tokugawa *bakufu* in the early 1700s. The descendants of those pioneering settlers continue to live along Oume Road. Collectively, they constitute (as of 1985) the minority (1 percent) "native" (*jimoto, tochikko*) sector of Kodaira, in contradistinction to the majority (99 percent) "newcomer" (*ten'nyūsha, kodairakko*) sector. "Newcomer," generally speaking, refers to those white-collar and blue-collar individuals and families who settled in Kodaira from the late 1950s onward. As I substantiate in the chapters that follow, antinomy between natives and newcomers—partly expressed as competing appropriations of *furusato*—provides the dialectic that energizes *furusato-zukuri* in Kodaira.

The name "Kodaira" was coined in 1889 for the new administrative village (*gyōsei mura*) created when seven smaller villages—the "Kodaira Seven"—were amalgamated under the auspices of the Meiji government's centralization program. Kodaira was made a town in 1944 and a city in 1962. The oldest of these seven villages, Ogawa-*mura*, was reclaimed from barren land in the 1650s by its namesake, the farmer Ogawa Kurobei. The other six villages were reclaimed about seventy years later, in the 1720s. Kurobei is now eulogized by city hall as the civic ancestor of all Kodaira residents, who are urged in the local press and other media—in altogether anachronistic terms—to follow

Kurobei's example and usher the city into its "second reclamation" period.

City hall is keen on restoring to the sprawling "bedroom town" (*beddotaun*) the harmony and camaraderie that allegedly characterized life and work in the seven original villages. Kodaira's second reclamation was inaugurated in the early 1970s under the rubric of *furusato-zukuri*. Newcomers in particular are encouraged to adopt a "pioneer spirit," which city hall presumes motivated the first reclamation and settlement over three hundred years ago. The rhetoric encouraging newcomers to regard themselves as locals (*jimoto*) is countered by increased efforts on the part of natives to reclaim and maintain a special place for themselves within the suburban city.

In the following chapters, I explore and analyze the various contexts within which antinomy between natives and newcomers and competing appropriations of *furusato* are manifested. These include settlement patterns, festivals, religious consociations, ritual practices, and neighborhood associations. The order in which I have organized the six chapters is my first step in making visible the rhetorical strategies informing native place–making in Kodaira and Japan today. In this connection, at several points in the book I purposely shift from a formal to a more informal style in order to impart a sense of the flavor of my encounters and experiences in Kodaira.

In chapter 1, I introduce the concept and operations of native place–making (*furusato-zukuri*) and discuss the politics of nostalgia operating at the national and local levels.[5] My chief interest is in the ways in which "the Japanese" past and future are reconstructed and appropriated. The title of this chapter, "Nostalgic Praxis," refers to the process of *furusato-zukuri* as a project that involves remaking the past as the condition for bringing about a social transformation—something that is new. That the "something new" is conceptualized in terms of an "old village" points to the operations of *furusato* as a dominant trope deployed at the national level by the state to both regulate the imagination of the nation and contain the local.[6] In Kodaira "old village" is equated with a purported historical and affective core of the city, a core made visible as theoretical and material metonyms, from the "authenticity" of a "living history" to thatched-roof farmhouses and festivals.

Chapter 2 contains a description and analysis of the Kodaira citizens' festival, inaugurated in 1976 to authenticate the newly reclaimed Furusato Kodaira.[7] Into the terrain of the citizens' festival have been implanted nostalgic interpretations of village life and ritual activities in the

Edo period. It is productive, therefore, to analyze the structure of the citizens' festival in terms of its narrativity. As I elaborate in this chapter, the citizens' festival is both a symbol of Furusato Kodaira and a chronicle, or narrative emplotment, of the past and present social episodes that constitute the gradual making of that city.

Earlier I noted that the proper object of history is not the past but the past-present-future relationship. Significantly, it is under the auspices of *furusato-zukuri* that Edo-period village life has become an absorbing subject of study in Kodaira and elsewhere. In this connection, chapter 3 has two interrelated agendas. One is to analyze present-day remakings of "Kodaira's" past. The other is to construct from archival data a coherent literary portrait of the social, political, and economic circumstances of the Edo-period farm villages that were later amalgamated under the name "Kodaira." Knowledge of these villages and their settlement illuminates the topographical grounds for the integrity of the native sector. A comparison of the material and symbolic aspects of village-making centuries ago and *furusato-zukuri* today helps to contextualize the narrative of the citizens' festival.

The authenticating effect of the citizens' festival is achieved by the addition of palanquin shrines (*mikoshi*) lent and carried by native residents exclusively. Kodaira natives have sought to reclaim their place in the suburban city largely through religious and ritual channels, the subject of chapter 4. For example, their practice of denying shrine and temple parish membership to newcomers is one of the most explicit ways in which they maintain the integrity of their sector. In this chapter, I extend the twofold agenda of chapter 3 by exploring both the history of religious institutions in Kodaira City today and the conditions influencing the installation of shrines and temples in the newly reclaimed *shinden* villages. Another dimension of native-newcomer antinomy is provided in chapter 5, in which I explore the various forms of spatial and temporal placement and displacement experienced by natives and newcomers. The very construction and performance of the citizens' festival, moreover, highlight the differential representation of natives and newcomers in terms of their social, geographic, and symbolic place within the city. Neighborhood associations, their historicity and membership, signify another type of settlement pattern in the episodic making of Kodaira. Chapter 6 reviews the *furusato-zukuri* project, concatenating new examples and ones from the preceding five chapters with the theoretical concepts presented here.

In this book, I explore some of the images and places—such as the citizens' festival and historical landmarks—that have made the turn from mnemotechnic aids into topoi of discourses on the past-present-future relationship. On the whole, I am more interested in the construction of dominant images of and, by extension, dominant discourses about *furusato*. Public representations of *furusato-zukuri*—and not private memories of the past, regardless of their collective character—are my concern. Of course, by making problematic the dominant, I simultaneously draw attention to and thereby make visible the marginal. My focus, with respect to Kodaira City, on a dialectic of native and newcomer highlights the forces and relations that sustain the difference between the two sectors and at the same time shows how the newcomer appropriates the native and vice versa.

CHAPTER ONE

Nostalgic Praxis

Definitions

"Future society," it has been said, "is the flavor of *furusato*."[1] *Furusato* literally means "old village," but its closer English equivalents are "home" and "native place." Some of the questions raised about "home" might also be asked of *furusato*:

[W]hat is a home? Is it a place? A set of relationships? A group of possessions? A feeling state? There is no universal answer, nor is there even a simple answer to the question of where a person's home is. Not every person thinks of himself [or herself] as having one, and only one, home. Parents' dwellings and other houses, neighborhoods, towns, or countries may also be thought of as home and even referred to as "my real home." . . . "Home" may also refer to the roots of one's psychological life which may or may not be the same as one's behavioral life. (Hayward 1975, 8)

Neither "home" nor *furusato* is simply "an environment where a person's observable life goes on" (ibid.). As a landscape, the quintessential features of *furusato* include forested mountains, fields cut by a meandering river, and a cluster of thatched-roof farmhouses. *Furusato* also connotes a desirable lifestyle aesthetic summed up by the term *soboku*, or artlessness and rustic simplicity. And, as I will discuss, *furusato* is shaped by, just as it shapes, a "living historical" past. "Living history" has been defined as "the simulation of life in another time" (Jay Anderson, in Handler and Saxton 1988, 242), although at the crux of historical simulation is the concept of "authenticity" (ibid.). *Furusato-zukuri*, or "old village"–making (also native place–making), works to integrate present-day activities and interpretations with past events, and to set in motion the construction of an "authentic" image (flavor) of the future.

Furusato is one of the most popular tropes and symbols used by Japanese politicians, city planners, and mass media advertisers and programmers. The ubiquity of *furusato* derives from the manifold contexts in which it is appropriated, from the gustatorial to the political and economic. In this chapter, I will explore the transformational potential of *furusato-zukuri* and show how *furusato* has been deployed as a dominant trope to regulate the imagination of the nation and contain the local.

Since the 1970s, the evocation of *furusato* has been an increasingly cogent means of fostering insideness at local and national levels alike. Furusato Kodaira, for example, is enveloped by Furusato Japan. The process by which *furusato* is evoked into existence is *furusato-zukuri*, a political project through which popular memory is shaped and socially reproduced. The dominant representation of *furusato* is infused with nostalgia, a dissatisfaction with the present on the grounds of a remembered or imagined past plenitude. Since nostalgia is a barometer of present moods, I will explore the main exigencies occasioning *furusato-zukuri*.

The Time and Space of *Furusato*

Furusato comprises both a temporal and a spatial dimension. The temporal dimension is represented by the word *furu(i)*, which signifies pastness, historicity, senescence, and quaintness. *Furu(i)* also signifies the patina of familiarity and naturalness that objects and human relationships acquire with age, use, and interaction. The spatial dimension is represented by the word *sato*, which suggests a number of places inhabited by humans: a natal household, a hamlet or village, and the countryside (as opposed to the city). *Sato* also refers to a self-governed, autonomous area and, by extension, to local autonomy.

The written form of *furusato* also manifests its multivalent nature. 故郷 is the ideograph most commonly used today, but *furusato* frequently is rendered in *hiragana*, the cursive syllabary, as ふるさと (*Kōjien* 1978, 563, 895).[2] The characters provide ideographic cues structuring the visual (mind's eye) apprehension of *furusato*—namely, an "old village." The syllables *fu-ru-sa-to*, however, provide no such extratextual referents but, rather, represent the sound *furusato* itself as a thing. *Furusato* today is most frequently written in the cursive syllabary because the word is used in an affective capacity to signify not a particular place—a real "old village," for example—but, rather, the generalized nature of such a place and the warm, nostalgic feelings aroused by its mention and memory.

Moreover, even when the ideographs are used, the current practice is to superimpose syllables above or alongside them, to ensure that the compound is read as *furusato* instead of as its alternative Chinese-style reading, *kokyō*.[3] The ideograph, in effect, is divorced from its objective, extratextual referents and is available for use in a connotative capacity. Moreover, as a *yamatokotoba*, or "really real" Japanese word, *furusato*, unlike *kokyō*, appears to be natural, familiar, and culturally relative. *Yamatokotoba* denotes—with more than a hint of ethnocentricity, particularly when rendered in the indigenous *hiragana*—a native Japanese word as opposed to a Chinese loanword. Thus, whatever *furusato* names or is prefixed to presumably is suffused with cultural authenticity. In its connotative capacity, *furusato* is commutable.

Furusato appropriates a special past: *mukashi* 昔. *Mukashi* signifies a past of indefinite chronology and duration, and resonates with nostalgic overtones. It contrasts with *kako* 過去, a compound used to denote a definite, unambiguous, irretrievably "passed" past. *Mukashi*, on the other hand, alludes to the Good Old Days—to modes and contexts of sociability long since transcended, abandoned, or dismantled, but reconstructable and revivifiable in a selective form through nostalgia. Its nostalgic mode imbues *furusato* with a profound emotional appeal and aura of legitimacy.

The Japanese media are rife with references to *furusato*: the "flavor of *furusato*" (*furusato no aji*), the "forests of *furusato*" (*furusato no mori*), the "commonsensical wisdom of *furusato*" (*furusato no chie*), and the sobriquet Furusato Japan, to cite but a few. The mass media contribute to and exploit the ubiquity of *furusato*, and help to make consensual its popular imagination. The landscape depicted in illustrated Tamajiman-brand *sake* advertisements, for instance, consists of the quintessential features of *furusato* described earlier. An ode to *furusato* serves as a caption: "The scenery of the Tama range carries to you a warm smell and the nostalgic song of *furusato*. This evening, bring on a rush of memories with a cup of our *sake*." Such advertisements help endow rural topography with hallowed content, effectively furthering its sentimental appeal. The appropriation of *furusato* by *sake* advertisers is particularly apt, since *sake* is an indigenous alcoholic beverage made from rice, a crop redolent of nativist symbolism. One ancient nickname for Japan, in fact, is *mizuho no kuni* (land of fresh rice ears).

Enka, a type of ballad, similarly eulogizes the landscape of nostalgia. These popular songs, enthusiastically crooned at home and in bars by millions of Japanese *karaoke* (sing-along tape) aficionados, provoke tear-jerking memories of *furusato*. Lyricists resort most frequently to three categories of *furusato* symbols in order to facilitate this response. They are symbols of a rural landscape: dirt path, sky, fields, mountains; symbols of estrangement: train, train station, port, train whistle, soldier, letter; and symbols of an "old village" lifestyle: spinning wheel, lullaby, paper lantern, shrine festival (Mita 1980, 220–25). *Enka*, furthermore, are sung in a nostalgic modality, which involves such conventions as a minor key, slow tempo, wavering melody, and repetitious cadences (cf. Davis 1979, 82–83).

The cogency of *furusato*, as a sentimentally evoked topography, increases in proportion to the sense of homelessness experienced by Japanese individuals or groups. In this regard, Japanese social scientists—particularly those cited in this chapter—have suggested that, with the rapid urbanization of the countryside since the postwar period, the Japanese "can't go home again." Because of the urbanization of villages, both villages and cities have lost their distinctiveness as social environments—so that the nostalgia provoked by estrangement from an "old village" has become thin and insignificant (Minami 1980, 146). There is no particular place to go home to; consequently, there is no particular place to feel nostalgic toward. Homelessness today may be defined as a "postmodern" condition of existential disaffection: nostalgia for the experience of nostalgia. A diffuse sense of homelessness, then, may be seen as an important sociopsychological motive for the *furusato-zukuri* project and the symbolic reclamation of the landscape of nostalgia.

The literary critic Kobayashi Hideo (1902–1982) presaged the postwar experience of homelessness in an essay titled "Kokyō o ushinatta bungaku" (Homeless literature, 1933). Paradoxically, Kobayashi attributed his realization of the mnemonic construction of *furusato* to his own inability to conceptualize "old village" life, a condition he blamed on the fact that he was born and raised in Tokyo (Kobayashi [1933] 1975, 288). He was estranged not from a rural hometown but from the melancholy experience of estrangement from a rural hometown.

Today at train stations along the Yamanote Line, which encircles the heart of Tokyo, new Furusato Tokyo signs have been posted to direct people to shrines, temples, and historical landmarks in the vicinity. The Furusato Tokyo emblem consists of a red orb, symbol of the Japanese nation-state, across which is superimposed a blue rectangle inscribed in white with Furusato Tokyo. Posters for the 1984 Furusato Tokyo festival, inaugurated in 1981, featured the slogan "Kokoro no naka no Tōkyō e satogaeri suru hi" (The day to go home to the Tokyo in [your] heart-mind), reflecting the mnemonic construction of *furusato*. Unlike the *obon* (ancestors') festival in late summer and the New Year's festival, two occasions when vast numbers of Tokyo residents return to their natal households, the October event is an occasion for psychic mobility. Residents are encouraged to make a metaphysical return to their new hometown, Furusato Tokyo (*Minna no Tōkyō*, 1 December 1984; see also Furusato Tōkyō matsuri jikkō iinkai 1986; My Town Concept Consultative Council 1982).

Presenting the Past

Although the imagination of *furusato* is not constrained by the necessity of a physically present rural landscape, its current reification is shaped by a history of discourse about the countryside. There exists a literary genre of affective environmentalism, beginning in the eighth century with the mytho-histories *Kojiki* and *Nihon Shoki*, spanning poetry anthologies and Edo-period farm manuals, and persisting today in the form of domestic policy platforms, city charters, and *sake* advertisements, among other media and productions.

The confluence of affect and environment is especially evident in the newly revivalized work of Shiga Shigetaka (1863–1927), who identified the mountains, forests, valleys, and streams as the "original forces that nurture the Japanese sense of aesthetics, have nurtured it in the past, and will nurture it in the future" (in Higuchi 1981, 186). *Furusato-zukuri*, in this context, may be interpreted as a means of reproducing native/national aesthetics in the face of pervasive urbanization and environmental pollution. Shiga, moreover, in his recently republished magnum opus, *Nihon fūkeiron* (Treatise on the Japanese landscape, 1894), declared that nature is more beautiful in Japan than anywhere else in the world, and even insisted that foreign visitors to Japan were awestruck and humbled by the unparalled beauty of the archipelago. Written during the westernizing Meiji period, Shiga's widely read treatise was an important factor in the development of a national identity predicated on an "[a]ffection for the Japanese country-side and pride in its distinctive beauty" (Pyle 1969, 161) as well as on an awareness of Japan's dramatic emergence in international affairs.

Furusato-zukuri recalls, in spirit if not in substance, early-twentieth-century efforts to achieve a cultural and national identity in a modern-izing context; for, as historian Carol Gluck argues, "Japan's modern myths were made in and from the Meiji period" (1985, 16). There are, however, crucial differences between *furusato-zukuri* today and Meiji-period mythopoeia. Most important is the absence in the *furusato-zukuri* project of an appeal to the preservation of an agrarian economy. Farmers presently constitute less than 8 percent of the working popula-tion, as opposed to an average of 60 percent during the Meiji period, and agricultural production today accounts for less than 4 percent of the GNP (Nōrinsuisan daijin kankyoku chōsaka 1989, 10–11). The general design of *furusato-zukuri* projects throughout Japan, as I discuss shortly, deals not with an agrarian economy in crisis but with the re-creation of a villagelike ambience in cities, towns, and villages alike. Furthermore, the incommensurability between city and country per-ceived by the Meiji ideologues is resolved in the *furusato-zukuri* project as a dialectic of "tradition" and "modernity," as sobriquets such as Furusato Tokyo and Furusato Kodaira reveal quite literally.

Finally, the sociopsychological catalyst for *furusato-zukuri* today is a nostalgia for nostalgia. The emperor system, on the other hand, in-volved an ideology of national unity and identity premised on an agrar-ian system of both production and social relations (see Gluck 1985, especially chap. 6; also Havens 1974). For this last reason especially, *furusato* is not isomorphic with the Meiji construct *kokutai*, the organic national polity. The politics informing the *furusato-zukuri* project are those belonging to a "postmodern" society, in which "the form of hege-mony lies in the power to master signs of styles and periods, the ability to read/construct 'codes of distinction'. . . order and power do not have to be imposed, or authored, but are already embodied in the very order of objects as they are presented" (Stewart 1988, 232).

Furusato also appears to be a projection of what the ethnologist Ori-guchi Shinobu (1887–1953) referred to as the "eternal-land cult" of

Yamato, the ancient name for Japan from which *yamatokotoba* derives. Origuchi suggested that the name Yamato gradually evolved from signifying a "gateway where one enters the mountains" to the land entered through that gateway: "The fact is that the people of old regarded the area within the mountain gateway as being sunny and cheerful. . . . When one descended through the gateway, one came upon a fertile plain, a bright and happy land. It was generally thought that, once inside the gateway, one encountered no more barriers. Consequently, attention was focused on the gateway itself, and its name, *yamato*, came to be applied to the land of light and hope within" (in Higuchi 1981, 99).

The generic mountainous landscape now associated with *furusato* appears to be at once a gateway *and* the land inside. Current popular memories and interpretations of *furusato* provide a gateway to further understanding of "the Japanese" landscape of nostalgia.

Popular Memories and Interpretations

At the beginning of 1984, the *Asahi shinbun* (one of the three leading national dailies) solicited essays for a column on the subject of "new *furusato*" (*atarashii furusato*). (The very appearance of such a column attests to the significance and newsworthiness of *furusato*.[4]) The use of "new" suggests that the editors define *furusato* both in the narrow, literal sense of real "old villages" and in the broader, metaphoric sense of a lifestyle aesthetic premised on a nostalgic interpretation of Edo-period village life. Below are brief synopses of four essays selected for publication in the morning edition of 14 January 1984. Collectively, they indicate the potential of *furusato* as a basis for the codification of popular memory within the larger political project of *furusato-zukuri*. By framing the topic of social transformation in terms of *furusato*, the editors reinforce the dominance of this trope. While my interest here is in the dominant images that emerge in the essays, several individualized and idiosyncratic images are also evident.

First is an account written by a middle-aged woman, a homemaker. She distinguishes between the household's *furusato* (her husband's natal household) and her own *furusato* (each of the places where she herself has lived). Her *sarariiman* ("salary man," i.e., white-collar worker) husband was transferred several times, and so the family has resided in several cities. Her criterion for a "new *furusato*" is affective in nature: "When and if a kernel of confidence, trust, and dependency grows between you and your new neighbors, then a new *furusato* is born." For this woman, affect per se is more central to the re-creation of *furusato* than is the evocation of a rural landscape, although symbols of an "authentic" community generally derive from the countryside (Gluck 1985, 250).

An unemployed seventy-nine-year-old man, on the other hand, insists that two minimum necessary conditions must be met if a place is either to maintain or to achieve *furusato* status. They are "motherly love" and a "local dialect." "Without these conditions," he writes, "the *furusato*-feeling toward a place will evaporate, and regardless of whether it is a residence inherited from one's ancestors, it will float free, remembered only as a faraway place." This essayist recognizes the capacity of language for "generating imagined communities" and building "particular solidarities" (Anderson 1983, 122). His identification of "motherly love" with *furusato* is also of considerable importance in understanding the sociopsychological valences of *furusato* in postwar Japanese society, as I elaborate below.

The popular association of "mother" and *furusato* is so tenacious that social critic Matsumoto Ken'ichi insists that the two words are synonymous. However, because of the rampant urbanization during the postwar period wrought by rapid economic growth, *furusato* no longer exists as a "concrete entity" (*jittai*). Likewise, Matsumoto continues, with the concomitant predominance of urban nuclear families, "mother" no longer symbolizes the countryside (*inaka*), the farm village, the land and soil, or rice.[5] Because they have lost their external referents, he concludes, both *furusato* and "mother" are "dead words" (*shigo*) (Matsumoto 1980).

Matsumoto argues that both *furusato* and "mother" have been lost to the same intrusive forces: westernization, industrialization, and urbanization. His point is more fully understood, on one level, in light of *amae*, psychiatrist Takeo Doi's term to describe a dyadic relationship of mutual dependency modeled after the mother-child manifold, in which one presumes upon another's willing benevolence: the "child" demands to be indulged, the "mother" encourages indulgence (Doi 1986). On another—and, in my view, more cogent—level, Matsumoto's argument is an expression of the nostalgia exacerbated by the so-called "postmodern" malaise.

Insofar as "natal household" is among its various definitions, *furu-*

sato, by extension, is a place—not necessarily an old village—where one can *amae* without compunction. Both the elderly essayist and Matsumoto would have it that, as a place suffused with "motherly love," *furusato* cannot exist without "mother." Their interpretation of *furusato* can be explained in part by the following argument. Today in Japan, mothers (who are married, as opposed to single) overwhelmingly are perceived as the irreplaceable primary agents of their children's enculturation. But since 1984, nearly 60 percent of the 60 percent of women between thirty-five and fifty-four in the work force are married women, and the majority of these women are very likely mothers (Atsumi 1988, 54–55). This trend evidently disturbs many men and a few women,[6] including the proponents of *furusato-zukuri*, such as government and civic leaders. The strong connection made in the *furusato* rhetoric between "motherly love" and *amae* suggests that what most disturbs these people is the possibility that a "woman with an identity outside the family would not be compelled to find her self-worth only through the successes of her children; accordingly, a strong psychological impetus to induce *amae* in them would be lost" (Mitchell 1977, 78).

Accordingly, the *furusato-zukuri* project calls for the realignment of the female sex and the "female" gender role of the "good wife, wise mother," a twofold gender role invented by the patriarchal Meiji Home Ministry (Nolte and Hastings 1991; Koyama 1982; Mitsuda 1985).[7] Significantly, in Kodaira and elsewhere, home-based mothers are encouraged to collect local folktales and read them to their children, ostensibly raising the *furusato* consciousness of both parties (see Sakada 1984c, 300–302). Exponents of "old village"–making thus are keen on reviving and maintaining the synonymy of "mother" and *furusato* in the face of urbanization and, more recently, internationalization.

"Mother" names a gender role, a semantic construct unconstrained by the experiences (parturient or otherwise) of real females, who, moreover, are not all " female" in the same way . By declaring *furusato* and "mother" to be dead words, Matsumoto both unwittingly and ironically confirms the absence of external (physical and real-life) referents for these terms—although the nostalgic implication is that there once were such unified referents. The imagination of both *furusato* and "mother" is independent of the existence or absence of either; both constructs gain cogency from the process of privileging nostalgia and ideology over historical and experiential reality. Matsumoto blames human agency (in the guise of westernization and urbanization) for the death of *furusato* and "mother," but he fails to acknowledge the human agency responsible for the construction of these "dead words" and their referents in the first place.

Furusato-zukuri projects are premised on a nostalgia for an "authentic" community symbolized by *ofukuro-san*, one of the most affective expressions for "mother" used by males and evoked in a wide variety of sentimental media—*enka* (ballads), for example. *Ofukuro-san* literally means "bag lady" and, consequently, refers connotatively to the notion of females as repositories—in this case, repositories of "traditional" values deposited for safekeeping by the (male) engineers of *furusato-zukuri* programs. This term for "mother" is a telling throwback to the premodern reference to females as *ohara-san*, or "womb ladies," indicative of a belief in procreation as a monogenetic phenomenon, or the belief that the male sex role is the generative and creative one and that the male alone is responsible for the identity and subjectivity of a child. Female bodies, literally and figuratively, are the containers for male-identified "babies," from human infants to things such as values and ideologies.

When Matsumoto and others attribute the death of "mother" to westernization and urbanization, they are—in effect—alluding to the crumbling of male certainty about the virility of "traditional" values and providing a chauvinist incentive for cultural monogenesis (see Mattelart 1986). Although the same "traditional" values were eschewed in the immediate postwar period as backward, cumbersome, and encumbering, they are now being implanted into the landscape of nostalgia, the isomorph of which is the female body qua "mother," where they can be cultivated (gestated) and harvested (delivered). An ideology of sexual difference and gender-role segregation informs the image of a "back-to-the-future" old village redolent of "motherly love." By conflating *furusato* and "mother," nostalgic men—like Matsumoto, politicians, and the Kodaira City administrators—can proclaim the inclusion of precisely what is *excluded* from the cure for the "postmodern" malaise—namely, female-identified subjectivity and self-representation. Such men may be nostalgic for the Good Old Days, but they remain very much a part of the present.

A third contributor to the column on "new *furusato*," a housewife, identifies progress as the juggernaut that has crushed the élan of *furusato*. Her account is a personal one. She is discouraged by, but somewhat resigned to, the consequences of urbanization, to which *furusato* is all too vulnerable. The jarring image she evokes is one of rice paddies overlaid with concrete highways. She recognizes, however, that people (in this case farmers) themselves ultimately are to blame, for their desire to profit from land sales only hastens urbanization (regardless of their concrete socioeconomic motives for giving up the hoe).

A final essay was submitted by a middle-aged man, a civil servant. He wonders whether the "my town" planned communities presently under development throughout Japan can ever be realized as "new *furusato*." Placing *furusato* within a rural setting, he argues that "campestral features such as nostalgia, pleasant scenery, compassion, and camaraderie cannot simply be reassembled and called *furusato*." His conditions for an "authentic new *furusato*" are presented as desirables and imperatives. He insists that

furusato should be a place where one can return whenever the urge strikes. And, ideally, it is a place where one's *kokoro* [heart-mind, conscience] finds repose and where daily-life routines are grounded in compassion. Second, it should be a place where customs and traditions are highly valued. The history of a town or village should be transmitted through story from generation to generation, and this in turn should be the source nurturing familistic ties and a feeling of regional solidarity. Third, an authentic *furusato* is not likely to be realized on the basis of an academic blueprint implemented by government offices. Residents themselves must determine self-consciously just what is *furusato*.

Ironically, and perhaps because he is a civil servant, this last essayist's criteria of and for a "new *furusato*" are virtually identical to those recommended by central- and local-government, and civilian, proponents of *furusato-zukuri* projects. Also evident here is an appeal to self-government or local autonomy (*jichi*), and the notion of the rural village, along with the "good wife, wise mother," as repositories of authentic and authenticating social values.

Furusato-zukuri projects are often categorized under the epochal rubric *chihō no jidai*, or "age of localism." Since the late 1970s, when the expression was coined, a vociferous debate has been waged as to whether "age of localism" euphemistically disguised the collapse of local autonomy or marked a departure from and a viable alternative to Tokyo-centrism (see Yamaguchi 1981). For instance, Isomura Eiichi, chair of the Japan Urban Studies Association, contends that *chihō no jidai* actually names an "age of cities." That is, the slogan reflects a move on the part of regional cities to emerge from the shadow cast by Tokyo and assert their "unique" characteristics (Isomura 1981, 16, 208). While this is not the place for an extended discussion on the vicissitudes of local autonomy in Japan,[8] it is pertinent to note that, in the Meiji period as in the present examples, *chihō* was variously defined as the "opposite of cities" and/or any place outside Tokyo. Moreover, like *furusato* today, *jichi* in the early twentieth century possessed a double meaning: it emphasized localities' administrative self-governance and at the same time "tied the *chihō* as closely as possible to the center" (Gluck 1985, 193).

All but one of the above essayists equate *furusato* with a nonurban setting, and key *furusato* components—nostalgia, pleasant scenery, local dialect, compassion, camaraderie, motherly love, enriching lifestyle—are described as qualities endemic to the countryside. The remaining essayist does suggest that *furusato* and city are compatible, insofar as neighborly trust and dependency are the foundation for a "new *furusato*." All but the first essayist, however, suggest that "new *furusato*" evokes the affective relationships and sociabilities presumed to have mediated and moderated life in "old villages."

Another perspective on the subject of "new *furusato*" is provided by a survey conducted in October 1985 by the newly established (May 1985) Furusato Information Center in Tokyo. The center was founded under the auspices of the Ministry of Agriculture, Forestry and Fisheries to facilitate the rehabilitation of depopulated rural communities through the creation of city-country networks.[9] Its operating budget for 1985 was about 450 million yen, part of which was spent networking with over 1,700 cities, towns, and villages; sponsoring symposia; installing a *furusato* information "hot line"; distributing pamphlets, newsletters, and guidebooks; and conducting a survey on *furusato*, its image and efficacy (*Furusato jōhō sentā-dayori*, 1986; Nakajima 1986).[10]

Part of the center's survey required the 1,920 female and male respondents to offer words they associated with *furusato*. *Inaka* (countryside) overwhelmingly was the respondents' first choice, followed by *shizen* (nature), *yama* (mountains), and *kawa* (rivers). More than public opinion per se, these results seem to reflect the generic image of *furusato* popularized in a variety of mass media and adopted by consumers. Other *furusato* synonyms included *atatakai* (warm, intimate), *shusshinchi* (birthplace), *ryōshin* (parents), *haha* ([my] mother), *soboku* (naive, pristine, simple), and *kokoro ga yasumaru tokoro* (place where the heart-mind finds solace), in that order (Furusato jōhō sentā 1986, 16–17, 48).

The language of the "new *furusato*" essays and the center's survey strongly suggest that old village-ness is signified through antithesis. *Furusato* is not limited to an actual rural place, nor does it presuppose an agricultural lifestyle. It is, rather, everything that suburbs and metropoles are not. Compassion, camaraderie, tradition, and even motherly love are presumed absent from postwar urbanized society, with its preponderance of nuclear families and mothers working for wages outside their homes. Nearly half of all Japanese live within fifty kilometers of the three largest cities (Nagoya, Osaka, Tokyo), on 1 percent of the land, and over 75 percent live in urbanized areas. For them, the image of an old village offers an appealing alternative to overcrowded, impersonal living conditions. Moreover, unlike the Edo-period farm village, with its harsh system of sanctions (such as *murahachibu*, or ostracism), the "new *furusato*" is represented as a benevolent community emerging from the nostalgic imagination of "homeless" Japanese. The grand design of the "new *furusato*" programs in suburban cities throughout Japan is the creation of a villagelike ambience (see Sakada 1984b, 1984d; Tamura and Mori 1985). Recognizing that native place-making mostly is a matter of reclaiming mental and cultural terrain, proponents of *furusato-zukuri* aim to cultivate and harvest that terrain, or the landscape of nostalgia.

The Landscape of Nostalgia

In his treatise *Bungaku ni okeru genfūkei* (Original landscapes in literature), Okuno Takeo offers a nativist explanation as to why "old village" is such a ready model of and for cultural renewal. The Japanese, he claims, are historically a farming people; therefore, despite a century of industrialization and urban growth, they "are subconsciously and collectively imprinted with the image of farm (paddy) villages and their environs" (Okuno 1975, 72). Since *furusato* is, according to Okuno, an *Ur*-landscape permanently etched on the *kokoro* of ethnic Japanese, it can be evoked through the agency of nostalgia. Okuno's ideas illustrate effectively the cultural mythopoeia and appeal to popular memory informing *furusato-zukuri*.

Nostalgia figures as a distinctive way of relating the past to the present and future by juxtaposing the "uncertainties and anxieties of the present with presumed verities and comforts of the . . . past" (Davis 1979, 10). Nostalgia is not a product of the past, for what occasions it resides in the present, regardless of the sustenance provided by memories of the past.

To refer to the past, to take account of or interpret it, implies that one is located in the present, that one is distanced or apart from the object reconstructed. In sum, the relationship of prior to present representations is symbolically mediated, not naturally given; it encompasses both continuity and discontinuity. (Handler and Linnekin 1984, 287)

Nostalgia is provoked by a dissatisfaction with the present on the grounds of a remembered or imagined past plenitude. The proponents of *furusato-zukuri* acknowledge the newness of the old, as evinced by the oxymoronic term "new *furusato*." The prefix *furusato* is used to identify and distinguish things purportedly indigenous to Japan. But the sobriquet Furusato Japan also attests to the ruling Liberal Democratic Party's (LDP) recent appropriation of *furusato-zukuri* as an administrative model of and for a "new" national culture.

Furusato-zukuri was adopted in 1984 by the LDP as the affective cornerstone of domestic cultural policy. The new policy, referred to as "Nippon rettō furusato ron" (Proposal for Furusato Japan), was introduced that year in a televised speech by the finance minister, Takeshita Noboru. In 1987 Takeshita succeeded Nakasone Yasuhiro as prime minister, and appropriated *furusato* as the trope for his own political platform. Although he resigned in 1989 following charges of corruption, Takeshita's brainchild, the Furusato kon no kai (Spirit of Furusato Association), was adopted by the present (1989) prime minister, Kaifu Toshiki, as his personal advisory committee.[11] Political factionalism aside, the LDP as a whole regards *furusato-zukuri* as the means by which to forge a new "cultural state" (*bunka kokka*) in tandem with a "new Japanese-style welfare state" ("Nihonsei no atarashii fukushi kokka") (Takeshita and Kusayanagi 1986, 10; see also Shōwa 59-nen tō undō hōshin 1984).

Tanaka Kakuei, the former (and now incapacitated) prime minister, spearheaded LDP interest in *furusato-zukuri* with his 1973 bestseller, *Nippon rettō kaizō ron* (Proposal for remodeling Japan). Takeshita simply replaced "remodeling" with *furusato* in appropriating his former mentor's title. In his book, Tanaka bemoaned the fact that "for an increasing number of people, *furusato* is but a small apartment in the city," and worried that "the present state of affairs will make it difficult for the Japanese people to transmit their superior qualities and wisdom to the next generation." His proposed program of decentralizing industries and increasing transportation networks was aimed at creating "what the Japanese people want most . . . a beautiful, livable land and an untroubled future" (Tanaka 1973, i–ii). Tanaka's proposal—already undermined by the disclosure that his associates had been informed of details which enabled them to speculate in local real estate—was rendered economically moribund by the "oil shocks" of the early 1970s.

Where Tanaka had focused on remodeling the physical landscape, the LDP seems to be interested in exploiting the affective potential of *furusato-zukuri* toward the creation of a politically symbolic landscape of nostalgia. The adoption of the term *furusato* signals the reorientation of domestic policy from a preoccupation with strictly material needs to a preoccupation with the affective dimensions of materialistic well-being. This shift is evident in the savings bonds advertisements discussed shortly. Its folkish, nostalgic connotations imbue the *furusato-zukuri* project with an emotional appeal and a legitimacy sanctioned by "tradition." But, as I discuss later in the context of advertising, the "tradition" evoked by *furusato* does not depend on an objective relation to either the past or the countryside.

As something perceived as broadly "Japanese," *furusato* appeals to a wide spectrum of political interests, from the right to the left. The postwar revaluation of local practices was promoted from the early 1950s by localists and "antigovernment" forces,[12] although the favored expression then for "authentic" community was not *furusato* but *kyōdōtai*, a concept I discuss at length in chapter 3 (Irokawa 1978). Today *furusato* is evoked both by local environmentalist groups, who are opposed to chemical fertilizers and pesticides,[13] and by the conservative LDP. Actually, the LDP adopted *furusato* only after its rhetorical and symbolic usefulness had been established by local and regional agencies. The promotion of *furusato-zukuri* offers the party an efficacious way of addressing troublesome political, social, and environmental issues under a single rubric.

Public opinion polls conducted over the past decade by the prime minister's office and private agencies reveal that the respondents harbor pessimistic views about the future of their society. Rural depopulation and environmental pollution are seen as especially worrisome and are associated with high economic growth. The central government regards such views as the consensus of popular opinion. In a poll published in February 1984, six months before Takeshita's "Proposal for Furusato Japan," 50 percent of the respondents felt that Japanese society would become more hectic and unstable in the future. The results were used in formulating the Fourth Comprehensive National Development Plan now in effect (*Japan Times*, 5 February 1984; Yano-Tsuneta Kinenkai 1985, 35, 313–17). In response to the worries expressed in such opinion polls, the Association of National Trust Movements in Japan was founded in 1983. The objective of the association is to prevent the "destruction of environments of scenic or historic value through indiscriminate development or urbanization" (Kihara 1986, 190). In conjunction with the aims of *furusato-zukuri*, the preservation of historical landmarks and nostalgic landscapes also constitutes an effort to reinvent a "traditional" style of social relations.

Japanese political and social commentators (*hyōronka*) tend to attribute the current preoccupation with *furusato* to the oil shocks of the early 1970s. "Oil shocks" is a now clichéd expression for the reactions of Japanese people to the dramatic rise in the cost of petroleum. It is argued that this development reminded them—or, rather, was used to remind them—of their chronic dependence upon imported raw materials, and led to a revaluation of "tradition" with a view to attaining self-sufficiency.

Self-sufficiency in the context of *furusato-zukuri*, however, actually embodies less an effort after political and economic independence than the pursuit of an "authentic" community in contradistinction to internationalization. As Befu has discerned, "the very processes of Japan's internationalization induce its separateness from the rest of the world and cause Japan to assert its cultural autonomy" (1983, 261). Sociologist Isamu Kurita agrees, and has argued that the search for an "Exotic Japan" by Japanese today was stimulated by the internationalization of postwar culture:

[T]he very international-ness of the life-style makes the traditional Japanese arts appear quite alien and exotic. We look at our tradition the way a foreigner does, and we are beginning to love it. It is the product of a search for something more "advanced" and more modish than what we have found in our century-long quest for a new culture.[14] (1983, 131)

What the oil shocks signaled was the end of high growth produced by the "economic miracle" of the 1960s. High growth itself could no longer be regarded as a political panacea, and political confrontation with the sociocultural costs of rapid economic growth could no longer be postponed. The end of the "economic miracle" meant the end of big spending programs, such as free medical care for the elderly and welfare support for children and disabled people. Furthermore, the crisis precipitated the decline of progressive politics and the concomitant strengthening of conservative (LDP) influence. The LDP has since co-opted the formerly progressive issues of pollution, welfare, and citizen participation (Samuels 1983, 214–19; Shōwa 59-nen tō undō hōshin 1984).

The nostalgic experience is particularly intense where the sense of vexation and insecurity is not just limited to the present but is expected to color the future as well (Zwingmann 1959, 199). Since nostalgia is a barometer of present moods, the ubiquity of *furusato* would seem to bespeak a chronic, pervasive anxiety on the part of many Japanese people today. Anthropologist Mitsusada Fukasaku echoes this anxious sentiment with his remark that the Japanese "can't go home again." He argues that

traditional patterns of life and thought are no longer possible, because Japan is no longer geographically isolated from the international community, [because] agriculture is no longer the basis for the Japanese economy, because Japan's once beautiful nature has been destroyed by pollution and urbanization, and because the traditional culture has been completely commercialized. (in Wagatsuma 1975, 330)

Although Fukasaku insists that the people of Japan will begin to create "a new culture of their own," he does not venture any suggestions about the form and content of this "new" entity. The "new" culture—the "authentic" community—appears as a state-regulated project in which the nostalgia for nostalgia is manipulated, on the one hand, to mask human responsibility for socioecological change and, on the other, to create a collectivist mythopoeia predicated on the reification of the "old village." "Old villages" are presumed to have existed in harmonious tranquility until vitiated and transmogrified by outside forces—such as westernization, industrialization, and urbanization. In the *furusato-zukuri* literature, change for the worse is described as precipitated by external agents. Change for the better, on the other hand, is presented as a wholly Japanese undertaking, a rallying against intrusive foreign agents. This distinction is evident in the verbs used to denote change. Change for the worse is denoted by passive expressions containing the intransitive verb *naru* (to evolve, to become, to be). *Naru* brackets, deflects, and conceals intentionality: creation is presented as an irruption, an epiphany, a release of what already is there.

Naru contrasts with *tsukuru* (to make, to build), a transitive verb that denotes intentional, purposeful action. *Tsukuru* is linked with *furusato* to form the compound *furusato-zukuri*. Unlike *naru*, *tsukuru* acknowledges that creation is a form of labor, a conscious construction. *Naru* elides or renders unproblematic the sociohistorical conditions of production; things simply enter the realm of present actuality from somewhere in the past. Thus, when the administrators of Kodaira bemoan urban sprawl, they couch their complaints in *naru* expressions: Kodaira "has become" a sprawling bedroom town lacking integrity. In this way, the administrators can avoid blaming specific persons and groups for the city's problems and instead exhort residents "to actively make" Kodaira into a place "we can call *furusato*." Similar rhetoric and a preponderance of *-zukuri* compounds characterize the LDP's 1984 platform.[15]

"Old Village" Villages

As a local-level policy, *furusato-zukuri* is not limited to cities faced with the untoward consequences of urban sprawl. It is also implemented in rural villages as a strategy to check depopulation. The term *furusato-mura* ("old village" villages) designates depopulated villages seeking to attract "honorary villagers." Honorary villagers are long-term tourists from the city who can enjoy picking mushrooms and bracken, slopping hogs, and transplanting rice seedlings without having to actually depend on agriculture for a living. Neither do the native villagers, since tourism is regarded as a more lucrative and desirable enterprise.

The Furusato Information Center functions as a clearinghouse for both prospective *furusato-mura* and honorary villagers. An example of typical copy prepared by a "village" for perusal by urban clients and publicized by the center is translated below. The site in question was newly renamed Kōzuke-*mura*, after the pre-Meiji name for the area now encompassed by Gunma prefecture. This profile recalls Origuchi's discourse on Yamato as a gateway.

Pursue the romance of "Kōzuke-*mura*," Gunma's secret frontier (gateway). The pristine currents of the "Kannagawa" flow through the center of the village, which is encircled by mountains. Ninety-four percent of the land abounds in beautiful forests—which is why it is called "Gunma's secret frontier." Kōzuke-*mura* has a history spanning more than 200 years: the Kurozawa family house was designated a national treasure. . . . Petrified rocks impart the romance of the Age of Dinosaurs. Many natural monuments—national and prefectural treasures—are found here.

Moreover, traditional seasonal events . . . and folk arts . . . are still passed on from generation to generation in their original form.

Natural wonders and pure traditions have been preserved in their original state. Those things unnurtured in a city, like a "restful heart-mind" and "poetic sentiment," are reawakened here. (in Nakajima 1986, 105)

Most of the so-called traditional village activities performed in *furusato* villages are either recently invented or newly revived as recreation for domestic tourists. Among them are festivals, *kagura* (Shinto music and dancing), folk kabuki, storytelling and folksinging sessions, handicrafts exhibitions, nature hikes, and rice-pounding contests. Honorary villagers, who pay an average annual residency fee of about 10,000 yen, enjoy other amenities as well. Back "home" in the city, they are provided with *furusato* newsletters and local produce (*Asahi shinbun*, 13 March 1983; Furusato jōhō sentā 1985; Kawashima 1984, 121–26; Sakada 1984a, 353–419). Real villagers, on the other hand, are entrusted with the custody of an irreplaceable (if imagined) community; they are curators of the landscape of nostalgia.

For natives and honorary villagers alike, what is experienced is not village life but a villagelike life. Honorary villagers are encouraged to think of a given village as if it were indeed their "new *furusato*." This "as if" does not denote falsity but, rather, refers to an imagined community. It is not false, because it is "a part of social relations which has a definite effect. In living 'as if,' subjects do not live in illusion, this 'as if' is the reality of their existence as subjects" (Paul Hirst, in Strawbridge 1982, 132).

Furusato-mura provide access to another, more "authentic" future society, but the "old village" villages must also be sufficiently of this world to be accessible by public or private transportation. Japan National Railways (JNR, privatized in 1987 as Japan Railways) early recognized its potential to traverse past and present. From "Discover Japan" in the 1970s to "Exotic Japan" in the 1980s, JNR advertised its world-bridging services to "homeless" urbanites. In the Meiji period, "agrarian moralists" warned of the detrimental effect trains would have on rural life (Gluck 1985, 163). Today the railroad brings people back to both the countryside and a nostalgic frame of mind. What is ironic in this connection is that, whereas rail service to isolated rural stations is being phased out gradually, nostalgia-evoking steam engines are making newly scheduled runs as tourist attractions. Those who are unable to travel can take advantage of the post office's "*furusato* parcel post" (*furusato kozutsumi*) service, inaugurated in 1985. Customers can choose from a variety of regional foodstuffs and handicrafts, colorfully advertised in "*furusato* parcel post" catalogues. The parcels are then posted directly to them from local manufacturers. Domestic tourism is a cogent means of inducing nostalgia and occasioning the experience of an exoticized past. Railway companies, the post office, and developers of *furusato-mura* alike recognize that leisure, just now becoming an industry in its own right in Japan, is among other things an anodyne realm in which gratification is offered in compensation for the disturbing consequences of postwar urbanization.

Conclusion: The Making of Furusato Japan

Furusato-zukuri is employed by the state as a synonym for "cultural administration" (*bunka gyōsei*), which in turn signifies the reorientation of domestic policy since the "oil shocks" of the 1970s from a strictly materialist to a more affective focus. The present time is referred to in various media as an "age of affect" (*kokoro no jidai*), the rather premature rationale being that, since basic material needs have been more or less met, civil servants and city planners must attend to the emotional needs of the people (cf. Uruoi no aru machi-zukuri kenkyūkai 1984, 21–22). This slogan is illustrative of the symbolic and affective political context within which *furusato* ideology operates. Former Prime Minister Nakasone consistently expressed the need for "heart-mind accord" (*kokoro no fureai*) between political administrators and the people (e.g., Nakasone 1984). Nakasone's call for administrative reform was characterized as the "culturization of administration" (*gyōsei no bunkaka*), the complement of "cultural administration" (Aiba et al. 1985, 296–319; Andō 1984, 143–54; Mori 1985, 49–62).[16]

The "culturalization of administration" involves transforming the essential substance and nature of administration itself: decorating government offices with works of art; producing colorful pamphlets that explain administrative policy in jargon-free language accessible to the public; making government buildings available on weekends for public use, such as for hobby classes; broadcasting music from government buildings during holidays, to create a festive ambience; and nurturing affective relations between civil servants by promoting the use, in their memos, of the more warmly respectful suffix *sama* over the indifferent *dono* (Mori 1985, 56; see also Tamura 1985, 3–20, 52–61).

Implicit in the "culturization of administration" is the idea of admin-

istrating culture and "tradition." Both are evoked to signify and provoke a new "value consciousness" (*kachi ishiki*) informing the *furusato-
zukuri* project. Planners, bureaucrats, advertisers, and the polled public
seem to recognize implicitly that "traditional" aspects of culture and
social life do not constitute an objectively definable inheritance,
although they may be eulogized as such. Instead, they are negotiable
symbolic constructs continuously reinvented in the present—and, in
the case of *furusato*, through the agency of nostalgia.

At the local level, *furusato-zukuri* concentrates on reviving and in-
venting shrinelike festivals in particular. Shinto shrines formed the affective and (especially from the Meiji period through World War II) the
administrative nexus of "traditional" village society. The nostalgic value
of shrine festivals is attested by their frequent mention in *enka* lyrics and
their imitation in city festivals. The early 1980s mark the beginning of
a *matsuri būmu* (festival boom) in cities, although participation in regional festivals has been an objective of domestic tourism since at least
the early 1960s.

As an administrative policy, *furusato-zukuri* is both a reaction to
postwar changes and an attempt to control change by restoring a sense
of sociocultural continuity to something that seems to verge on the
discontinuous. The something is postwar Japan, which for the past
forty years apparently has proceeded along a trajectory at variance with
its emergent ideological antithesis: Furusato Japan of nostalgic, popular
memories. With a view to both resuscitating "the Japanese spirit" and
reforming the state, former Prime Minister Nakasone declared the imminent end of the postwar era. He announced that a new era—one divorced from the guilt of imperialist excesses, the humiliation of defeat,
the American Occupation, and, by extension, the oil shocks—must
begin.[17] Those institutions imposed upon Japan by SCAP (Supreme
Commander of the Allied Powers), such as the constitution and the
educational system, must, insisted Nakasone, undergo a total reevalua-
tion and be rendered more Japanese.

Furusato Japan is the dominant imagination of *post*-postwar Japan.
A series of savings bond advertisements published by the Ministry of
Finance cogently illustrates the political project that underlies this image. These advertisements constitute a visual representation of "cultural administration" and, in keeping with the "Proposal for Furusato
Japan," encourage the revaluation of "old village" practices. All of them
feature scenes from Shinto festivals. An early (1983) version, appearing
in the *Asahi shinbun*, consists of a color woodblock print of a shrine

Fig. 1. An advertisement for savings bonds issued by the Ministry of Finance in 1983, appearing in the *Asahi shinbun*.

festival in progress (fig. 1). In the right margin is a poem celebrating the tutelary deity of an archetypical "old village." The poem is sandwiched between the slogan "Ii naa. Furusato Nippon," which may be translated, with a touch of wistfulness, as "Ahh, it's so fine. Old Village Japan." The generic quality of this festive scene is further connoted by the use of the *hiragana* (i.e., *yamatokotoba*) form of *furusato* in the slogan.

A later (1985) edition of the same savings bond advertisement features photographs of costumed children taking part in their respective hometown festivals. Whether the festivals in question—such as the *hana matsuri* (flower festival) in Higashisakae-*chō*, Aichi prefecture (fig. 2)—are longstanding or recently revived is immaterial. The caption of these later ads reads "Watashi no furusato, watashi no Nippon," or "My old village, my Japan." This slogan unequivocally identifies native place with the nation and conflates localism and nationalism. In this connection, the syllables *fu-ru-sa-to* inserted alongside the ideograph effectively assimilate each "old village" featured within the larger and largest community, Furusato Japan. The caption determines and guides the reception of the photographic image: Furusato Japan may exist only within the framework of the advertisement itself, but the use of photographs of actual hometown festivals and faces helps to bridge the ideological distance between locality and nation.

These savings bond advertisements gloss over the often divisive and exclusionist nature of shrine festival participation at the local level, leaving unacknowledged the problematic relationship between local politics and the central bureaucracy. The festivals, photographed for commercial purposes, are severed from their singular, local contexts, and re-presented (re-membered) as metonyms of a national "authentic" community.[18] The *furusato* cities, towns, and villages throughout Japan represent concentric circles of insideness, each ringing its respective core constituency. They are encompassed in turn by Furusato Japan, the largest of the imagined communities. The invented microheritages of Furusato Kodaira and *furusato-mura* throughout Japan collectively constitute the proposed macroheritage represented by Furusato Japan; the local is a metonym of, and a metaphor for, the national.

The continuous generational transmission of local folkways is advocated quite literally in the above advertisements through the portrayal of children reenacting presumably historical festive rituals. This device effectively traditionalizes the new while simultaneously perpetuating seemingly old traditions. The advertisements also equate the survival of

わたしの故郷、わたしの日本。

いずれも額面5万円から、

源泉分離課税16％。

5年割引国債

中期2〜4年
10年利付国債

中期2〜4年
10年利付国債

（後）と特別（後）て、600万円まで非課税です。

花祭り（愛知県・東栄町）

国債

大蔵省

お求めは…証券会社、銀行、相互銀行、信用金庫、農林中金て。

Fig. 2. An advertisement for savings bonds issued by the Ministry of Finance in 1985, appearing in the weekly *Shūkan Asahi*.

"tradition" with the solvency of the central government. "Tradition," as I have explained, is a relationship of prior to present representations that is symbolically mediated and not naturally given. Neither pastness nor givenness defines something as "traditional." "Traditional" is "an arbitrary symbolic designation; an assigned meaning rather than an objective quality" (Handler and Linnekin 1984, 285–86). Although promoting sales of government savings bonds, the advertisements at the same time urge an emotional investment and participation in that exclusive community Furusato Japan. The implication is that nostalgia is as redeemable as government savings bonds, and that in the remaking of the past is the making of the future. The Furusato Japan advertisements offer Japanese citizens qua investors a cultural, cognitive bargain that the Ministry of Finance believes they cannot and will not refuse.

In promoting civic insideness by implicitly encouraging the staging of shrinelike festivals as a style of citizen participation, the central government (LDP) and local municipalities resemble their Meiji counterparts. But where the latter created shrine-centered administrative villages in a concerted effort to foster national spiritual unity,[19] the present government is expropriating local festivals toward a similar end. The outcome is both the cultural and political appropriation of the local by the national and the permeation of the national by the local.[20]

The nostalgic potential, sentimental value, and apparent historicity of *furusato* imbue it, and whatever it is prefixed to, with authenticity and cultural relativity. Furusato Japan conjures up a far more endearing image than does *bunka kokka* (cultural state), the abstract term popularized in the 1950s by Prime Minister Yoshida Shigeru (1878–1967) to characterize postwar Japan. Appropriated at different administrative levels and popularized in the mass media, *furusato* is evoked in nostalgic memories, just as "old village"–making incorporates the remembering of nostalgia. Prefixed to Japan, *furusato* facilitates the collective re-membering of a nation dis-membered by defeat in war and, more recently, by the uncertainties of an international, late-capitalist economy, which have rendered the "future" a vexing problem. In the following chapters, I discuss and analyze the significance and operations of *furusato-zukuri* in Kodaira City, beginning with the Kodaira citizens' festival.

CHAPTER TWO

New Festivals for Old

Reinvented Festivals

       A great many academic and popular texts have been published in Japan over the past fifteen years on things "traditional," from regional cuisines to *matsuri*, or festivals. Several of these texts are cited in this chapter. In addition, the "Leisure Wide" column in the *Asahi shinbun*, as well as other leading dailies, provides a listing of current festivals under the heading *matsuri*. Television stations regularly cover local festivals and broadcast special reports on "traditional" pastimes. For urbanites wishing to enjoy their leisure in a *matsuri* frame of mind, the Furusato Information Center provides detailed information on regional festivals and "traditional" events accessible to domestic tourists.

       The revival and invention of *matsuri* as authentically Japanese modes of group entertainment have, in turn, occasioned the traditionalization of the novel, such as *kodomo mikoshi* ("child" shrines).[1] "Traditional" (*dentōteki*) imbues whatever it is used to signify with positive and edifying value and cultural authenticity regardless of the actual history, vintage, or derivation of the thing or concept in question. The "traditional culture" (*dentōteki bunka*) boom, as it is referred to in the Japanese mass media, is further evident in the inauguration of wholly new *matsuri*, such as the Kodaira citizens' festival (*shimin matsuri*). Like other city festivals, it is modeled after shrine *matsuri*, with the ostensible purpose of creating an "old village" ambience within the suburban bedroom town. The Kodaira citizens' festival was inaugurated by and is conducted under the auspices of city hall and not a shrine, although local shrines lend the paraphernalia necessary to "authenticate" the event. The highlight of the festival is a parade of citizens new and old, who narrate literally and symbolically the historical development of Kodaira and its present social texture.

Citizens' festivals, generally speaking, are staged in cities throughout Japan as a conscious effort on the part of municipal governments to reclaim from inexorable urbanization the "old village" within the city. "Village" here is equated with the purported historical and affective core of a given city, evident today in metonymic terms: a thatched-roof farmhouse; a generations-old local product, such as a type of noodle or a handicraft; a stand of trees; an irrigation canal; *matsuri*; and so forth—all of which now evoke a past- and place-affirming nostalgia. *Matsuri* are perceived as a particularly cogent symbol of and condition for an "authentic" community.[2]

The Kodaira citizens' festival was inaugurated as an efficacious way for interested parties to occasion, maintain, and control the affective bases of social interaction, and not as the result of collective sentiments (cf. Smith 1975, 7). Moreover, as in the case of Kodaira City, this social interaction provokes and reinforces sectoral differences, which are cast in high relief in the citizens' festival parade. The parade is a social drama, which has "a habit of activating . . . 'classificatory oppositions'" (Turner 1982, 11); it is a dynamic juxtaposition—a dialectic—of native and newcomer. Therefore, unlike Inoue and his associates (1979), I do not regard Shinto shrine festivals as an ideal-type norm to which city festivals do not (or cannot) measure up. Whereas the majority of studies in English on Japanese urban ceremonial are about microlocal events (e.g., Bestor 1985; Littleton 1986; Sadler 1972), this chapter deals with a citywide festival. An analysis of the Kodaira citizens' festival contributes to an understanding of the rationale for the incorporation of affect and "tradition" in city-planning strategies.

Reclaiming the "Old Village" in the City

Matsuri are generally defined in the ethnographic literature as Shinto shrine–centered festivals, planned and performed by a given shrine's parishioner households (*ujiko*). Shinto shrine events (*gyōji*) formed the affective core of farm village society through the postwar period, an arrangement amplified by the Meiji government. Villages and shrines were amalgamated at the turn of the century to form shrine-centered administrative villages, in a concerted effort to centralize government policy and foster national spiritual unity (Fridell 1973). Shrine festivals also formed the affective nexus of castle-town (*jōka-machi*) society during the Edo period. In fact, the prototypes of the consumer-oriented urban citizens' festivals of today may be traced to the *matsuri* staged in the newly created capital city of Edo, where the de facto power of the merchant class was demonstrated in a variety of festive spectacles, from fantastical processions of licensed courtesans and their pimps to the rambunctious parades of elaborate palanquin shrines (*mikoshi*).

Although *matsuri* probably were originally performed quietly and at night (see Yanagita 1985, 41–52), Edo festivals were staged in the broad daylight in fairlike settings. A festival offered townspeople a chance to display and purchase new fashions and to consume great quantities of special dishes and alcoholic drinks. Today specialized *matsuri* garb itself is considered fashionable,[3] and the word *matsuri* figures prominently as a commercial signifier. The mass media provide countless examples of "used-book *matsuri*," "furniture *matsuri*," and "imported-wine *matsuri*," among others. There are also "family sports *matsuri*" and "hydrangea *matsuri*," in addition to "citizens' *matsuri*." Clearly, the word *matsuri* imbues used-book sales and sporting events with an extraordinary value previously associated with shrine ceremonies in particular. Moreover, *matsuri*, in a way reminiscent of the case with *furusato*, has been divorced from its primary referent and is now used in a connotative capacity.

What are the sociohistorical premises of the citizens' festival? In Kodaira, *furusato-zukuri* formally was initiated with the promulgation of the Kodaira citizens' charter (*shimin kenshō*) in 1972, on the occasion of the tenth anniversary of cityhood. The five-article charter, termed a "roadmap of civic life," begins with a preamble celebrating the pioneer spirit of the first settlers.

Three hundred years ago, the pioneers first put a spade to this then wasteland. We, the citizens of Kodaira, native and newcomer alike, have inherited their intrepid pioneering spirit. This charter was conceived to carry on, in that spirit, the making of Kodaira into a cheerful residential city.

1. Let's build a verdant city to which small birds will flock.
2. Let's build a city full of compassion and empathy toward the young and old alike.
3. Let's build a city characterized by punctuality and clockwork orderliness.
4. Let's build, smiling as we work, a city bursting with health.
5. Let's join together in enjoying civic life.

About the same time the charter was implemented, city hall began referring to the city as Furusato Kodaira, a name coined to imbue the suburban bedroom town with folkish familiarity.

In September 1975, three years after the charter was promulgated, the Council to Actualize the Citizens' Charter was organized by city hall to enforce the civic manifesto. The council consists of five "special sections," each named after the article of the charter it is responsible for bringing to fruition. The key activity overseen by the section in charge of the fifth article—the goals of which include the recovery of local history and the promotion of *furusato-zukuri*—is the annual citizens' festival.

According to city hall, the explicit purpose of the citizens' festival is to foster, among the city's diverse residents, camaraderie of the sort that presumably infused Shinto shrine festivals in the original seven villages. From the outset, the citizens' festival was ballyhooed as an occasion to "intertwine the hearts of 150,000 residents" and bring to experiential fullness Furusato Kodaira.

By the mid-1970s, Kodaira's administrators had decided that both concrete and symbolic actions were needed to unify the city's diverse population. Newcomers, who by 1976 constituted nearly 98 percent of the total population, allegedly lacked a sense of affinity with Kodaira, for only a little over 50 percent of newcomer households had definite plans to put down roots in the city. With the decline of big spending programs precipitated by the oil shocks, local self-sufficiency became a necessary pragmatic concern as well as an ideological position. A large permanent, and growing, population would ensure a tax base adequate to maintain and improve the standard of civic life in Kodaira City.

A sense of insideness among newcomers was also retarded by a simmering tension between them and the natives. In 1967 the tension finally erupted as a public issue that was widely reported in the city newspaper. The occasion was a round-table discussion that spring between four residents and newly elected Mayor Ōshima, who retired in 1983. One newcomer, a *sarariiman*, broached the matter by pointing out that there was bad blood between natives and newcomers, and he recommended that "citizens' forums" be inaugurated to enable both sides to communicate more constructively with each other (*KSH*, 20 May, 1 October 1967).

Ōshima, perhaps in acknowledgment of the political influence of the native sector, emphasized that his first priority was to implement a comprehensive agricultural policy in order to balance urbanization with the preservation of farmland. He added that he already had asked various women's organizations to include in their social agendas activities to help smooth out relations between natives and newcomers. Apparently, the mayor believed that native-newcomer antinomy was expressed primarily between men and that women were more capable of negotiating differences among themselves. The fact that Ōshima himself was not Kodaira born and raised may have increased his sensitivity toward the needs of the native sector.

As an example of the discord between the two sectors, the *sarariiman* brought to the mayor's attention the matter of fire drills. Although the fire brigade was short of hands, only natives were allowed to join; newcomers were excluded even from fire drills. Historically, households ostracized from village life were allowed to take part in fire-fighting and funeral services. In postwar Kodaira, however, the exclusion of newcomers from the fire brigade and from participation in fire drills suggests symbolically that they are not part of a community, since in a "real" community even ostracized households have access to fire prevention measures. The mayor countered by insisting that the newcomer had it all wrong; that natives, rather, were disappointed by the newcomers' lack of interest in these exercises. Many newcomers did want to participate, the *sarariiman* retorted, but they were not informed of when and where the drills would be held. Crucial information, in short, systematically had been withheld from newcomers by natives. Since then, fire drills have been conducted by the larger of the 380 neighborhood associations (*jichikai*) in Kodaira.

As I bring up again in subsequent chapters, the native sector's sense of its nativeness was stimulated, initially at least, mainly by the reactions of the adversarial newcomer sector (cf. Kamishima 1978; Suttles 1972, 53–65). Newcomers were similarly defined. Since the initiation of *furusato-zukuri* in the mid-1970s, however, nativeness—and not newcomerness—has been legitimated by city hall as a highly desirable identity in its own right. The concept of *furusato-zukuri* was introduced in part to foster, in newcomers especially, an emotional commitment to Kodaira, but city hall actually has exacerbated the antinomy between the two sectors. Even as city hall appropriates the native sector in its quest to locate the "old village" in the city, natives, on the other hand, feel constrained to reclaim, as a reparative strategy, the "really real" *furusato* within Furusato Kodaira. New publications lauding the achievements of Kodaira natives and their ancestors are widely distributed, and commemorative steles and signboards designating historical landmarks, including shrines and temples, help to magnify the natives' past in the present landscape. Once again, at the same time, these displays of nativeness are appropriated by city hall toward *furusato-zukuri* as examples of Kodaira's "living history."

In the Edo period, newcomers to Kodaira (that is, to one of the seven *shinden* villages) occupied a temporary status category that changed automatically to "old-timer" after certain communal services were rendered and several years of residence completed. Since the postwar period, "newcomer" has become a permanent status category. While newcomers eventually may come to feel "as if" they were natives, or express a local-place consciousness, nomenclature effectively has frozen the dichotomy. The 53 percent of newcomers who have expressed a desire to settle permanently in the city are called *kodairakko*, or "children of Kodaira," while natives are called *tochikko*, or "children of the soil." Placeness for newcomers resides in citizenship, but for natives it is grounded, like crops, in the land itself—or so these labels (in the local literature) presume to establish.

Natives not only have resented the "intruders" and the resultant urban sprawl—although they have been selling land to developers since the early 1920s—but have continued to exclude them from parish membership in Shinto shrines and Buddhist temples. The exclusion of newcomers was made clear to me in interviews with the head priests of the oldest religious institutions in Kodaira; it also was evident in their organizational structure. Unlike Kodaira's shrine festivals, which are limited essentially to native parishioners, the citizens' festival was conceived as an all-inclusive event staged on a citywide scale. The exclusive nature of local shrine festivals affected the public's initial reception of the citizens' festival: newcomers mistakenly thought that it too was a closed affair. Notices for the first several *shimin matsuri* therefore emphasized that the event was open to all residents regardless of seniority.

Scripting the Citizens' Festival

Prior to the actual staging of the citizens' festival, the city's thirty-two assemblypersons held a number of meetings to discuss the desirable form and content of the event. One Japanese Socialist Party (JSP) member took the initiative in raising both pragmatic and philosophical questions. First was the matter of sponsorship. Was the festival to be wholly subsidized by city hall, or should commercial and private funds be solicited? Next was the matter of its content. Should the festival encompass a hodgepodge of exhibits and activities? Should it epitomize a self-conscious localism? What sort of concept or vision of Kodaira was to be presented? What sort of place should the citizens' festival ideally occupy in the lives of Kodaira's residents? (*KGR*, September 1976, 137)

A native assemblyperson, who later served as speaker, replied that the citizens' festival would provide a means of fostering local patriotism. He remarked that the oil shocks several years earlier had sparked a positive revaluation of "traditional" (*dentōteki*) lifestyles and seasonal events. Moreover, there was a pressing need to raise a new generation of residents who would feel an attachment to Kodaira. A citizens' festival, he felt, would serve as the basis for the generation of a "consciousness of interconnectedness" (*rentai ishiki*). And for the benefit of bedridden elderly residents and members of Kodaira households living elsewhere in Japan, he, with the mayor's help, planned to negotiate with a television station to have the festival filmed and eventually broadcast.[4] Through the mass media, local patriotism could be nurtured and civic consciousness raised, and the city would become widely known (*KGR*, September 1976, 139–40). While the Kodaira citizens' festival has yet to be televised, videos are made of each one, and a rotating exhibition of festival pictures taken by local photographers is held each year.

The superintendent of schools added that the plan to inaugurate a citizens' festival was based on the interest expressed by certain (unnamed) groups over the past several years. A citizens' festival, he declared, would not be merely an entertainment but, in its capacity as a "public place for interpersonal exchange" (*kōryū no hiroba*), would effectively help to forge affective links between natives and newcomers (*KGR*, September 1976, 142–43). *Kōryū no hiroba* is one of the many variations on a theme of *ba*, or public place. A more colloquial version is the cliché *fureai no hiroba*. *Fureai* implies actual contact—touching, brushing—between people, whereas *kōryū* is the more technical term for exchange or interchange. According to Nakane, a *ba*, or "frame," "sets a boundary and gives a common basis to a set of individuals who are located or involved in it" (1973, 1). Her definition, however, essentially is limited to the physical boundaries demarcating groups within (literally) concrete institutions, such as large companies and universities. As exemplified by the Kodaira citizens' festival, *ba* boundaries may also be fluid, temporary, and affective in nature.

The logistics of the first citizens' festival were almost casual in comparison to the hierarchy of bureaucratic tasks that characterized the ninth. The first three festivals were administered by the Culture Division of the Social Education Department. Then, in 1981, the Civic Life Department was created, and a committee under its jurisdiction, the Citizens' Festival Executive Committee, was established to emphasize the festival's importance as a civic event. The remaining conflict of interest between the league and the committee was resolved in 1982, when it was agreed that the chair of the Culture Division would serve concurrently as head of the executive committee.

Six years after the citizens' festival was inaugurated, several assemblypersons professed to remain unclear about its administration and purpose. One assemblyperson, a member of the Democratic Socialist Party (DSP), for example, was curious about the division of labor between the Culture Division and the executive committee, since he had just discovered that both were chaired by the same individual. He demanded an itemized account of how the nearly 4,000,000 yen budgeted for the eighth festival—four times the amount budgeted for the first festival—had been disbursed. Were funds for the portable toilets, telephones, electricity, and police patrol included in the budget? The DSP assemblyperson advocated an increased festival budget. His rationale was along "socialist" lines; that is, he adamantly opposed the recently proposed idea of turning the citizens' festival into a profit-making venture. It would not be fair, he argued, to extend support to the business sector while admonishing the people to fund their own events in the name of spontaneous populism. A *matsuri* by his definition was not a commercial operation (*KGR*, December 1982, 236–39).[5]

Responding to the DSP assemblyperson, Mayor Ōshima ran through a list of key festival expenditures. They included substantial honoraria to local landlords for the use of their property; funds for programs and posters; and remunerations to construction, sewage, electrical, and communications agencies. The festival budget for that year also included prize money awarded to the winner of the "Kodaira Citizens' Festival Song" contest.[6] Ōshima acknowledged that some financial support was necessary to popularize the annual event; but, he added, since public participation was "supposed to be spontaneous" ("spontaneous" being a euphemism for voluntary), each group should bear its own costs (*KGR*, December 1982, 237). The groups in question primarily are neighborhood associations, whose leaders appropriate members' dues toward funding the citizens' festival.

Unless they have read the proceedings of the assembly, the 150,000 residents whose solidarity the citizens' festival was designed to promote are unaware of the backstage politicking. For most, the *shimin matsuri* is an occasion to browse and munch on fried noodles, candied apples, *okonomi-yaki* ("omelettes"), and other typical festival fare. Apart from the "festival headquarters," staffed by members of the planning committees on hand to distribute programs and to comfort lost children, the only other visible presence of city hall is the appearance of city officials in the third segment of the parade. One native assemblyperson proposed, in 1981, that all thirty-two assemblypersons should parade together to emphasize the city's seriousness in promoting *furusato-zukuri* (*KGR*, September 1981, 128). His proposal was voted down. The invisible presence of city hall is everywhere, however, from the festival's site along city-owned Akashia (Acacia) Road to the flea market sponsored by the welfare center. And, of course, the festival itself is an annual creation of city hall.

Before I proceed to an analysis of the ninth citizens' festival, a brief review of the construction of the eighth one (1983) is instructive.[7] The executive committee met officially twice prior to the festival and once after the event to reflect on its successes and its shortcomings. Representatives from each of the participating groups also attended these meetings. In addition, a temporary steering committee was established, and its members met before and after the festival. The division of labor between the executive and steering committees may be summarized as follows: the executive committee articulates the concept of the citizens' festival, elects officers, decides on a date, and attends to advertisements; the steering committee supervises the election of section chiefs, prepares budget estimates, and arranges safety provisions.

City hall budgeted 3,800,000 yen for the 1983 citizens' festival, which was augmented by 335,000 yen in contributions from the

Kodaira Rotary Club and other philanthropic societies. Monies allotted toward the festival by the neighborhood associations varied according to the size of the association and the extent of its members' participation in the event. The city's largest association, with over 1,800 members, earmarked 133,800 yen, which was used to provide two children's groups with costumes and art supplies (Gakuen Nishi-*chōkai* 1983; *KSH*, 1 October 1983).

Kodaira's Ninth: The 1984 Citizens' Festival

The highlight of the annual citizens' festival is a four-part parade staged along a one-kilometer stretch of Akashia Road. In addition to the parade, on which I focus exclusively, the festival consists of numerous "corners," as ad hoc exhibits and stalls are called. The 1984 event, held on Sunday, 21 October, included an all-day local talent show, as well as a *karaoke* (sing-along cassette tape) competition; a blood donation corner; a children's forum featuring arts and crafts demonstrations, a singing-in-sign-language stage, and a sketching corner where youngsters were encouraged to draw pictures of the event for the annual citizens' festival art exhibition; a horticultural and *bonsai* fair, and a fresh-produce market; a rice-pounding demonstration; a Chamber of Commerce corner stocked with electrical devices and other manufactured goods; food, candy, and toy stalls; and a one-day zoo consisting of a gravel lot filled with small caged animals and one Shetland pony.

It is the parade, however, that is the subject of my description and analysis. The parade of the ninth citizens' festival was divided into four parts: children's groups, women folkdancers, Western-style marching bands, and a "traditional" palanquin shrine procession. (This four-part division also characterized the preceding eight festival parades.) It began at the intersection of Oume Road, along which the first homesteads were founded, and terminated at the Kodaira Danchi, a high-rise complex constructed in 1965 to accommodate the growing newcomer population (see the program guide, fig. 3). The parade along Akashia Road symbolically reenacts or emplots the making of Kodaira, a continuous process initiated by the Edo-period land reclamation programs and currently maintained in the name of *furusato-zukuri*.

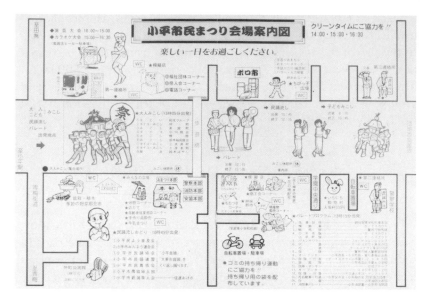

Fig. 3. Ninth Kodaira citizens' festival program guide. The four-part division
of the parade is clearly indicated.

"CHILD" SHRINES

The 1984 parade, which opened to the boom and
crackle of fireworks, was several hours in duration. In the lead were
children's groups, whose members shouldered handmade palanquin
shrines called *kodomo mikoshi*, or "child" shrines. Real *mikoshi*—"adult"
shrines, in citizens' festival jargon—are elaborate constructions. Carried
on a framework of poles, the shrines, which usually weigh hundreds
of kilograms, are built of lacquered wood decorated with shiny metal
fittings, elegant brocades, and colorful tassels, and are commonly
topped by a golden phoenix.

Over a thousand children officially took part in the 1984 procession;
all were clad in *happi* (short wrap-around jackets) and most wore a
colorful headband. Each "child" shrine was preceded by a sign bearer
identifying the group by club, neighborhood association, or school district. A few of the *kodomo mikoshi* were of a conventional shape, albeit
constructed from milk boxes and juice cans and painted in rainbow
colors. Most were effigies of cartoon characters; three "child" shrines
were likenesses of that perennially endearing rodent Mickey Mouse.
Two groups had fashioned "shrines" in the shape of the Australian

frilled lizard, a creature appearing widely in television commercials that year (fig. 4). There was also a pink elephant *mikoshi*, a local tribute to the two baby elephants presented to a Japanese zoo by the Indian government. Parents (mostly mothers) and club directors clustered solicitously around the "child" shrines, urging on their young charges with shouts, shrill whistles, and flailing arms. While not all the adults who joined in hoisting the "child" shrines were newcomers, the only palanquin shrines that newcomers are allowed to carry are the "child" shrines, an issue I will return to when discussing "adult" shrines. Regardless of their novelty, these effigies are still referred to as *mikoshi*, for the festival's organizers maintain that novelty is quite acceptable in the service of tradition, in this case shrine bearing. Significantly, a sign carried by a children's group representing a largely white-collar neighborhood was inscribed with the slogan "Let's make a *furusato* for ourselves."

That the citizens' festival parade should begin with a "child" shrine procession is not fortuitous. The primary beneficiaries of the "new *furusato*" symbolized by the festival are the city's children, especially the (post–oil shock) Kodaira-born among them. They are the youngest *kodairakko*. A poem entitled "Kodairakko," which was published in the 1975 New Year's edition of the city newspaper, marks the first appearance of the term. Its three verses celebrate the "fighting spirit" of the city's youngsters.

Kodairakko

Hey, come on! Get together, *kodairakko*!
It's time to go for a run.
A brisk wind is blowing from Chichibu,
But hard as it blows, we won't give up.
Fight! Fight! That's how we'll run.

The branches of the chestnut trees are waving,
The branches of the *nashi* are waving too.
The tops of the zelkovas are waving.
Fight! Fight! That's what they yell,
Those energetic *kodairakko*!

Fight! Fight! Hearing that yell,
The buds sprout, the flowers bloom;
They grow abundantly and bear fruit.
A dream that *kodairakko* will flourish.
A dream that *kodairakko* will thrive.

Fig. 4. A "child" shrine in the shape of an Australian frilled lizard. (Photo by author)

Youthfulness is celebrated not for its own sake but as a product of a healthful family life. The theme of forging a "new *furusato*" is conjoined with the aim of eradicating juvenile delinquency through the re-creation of a holistic social life grounded in the ideal of *danran*, which means "happy and harmonious home circle." Between August and October of 1984, a total of 1,882 juvenile delinquents were appre-hended for drug (i.e., stimulants) abuse, shoplifting, vandalism, and vagrancy. This figure represents about 7 percent of the 26,581 youths (fourteen to nineteen years old) in Tokyo metropolitan prefecture taken into custody that year (*KBH* 1984; *TSK* 1985). The prevention of juvenile delinquency was a much emphasized theme in the third seg-ment of the parade. Like children, Furusato Kodaira must be care-fully nurtured to a healthy maturity. Sloganized, this administrative policy might be rendered "*kodairakko* energy, *tochikko* values" or, from a more practical perspective, "*kodairakko* taxes, *tochikko* stability."

DANCING MOTHERS AND KODAIRA ETHNICS

Following the "child" shrines were six blocks of female folkdancers moving forward rhythmically to the alternating strains of the "Kodaira *Ondo*" and the "Greater Tokyo *Ondo*," which were broad-cast throughout the day as well.[8]

Kodaira *Ondo*

Ha-aa. Long ago in Musashino was Ogawa village, you know.
A post station along an avenue of zelkovas. (As for now,)
Now there are seven: Kami-Naka-Shimojuku, Kubō Slope—hey now!
(Throngs of people)
Enjoying a cool moonlit eve in Misono.
(Kodaira is a good, fine place!) You bet!
(Kodaira is.)

Ha-aa. Come now, let's sing; make a circle and dance, you know.
Flower of Koganei, along the canal. (As for fragrance,)
Fragrant are Gakuen, Tsuda College, Arts College, Hitotsubashi.
(Now then), Shinmei-*gū*.
The Seibu line carries your dreams.
(Kodaira is a good, fine place!) You bet!
(Kodaira is.)

Ha-aa. Come now, let's sing; make a circle and dance, you know.
To the east, Tsukuba; to the west, Mt. Fuji. (And in between,)

(Now then), avenue of buildings.
Strike up the *ondo* and build up the town.
(Kodaira is a good, fine place!) You bet!
(Kodaira is.)

( ) = chorus
Lyrics: Yokozawa Chiaki
Music: Hayama Tarō

The six groups averaged between 70 and 150 members, mostly women between forty and sixty-five years of age for whom folkdancing was a weekly pastime. I recognized among the dancers several of the clerks at a local supermarket. One of them later told me that her group practiced once a week and also performed at various festivals and functions elsewhere in Tokyo. For over an hour, row after row of dancers clad in decorative kimonos filed by, swaying and stepping in perfect unison. Their expressions were sober, crinkling into brief smiles only at the sight of an acquaintance among the appreciative spectators (fig. 5).

Trailing a slight distance behind these six groups was a seventh, the women of the Niigata prefectural association, dancing the "Sado *okesa*," a style of folkdancing that originated in Sado Island. They had not participated in the past several festivals. Whereas the other groups were identified by modest hand-carried signs, the Niigata women announced their presence in a bold way. They were preceded by a sound truck outfitted with several large white panels, bordered with colorful pom-poms, on which was brushed the name of their association in giant red characters.

When each group of dancers reached the end of the parade route, they broke rank. A few fell back to mingle with their friends, who graciously "oohed" and "aahed" over their performance and enviously fingered the dancers' festive kimonos.

It is fitting symbolically that the "child" shrine procession should be followed by one featuring older women. In the first place, females—wives and mothers especially—are regarded by city hall as a "class" of resident and are acknowledged collectively as the nexus between the private household and the public neighborhood or society at large. They are also regarded as mediating between past and present, "tradition" and "modernity." Wives and mothers negotiate these counter-posed domains through their husbands and/or children. Women's groups, to a certain idealistic degree, function as extensions of the household, as the ancestors' festival dance (*obon*) in Kodaira illustrates.

The *obon* dance, jointly organized by the women's and youth groups

Fig. 5. Female folkdancers. (Photo by author)

of participating neighborhood associations, is highly valued as an opportunity to instill in youngsters an appreciation for "traditional" entertainment. Rehearsals are held, for sloppy dancing on the two nights of the festival would "exert a bad influence on the impressionable youngsters" (*KCH*, 1 July 1958). Similarly, groups of mothers are made responsible for collecting and publishing local lore and folktales, which are considered to be of socially redeeming value for children. In the context of the citizens' festival, the polished female folkdancers collectively are idealized as the civic materfamilias of *kodairakko* and, as such, symbolize the operations and consequences of the dominant ideology of the "family system."

The "family system"—which refers to the tendency to extol the patriarchal household as the center of state, national, corporate, and social structures (cf. Maruyama 1969, 36)—relies on the social import and utility of the mediational role of wives and mothers. This system does not accord females qua females high status; rather, it is the "female" gender role of mediation that is acknowledged. Not rights and respect but, instead, service to the patriarchal household and, by extension, to the state is the subtext here. Although the "male:public::female:private" equation has been roundly critiqued and dismantled by feminist theorists,[9] it nevertheless informs the dominant representation in Japan of men's and women's social spaces, and so it is in reference to this equation that I explore the sex-gender dynamics of the "family system."

The private/public distinction is usefully regarded as a "culturally constructed continuum which gives rise to different patterns of male power and control" (Brittan and Maynard 1984, 130). "Male power and control" refers to a man's potentially unlimited access to manifold public spheres of interest, as well as to a private household. Contrarily, the housebound married woman is triply circumscribed by the "female" gender roles of "mother," "housewife," and "wife," and their respective activities of childraising; cooking, cleaning, and washing; and sexual services. However complementary the private/female and public/male domains appear or are presumed to be, the actual relationship between the two domains is neither symmetrical nor equal. From a man's perspective, the continuum is continuous, but from a woman's perspective, it is discontinuous. A husband has the opportunity to take on domestic chores, but a wife cannot assume at will her husband's work, although the quality of her wifely role can affect the quality of his work and, by extension, the social standing of the household. The implication is that the work married women do in their homes is invisible and becomes apparent only when it is not completed or is managed improperly. It is only when something goes wrong with the system—increased incidences of school vandalism, drug abuse, juvenile delinquency, and so on—that the mediational role of wives and mothers is acknowledged (Atsumi 1988; Brittan and Maynard 1984, 131; *Japan Times*, 31 December 1983). Significantly, during his tenure, Mayor Ōshima attributed to women a greater capability than men to negotiate differences, and he asked various women's organizations to help mediate strained relations between natives and newcomers. As I pointed out in chapter 1, the gender ideology informing *furusato-zukuri* projects supports the practice of gender-role segregation, whereby married women, in the capacity of wives and mothers, are to nurture "old village" consciousness within their families.

Some of the female folkdancers represented another aspect of *furusato-zukuri* in Kodaira, that of "prefectural ethnicity." The Niigata women danced to their own tune, as it were, at the ninth citizens' festival, a reminder of the residents' diverse backgrounds and the we/they dichotomy at work. Their dance, the "Sado *okesa*," may be construed as a symbolic expression of their "ethnic" identity, the boundaries of which are drawn, for the sake of convenience, at the prefectural level. It is an expression that is at once condoned and moderated—condoned in the sense that the citizens' festival was designed as a forum for interpersonal exchange, and moderated in that the ultimate purpose of such commingling is the creation of Furusato Kodaira. The diverse ethnicities of nonnatives are celebrated not for their own sake but as resources to be assimilated and appropriated toward the task of *furusato-zukuri*. Along with native-newcomer, another dialectical relationship complicating the narrativity of the festival parade is Kodaira-prefecture ethnicity.[10] Thus, the female folkdancers qualified themselves as members of *Kodaira's* Niigata Prefectural Association.

The several prefectural associations in Kodaira were established in the 1970s by concerned "ethnics" as one expression of the localism accompanying the post–oil shock revaluation of regional folkways. Prefectural associations offer to newcomers what parishes and consociations offer to natives; namely, support and camaraderie. Although members of these associations come from different cities, towns, and villages within a given prefecture, it is from their position as Kodaira residents that the prefecture itself is regarded as a local place in common. Logistically, too, the prefecture is a desirable boundary. Many of the associations are involved in interprefectural trade and tourism, the efficiency of which would be hindered were ethnic boundaries drawn on a smaller scale.

Beginning with the first citizens' festival, stalls stocked with prefectural specialties have been set up in a "corner" devoted to "specialty shops of the prefectural associations."[11] As explained in the city newspaper, "The main theme of this first citizens' festival is: Let's build ourselves a *furusato*! Seizing the opportunity to mingle constructively and positively, members of the prefectural associations will perform regional dances and sell regional products" (*KSH*, 1 October 1976).

As Mayor Ōshima declared in a *Tōkyō shinbun* interview at the time, "Our plan is to build a unique *furusato* enriched by the local color of the prefectural associations." In that same article, the chair of the Fukui prefectural association proudly affirmed his pride in that prefecture and expressed a desire to "introduce the songs of Fukui packhorse drivers to all Kodaira residents." His gang of seven horse riders performed at the second citizens' festival, and he recalled thinking at the time, as the horses pranced up Akashia Road, "What a real *furusato*-style adventure it would be if the horses bolted!"

These are among the ways in which the affective compass of Furusato Kodaira is stretched to assimilate the different prefectures. The citizens' festival not only is an occasion to "intertwine 150,000 hearts" but also provides an opportunity to redraw affective boundaries—so that Kodaira ethnics can demonstrate their prefectural affinities without slighting their Kodaira identity. Although these affective boundaries transcend the city's administrative borders, the territory encompassed is none other than Furusato Kodaira.

One other ethnic participant in the citizens' festival since 1978 has been Obira, Kodaira's sister-city in Hokkaido. Obira, a town on the northwest coast of Hokkaido, briefly enjoyed the limelight in June 1984, when the hull of the *Taitō-maru* was discovered by salvagers. In 1945 the ship was sunk by an unidentified submarine while en route to Japan from Sakhalin with a cargo of seven hundred expatriates. Radio, television, and English newspaper reports of the discovery consistently referred to "Kodaira," and, indeed, local legend has it that sister-city relations between Kodaira and Obira were initiated because they share the same name characters.

The population of Obira, which became a town in 1978, has been declining steadily at a rate of about 10 percent a year; in April 1984, it totaled 6,163 persons. That same year, Obira's administrators came up with the slogan "Obira is where Kodaira's dreams can come true." Their intention was to make Obira the giant-sized backyard of Kodaira, and a program has been under way since the early 1980s to encourage their urban counterparts to invest in forestland named "Kodaira's/Obira's forest" (*Obira*, April–May 1984). This is only one of the many similar "*furusato* reforestation" schemes jointly implemented by urban and rural sister-cities throughout Japan.

A dearth of eligible women has prompted the young men of Obira to seek brides from Kodaira. In this connection, it was significant symbolically that during the ninth citizens' festival the Obira town flag was carried by a group of girl scouts. After all, eligible young women from Kodaira have been urged to wear the Obira colors, so to speak.

The executive committee's report on the 1983 festival notes that the Obira sales corner turned a several-million-yen profit. Although the report cites only the figures for Obira, the same success probably was not enjoyed by the prefectural associations, as hinted by a prefectural association member and a DSP assemblyperson, who remarked that the associations operated in the red but "did not expect to profit anyway, since profit mongering is contrary to a festival spirit" (*KGR*, December 1982, 239). It seems that, whereas the participation of Obira is acknowledged and supported officially, the presence of the prefectural associations is taken for granted, despite Mayor Ōshima's enthusiastic rhetoric during the first citizens' festival.

WESTERN-STYLE MARCHING BANDS

The novel "child" shrines ushered in the folkdancers in the first half of the festival; a Western-style parade preceded the "adult" shrines and opened the second half. Making their first appearance in the citizens' festival, the Konjō High School brass band led off the hour-long parade of marchers with the rousing tune of the "Kodaira Citizens' Festival Song."

Kodaira Citizens' Festival Song

Gather, everyone! Gather,
At the glorious festival site;
Even the blue sky is aglitter.
The Kodaira people's, the Kodaira people's;
The Kodaira people's joyful cheering.

Everyone is happy; linking arms,
Living peacefully—this merry site.
Flutes, and drums, and dancing too.
The Kodaira people's, the Kodaira people's;
The Kodaira people's footsteps ringing.

Dreams are big in Kodaira;
All of ours together, this festival site.
Hope is winging toward tomorrow.

The Kodaira people's, the Kodaira people's;
The Kodaira people's forward marching.

Music: Morikoshi Kazuko
Lyrics: Kodama Yukiko

The horn players, in their well-tailored red, white, and blue uni-
forms, were followed by a troop of boy scouts and their den fathers,
dressed for a jamboree. Equally well turned out were the four mounted
police officers on their huge, gleaming thoroughbreds. Next was
another boy scout troop, this one bearing the Kodaira flag, and behind
them the girl scouts, in baby-blue shifts and bobby sox, with the Obira
flag.

My favorites were a smart-stepping drill team who billed themselves,
enigmatically, as a "rhythm baton" and moved on down the road to a
peppy Beatles' medley. The coed troop of fifty, outfitted in tennis gear
and Stetson hats, had seemed more inspired the year before, when they
tittupped to the beat of the American rock song "Gimme Some Love."
Like the Niigata dancers, they came equipped with their own sound
system: two giant speakers mounted on the luggage rack of a Mitsu-
bishi van. They performed fifth in line, enlivening the rather tedious
string of boy and girl scout troops preceding and following them.

Next came the police officers' drum corps, the women dazzling in
their bone-white miniskirts and go-go boots, tricolors snapping in the
persistent Musashino breeze. Right behind them was the shiny red Nis-
san convertible carrying the mayors of Kodaira and Obira and the
speaker and chair of the city assembly. The Kodaira officials wore green
happi trimmed in blue, and the Obira mayor wore a blue one bordered
in green. In view of the constant and explicit symbolic counterpointing
throughout the citizens' festival—from its express theme of joining natives and newcomers, to the alternation of novel and "traditional"
performances—this color reversal clearly was intentional.

Sandwiched between the red car and a white convertible carrying
Miss Kodaira were a troop of cub scouts, a drum-and-fife corps from a
local elementary school, and the Kōsei Group's[12] cheerleading squad.
Miss Kodaira and her "court"—the former Miss Kodaira and the 1984
runner-up—were swathed in scarlet robes and wore crowns the size of
busbies (fig. 6). They were all smiles as they waved politely to the spectators. When a couple of young men yelled out, "Bijin da!" (Hey,
beauties!), the three women blushed and looked the other way. Meanwhile, I continued to ignore the constant "haro, haro" (hello, hello)
from the thronging children.

Fig. 6. Miss Kodaira and her "court." (Photo by author)

Behind the "royal coach" filed another large group of *kodairakko*: the traffic safety unit and the Young Misses, the latter a girls' club making its festival debut. The youngsters were followed by a squadron of Toyota sedans, adorned with pink and purple pom-poms, ferrying members of the Kodaira fathers' and mothers' associations. They exploited the publicity by broadcasting crime-prevention slogans, singling out in particular the vexatious motorcycle gangs (*bōsōzoku*) whose one thrill in life, it seems, is to roar through sleeping neighborhoods on mufflerless motorcycles.[13] Trailing behind the sedans was a "reformed" delinquent on a tame Honda 50 bedecked with paper flowers and balloons. The sign fixed to the back of his leather jacket read, "Banish motorcycle gangs."

The parade of more than one thousand marchers ended with a fleet of fire trucks rumbling down Akashia Road. Affixed to the ladder of the lead truck was a large golden globe. When the massive vehicle reached the festival headquarters, it stopped and its telescoping ladder was raised as high as it could go, whereupon the globe burst open, showering the delighted onlookers with confetti and rainbow streamers. Once the fire trucks had rumbled on, the crowds poured back into the street, using the intermission before the onset of the "adult" shrines to bargain and browse.

The image of cityhood extolled in the third segment of the parade is distinctly Western, in contradistinction to the preceding "child" shrines and folkdancers and to the "adult" shrines that follow. It is also a non-civilian image, given the dominating presence of the police force, crime-prevention associations, girl and boy scouts, and fire fighters. Only the participation of the Self-Defense Forces was missing, although their brass band had marched in the first several citizens' festivals. Two weeks earlier, the forces had held a festival to celebrate the thirtieth year of their Kodaira base. The highlight of this festival was a mock battle replete with percussion bombs and flamethrowers. Afterward, their appetites whetted, the youngsters among the spectators were treated to a display of heavy artillery, over which they clambered delightedly.

When Kodaira earned city status in 1962, the local headlines proclaimed that "Kodaira City is born!"—as though an entirely new entity suddenly had appeared. Awesome powers were imputed to the new suffix *shi* (city). The addition of *shi* to Kodaira meant that residents "could soon look forward to the best in welfare facilities, obstetric clinics, day-care centers, trash disposal, and water, sewage, and gas systems." Moreover, "only as a city can Kodaira begin to forge its own identity and spearhead development in the North Tama district" (*KCH*, 25 January 1962). The initial theme of cityhood was sloganized as "A city that must think of the future and not dwell on the past" (*KSH*, 1 October 1962). But by the mid-1970s, when the citizens' festival was inaugurated, the desirability of rooting the present and locating the future in a newly revalued and reclaimed past took precedence, as revealed by the festival's twofold theme of restoring *furusato* to Kodaira and Kodaira to *furusato* (*KSH*, 20 June 1976).

Cityhood officially was celebrated on 1 October 1962, with speeches by the home affairs minister and the governor of Tokyo. Later in the afternoon, a parade of fifty "float cars," led by the Air Self-Defense Force band, traveled the length of Oume Road, looping briefly to traverse, and thereby incorporate into cityhood, the other main, historical thoroughfares. This quasi-military celebration contrasted sharply with the ceremony marking townhood on 1 November 1944. Instead of a military band, the featured entertainment was "traditional" and included *manzai*, or witty dialogues; *ryōkyoku*, musical tales; *rakugo*, comic stories; and *kayōkyoku*, popular songs. It was, reportedly, "a peaceful day during a time of war" (*KC* 1959, 457).

From the start, then, the conceptualization of cityhood has been permeated with noncivilian and even military elements that have been carried over and incorporated into the citizens' festival parade. That the townhood ceremony was such a relaxed affair, and the cityhood celebration so formal and strictly coordinated, may be interpreted as follows. Townhood was granted during a tense period of national mobilization, to facilitate the dissemination and implementation of central authority (*KC* 1959, 543). Law and order were not problematic then; peace was, and "a peaceful day" is what the townhood ceremony offered. Cityhood, on the other hand, accompanied rapid population and industrial growth, and a resultant impersonal urban sprawl, to which was attributed "lawlessness," identified in the city newspaper as amphetamine abuse, high blood pressure, tardiness (i.e., "Kodaira Time"), juvenile delinquency, traffic violations, and environmental pollution. The new city was perceived as needing law and order. Thus, the citizens' festival parade—with its mounted police; fire trucks; multitude of obedient, uniformed girls and boys; crime-prevention and traffic-safety squads; and token, reformed juvenile delinquent—both epitomizes and promotes civil discipline and law-abidingness. Significantly, the "Kodaira Citizens' Festival Song," introduced at the seventh festival, contains no references to Kodaira's past but, rather, eulogizes the concepts of citizen (*shimin*) and public place (*hiroba*).

Finally, there is Miss Kodaira, the city's anthropomorphic emblem. Its logotypic emblem (fig. 7) was created in 1959.[14] Among other things, Miss Kodaira symbolizes Kodaira's spatial articulation with Tokyo metropolitan prefecture; for, after winning the city crown, she goes on to compete in the Miss Tokyo contest. She is the brainchild of the Chamber of Commerce, which sponsors the competition in co-

Fig. 7. Kodaira's logotypic emblem. The design is based on the two characters for Kodaira, 小 and 平.

operation with city hall and the *Tōkyō shinbun*. The first contest, held in October 1977, attracted seven contestants; by 1981 there were twenty-two aspirants. The young women, many of them students at prestigious Tsuda Women's College, and most—like newcomer residents in general—blithely ignorant about Kodaira, are "judged" on the basis of looks, character, and intelligence—in that order. In contrast to women's appearance at the more internationally renowned "cattle auctions," the Kodaira women pose in coordinated jogging outfits. During her year-long reign, Miss Kodaira is obliged to pay a visit to sister-city Obira, appear in the citizens' festival, and graciously host various city functions. Here too is evident the perception of females as diplomatic mediators.

That Miss Kodaira rides in a white car and the city officials in a red one is of some significance. Red and white are the standard colors of dynamic opposition in Japan, a convention popularly attributed to the protracted Genpei wars in the twelfth century, in which the ultimately victorious Genji clan fought under a white banner and the vanquished Taira under a red one. Thus, for example, the annual star-studded singing contest televised on New Year's Day is divided into red and white teams. In the context of citizens' festival rhetoric, the counterposition of red and white symbolizes not conflictive opposition but, rather, dynamic interaction—most prominently, that between the administration (red) and residents (white), on the one hand, and natives (red) and newcomers (white), on the other.

Dynamic interaction, in fact, was the much-evoked theme of the Ōshima administration, during which the citizens' festival was inaugurated. Soon after his election in 1967, Mayor Ōshima announced his intention to "govern in accord with the people's will." Toward this end, he created a "Letters to the Mayor" column in the city newspaper and convened regular meetings with members of the public. He also bicycled around Kodaira to observe firsthand the progress of utility and other municipal projects. Ōshima at one time even authored his own newspaper column, through which the former Chinese classics scholar imparted his hybrid "Confucian-progressive" political philosophy.

"ADULT" SHRINES

Last in the parade came the palanquin shrines shouldered boisterously by *tochikko* (fig. 8). The cavalcade of natives began with an *oharai*, or purification ritual, for which a local Shinto priest was

Fig. 8. An "adult" shrine. (Photo by author)

hired to wave a wand of *gohei* (folded strips of sacred white paper) in
front of the parked shrines. A similar ritual was conducted for the
"child" shrines. Performed at both the outset of the parade and prior to
the "adult" shrine procession, the *oharai* signified the "traditionality"
and "authenticity" of the citizens' festival and served as its chartering
enactment—signified but not sanctified; for the absence, as I will discuss, of Shinto deities from even the natives' portion of the festival
precluded the religious legitimation of the event. The civic legitimation
of the festival, on the other hand, was signified by the inclusion of city
officials riding high in a red convertible.

The natives' parade alternated between palanquin shrines and drums
(*taiko*) mounted on wheeled platforms. The drums served as figured
bass to the contrapuntal "wasshoi, wasshoi" (heave ho, heave ho) of the
shrine bearers. No shrill whistles and harried shouting here. Unlike the
preceding three processions, the native shrine bearers took an intermin-
able time wending up Akashia Road, mostly on account of the nature of
shrine bearing: one step forward, two backward, and ninety-seven side-
ways! Whether it was the great weight of the elaborate shrines, or the

bearers' inebriation, or both, the natives were the most expressive performers in the parade. The crowd loved the heaving, squashing, groaning, grimacing, laughing, carousing, yelling, and shoving. But the best was yet to come. Instead of melting, one by one, to a finish, the shrine bearers deliberately caused a crushing pileup, sending the delighted bystanders fleeing to the safety of the guardrailed sidewalk with the shrines in reckless pursuit. The spectators were thrilled by the display of festival mayhem (*matsuri sawagi*). This was more like a "really real" festival, raucous and rambunctious! As I groped my way out of the pulsing rush-hour throngs, I overheard one adventurous elderly woman exclaim, as she pushed and shoved and clutched indiscriminately, "You don't know whose hand you'll come out holding!"

The natives' shrines, as I have noted, are referred to as *otona mikoshi*, or "adult" shrines. They are not called such outside the context of the citizens' festival—the context necessitates the naming. The prefix *otona*, or adult, signifies both "real thingness" (as opposed to pink elephants and Mickey Mouse) and "native" (as opposed to newcomer). Adult newcomers may help shoulder only the "child" shrines. The portable "adult" shrines are the property of natives. Each one of the *taiko* and *mikoshi* is inscribed with the name of the parish or native coterie to which it belongs.[15] Lent by the natives to the city for a day, the giant drums and palanquin shrines imbued the ninth citizens' festival with verve, a "traditional" ambience, and sensorial authenticity.

"NEWCOMER" SHRINES

A *mikoshi* is the temporary abode of a given shrine's deity (*kami*), and in a shrine festival it is carried through the parish territory so that the mobilized deity may purify the area. ("Deity" is an inadequate but convenient translation of *kami*, the generic term for both ancestral spirits and the vital essence infusing animate and inanimate phenomena alike.) A given shrine's deity guards and blesses its own parish territory exclusively. Akashia Road is not included within a native parish; therefore, the "adult" shrines featured at the citizens' festival do not house a *shintai*, or *kami*-body. Similarly, the purification ritual at the outset only simulated the *oharai* performed at a Shinto shrine or in the presence of *kami* evoked for that ceremony.

Kodaira natives are aware of the deities' absence from the *mikoshi* and consequently refer to the citizens' festival as bereft of authenticity, the implication being that a "real" (shrine) festival is contingent upon a supernatural presence. One participant interviewed at a shrine festival remarked that "without *kamigakari*, festivals are no fun" (Matsudaira 1980, 98). (*Kamigakari* refers to both the process of becoming possessed by a *kami* and the individual possessed.) The same person also remarked that one "can't *kamigakari* at city hall–sponsored festivals" because the deity is not present. At the Kodaira citizens' festival, the countless cans of beer quaffed by the bearers at the two half-hour rest stops apparently compensated for the absence of *kami*. Historically, alcohol (*sake*) has been a standard feature at festivals, especially at the social gatherings following a *mikoshi* procession. City hall apparently had considered banning alcoholic beverages but realized that without beer the "adult" shrine procession in particular would lack the essential zest.

None of the dozen or so newcomers I queried at the 1984 citizens' festival were aware that the "adult" shrines were *kami*-less. Generally speaking, deities and shrine structures tend to be conflated in Japan, but in this instance a clear distinction was made between the two. This distinction was dispensed with altogether in a 1985 editorial in the *Asahi shinbun* (14 July) addressing the issue of portable shrines without *kami*. Evidently the popularity of shrine bearing in city festivals throughout Japan has created a demand by urban newcomers for *mikoshi* rentals, despite exorbitant rates ranging from 600,000 yen to 12 million yen for several days' use. (According to a recent advertisement, *mikoshi* kits are also available, enabling interested groups, as opposed to specialist carpenters, to construct their own shrine for about 53,000 yen [*Asahi shinbun*, 16 July 1986].) "We Japanese thrive on festivals," the editorial closes, "and so it is a good thing that rental shrines are available. Since the *kami* are invisible in traditional shrine festivals anyway, their absence from rental shrines does not diminish the joys of shouldering *mikoshi*."

Shrine kits and rentals signify not only the popular construction and commodification of "tradition" per se but also the virtual expropriation by city halls and newcomers of "traditions" hitherto maintained by exclusively local native parishes or coteries. It has been remarked, in fact, that "traditions" such as the making and carrying of *mikoshi* "henceforth will be perpetuated by all interested parties" (*Asahi shinbun*, 16 July 1987). In Kodaira the "adult" shrine segment of the parade is so popular that city hall is considering the feasibility of providing newcomers with a *mikoshi* of their own—possibly a rental—to shoulder in the annual citizens' festival. Should the administration follow through on this plan, city hall would, symbolically, approximate a shrine with a citywide parish consisting of newcomers. According to this logic, newcomers would be carrying the city's palanquin shrine, in a festival financed and managed by city hall, as an outward expression of their *kodairakko* identity and commitment to the making of Furusato Kodaira. This potential development bears similarity to the ancient concept of *saisei itchi*, or fusion of Shinto rites and government, revived by the Meiji government and maintained until 1945. Symbolically at least, a city hall *mikoshi* would be comparable to a confluence of creed and civic-mindedness. The public relations director[16] of the Kodaira citizens' festival mentioned that the controversial implications of this symbolism have figured largely in postponing the acquisition of a newcomers' *mikoshi*.

In Kodaira the natives' domination of the most "traditional" event in the citizens' festival was underscored by the participation as shrine bearers of natives from neighboring cities. (That they are indeed from outside Kodaira was evident from the place-names printed on the lapels and backs of their jackets.) Apparently the festival's organizers—a committee consisting of a majority of natives—did not perceive the presence of these outsiders as contradictory to the aim and purpose of the event, which was to "intertwine the hearts of 150,000 residents" and "make Kodaira a place newcomers can call *furusato*." The festival's public relations director, himself a *tochikko*, told me that outside natives are invited because the festival's organizers want to make sure that there will be enough (native) bodies to parade the *mikoshi* in a properly rambunctious style. Kodaira's newcomers are not regarded as suitable candidates for this task. The "adult"/"child" distinction between natives and newcomers pertains here as well in a figurative sense, suitability implying "adult" (native) status.

Evident as well is the natives' reluctance to share participation in "their" local practices. Parish exclusivity and even token religious activity—as in the case of the *kami*-less "adult" shrines—are the most effective means at their disposal for (re)defining their distinctive if diminished place within the city. Like the fire brigade incident over a decade earlier, the citizens' festival occasions the exposure, in high relief, of antinomy between natives and newcomers. Significantly, a fire brigade was included in the 1985 lineup to mark the tenth anniversary of the citizens' festival. The Kita-tama shōbō-mutsumi, an all-male native coterie from the northern part of Tokyo metropolitan prefecture, was hired to perform the acrobatic stunts historically associated with fire fighters. The team, which practices these stunts as a hobby, performed twice: before and after the Western-style marching bands. The public relations director explained that the acrobats deepened the "traditional" ambience and "authenticity" of the citizens' festival. But given the frictional exchange between natives and newcomers in the past over the issue of fire fighting, the presence of the fire brigade also symbolically deepened the divide between Kodaira's two main sectors.

Whatever civic camaraderie is occasioned by the festival is predicated not on the blurring of differences between natives and newcomers but on the display and recognition of those differences. The citizens' festival parade symbolizes the city's demographic topography. The signs and labels carried and worn by the performers ensure that each group is not abstracted from geography but, rather, is more precisely identified with a specific social sector and/or geographic location. *Tochikko* parishes and coteries are identified by inscribed drums and shrines; *kodairakko* associations and clubs, by the signs carried by children. What is emphasized in the parade is the social and status classification of each participating group. The official public relations media for the festival hint as much, for the image of civic camaraderie is one of "intertwined hearts," as opposed to "fused hearts" or other references to oneness. Administrators draw attention to Kodaira's native sector as a "living historical" culture, in an attempt to portray the bedroom town as a palatable "new *furusato*" for the newcomer majority, whose permanent residence is necessary for the city's socioeconomic stability. The hearts of 150,000 residents notwithstanding, the citizens' festival, and by extension Furusato Kodaira, is predicated on the dynamic interaction of the native and newcomer sectors.

Ceremonial Precedents and Legacies

A comparative review of the ill-fated townspeople's festival staged during the 1950s effectively illustrates the importance of both the *furusato* rhetoric and the native-newcomer antinomy motivating the citizens' festival. Articles in the town newspaper describe the townspeople's festival (*chōmin matsuri*) as plagued from the start by erratic planning and competitive strife. Dubbed the "first such event in Kodaira," the townspeople's festival was a tripartite affair divided into (1) a cultural exhibition, at which local historical materials were displayed along with the works of Kodaira's litterateurs and artists; (2) an industrial exhibition, featuring agricultural products and handbooks of farm household management; and (3) a sports meet. This last event, which I will focus on, most corresponds to the citizens' festival parade, while the the first two correspond to the various "corners" and exhibitions that impart a fairlike character to the citizens' festival as a whole. Held in November at a junior high school, the sports meet included track-and-field events and tugs-of-war between rival school teams, neighborhood associations, and groups of natives representing the Edo-period village divisions. Prior to the redistricting of Kodaira in 1962, the town's districts were based upon the internal organization of the original seven villages. Only Ogawa-*mura*, the oldest village, has retained its geographic integrity, as the new districts were simply superimposed upon the village's existing structures.

The sports meet apparently exacerbated a parochial conceit which ultimately undermined the pan-Kodaira identity that town hall had intended it to foster. In retrospect, it seems clear that the townspeople's festival lacked a powerful symbolic topos, such as *furusato-zukuri*. Also missing was the dynamic interaction of native and newcomer that motivated the citizens' festival. Kodaira's population in 1951, when the townspeople's festival was inaugurated, was one-sixth of that in 1976, when the citizens' festival got under way; and the town's internal boundaries still coincided with those of the seven villages. Farmers, who comprised 30 percent of the population in 1951, had yet to feel threatened by newcomers, whose entry peaked in 1963. By 1976 farm households made up only 2 percent of the population, and the rationalization of boundaries had significantly undermined the geographic basis for parochial rivalries. Instead, occasioned by the pervasive *furusato* rhetoric, nativeness itself emerged as a transcendent common identity, and its expression has become a means by which Kodaira's indigenes have attempted to control the circumstances of their minority existence.

One of the reasons given for terminating the townspeople's festival in 1954 actually served to forge a common identity among the native population. This was the central government's plan, launched nationwide in the fall of 1953, to merge small towns into larger administrative units. Kodaira and the neighboring towns of Koganei and Kokubunji were selected for amalgamation. The main obstacle to the proposed merger was the opposition of the agricultural sectors of Kodaira and Kokubunji, which organized a vociferous lobby and eventually succeeded in preventing the amalgamation. As described at the time, "the

planned merger fell through on account of the natives' town patriotism" (*KC* 1959, 689–95; *KCH*, 9 May 1954; *KHS*, 1 January 1981).
Although local patriotism today is condoned and praised as a virtuous
attitude, in the 1950s it was disparaged as "rustic conservatism," and
attention was drawn to the fact that all but the native (farm household)
sector were in favor of the amalgamation (*KCH*, 9 May 1954). Thus,
the merger dispute occasioned a crisis provoking Kodaira's natives to
mobilize and act in unison against those who favored the merger. The
consequent climate of divisiveness thwarted the resumption of the
townspeople's festival, and the we/they dichotomy between natives and
newcomers has persisted to the present day.

Conclusion: Toward Festival-Mindedness

Most but not all residents are as enthusiastic as city
hall about the citizens' festival. Among the criticisms of the annual
event uncovered in a 1982 survey published in the city newspaper was
the complaint that the event was "not all that it is made out to be;
namely, a festival for all to participate in" (*KSH*, 20 December 1982).
One respondent substantiated this charge by noting, "[My] neighbors
never talk about the citizens' festival and [I] only found out about
it through the city newspaper." Partly to encourage residents to talk
about the festival, city hall has included as a postfestival event an exhibition (at the central citizens' hall) of drawings and photographs of
the *shimin matsuri*. The drawings are by children who participated in
the "sketching corner," using paper and crayons provided by city hall.
The photographs are submitted by the city's amateur photographers,
and city hall staff members also make a video film of each year's citizens'
festival. Ideally, preparation for the exhibition, and for the *matsuri* as a
whole, and participation in both the exhibition and the *matsuri* deepen
the residents'—native and newcomer alike—sense of place by inducing
popular memories. The place ostensibly occasioned in this fashion is
Furusato Kodaira, a mnemonic landscape inhabited by harmonious
families and compatible neighbors.

City hall recognizes the potential of *matsuri* to occasion *furusato*-
mindedness and apparently is aware of the destructive capacity of festivals as well. Apart from natives' opposition and the *saisei itchi* implications, city administrators are reluctant to introduce a newcomers'

mikoshi because of the often dangerous rowdiness accompanying their presentation. As early as the eighth century, palanquin shrine bearing has been associated with protest riots, and in recent history "wasshoi, wasshoi" has been adopted as the chant of student and labor demonstrators. An incident at the 1976 Kobe festival illustrates the danger that can turn a *matsuri* into a tragic event. A newspaper photographer was killed in the mayhem that erupted at the *mikoshi* terminus. Youths from a Kobe gang, "who were looking for great outbursts of energy and experiences of mass elation," were held responsible for instigating the homicidal turmoil on that occasion (Inoue et al. 1979, 181). The *mikoshi* in the Kodaira citizens' festival are paraded by natives exclusively, whose raucous behavior is counterbalanced by their seniority, community responsibility, and local patriotism. Newcomers in general, on the other hand, are believed to lack these tempering attributes.

Although the *furusato* rhetoric enwreathing the citizens' festival is not unique to Kodaira, historical and contemporary circumstances have made *furusato-zukuri* a particularly cogent topos in that city. The reclamation of the original seven villages from barren land is cause for the celebration of the pioneering spirit of the first settlers and the encouragement of the second reclamation of Kodaira by postwar newcomers. The tenacity of the native sector, in the wake of the massive influx of newcomers since the 1950s, has enabled city hall to appropriate Kodaira's "living history" as part of its program to make the city a more palatable "new *furusato*" for newcomers.

There are other festivals held throughout the year in Kodaira, ranging from local shrine *matsuri* for parishioners to *chō* (district)-level festivals held at citizens' halls for, primarily, mothers and their children. Only the citizens' festival, however, is advertised as the affective core of Furusato Kodaira, a community constructed from the dynamic interaction of old and new, and perpetually in the making. Activities and ambiences that were formerly the province of natives alone are now administered by natives, albeit under the auspices of city hall, for the collective benefit of all Kodaira residents. In Kodaira City, the tenacity of the native sector in particular and the viability of *furusato* rhetoric in general have made possible the interdependence and the relative autonomy of natives and newcomers. This is precisely the sort of "new" community of and for which the Kodaira citizens' festival is a model.

In 1962, when Kodaira attained city status, all eyes were focused on the immediate present; Kodaira was envisioned as a modern city of high-rise buildings and paved roads. No one then would have guessed that less than twenty years later city hall and Kodaira residents would look nostalgically to the agrarian past in search of inspiration for an "authentic" community.

An exploration of the citizens' festival and the symbolic terrain of Furusato Kodaira provokes curiosity about how *shinden*-village society, from which their inspiration was drawn, was constructed and organized. That is the subject of chapter 3, which deals with "Kodaira's" beginnings in the seventeenth century as a cluster of newly reclaimed farm villages. A review of the area's historical patterns of settlement, moreover, will yield a deeper understanding of the present texture of the city and the basis for the postwar antinomy between natives and newcomers.

CHAPTER THREE

The Making of Kodaira

Community through Nomenclature

The proper object of history is not the past but the past-present-future relationship. Thus, it is under the auspices of *furusato-zukuri* that the land reclamation program engineered by the Tokugawa *bakufu* has become an absorbing subject of study in Kodaira. As I noted in the Introduction, this chapter has two related agendas. One is to analyze various remakings of "Kodaira's" past; the other is to construct from archival data a coherent literary portrait of the social, political, and economic circumstances of the Edo-period farm villages that were later amalgamated under the name Kodaira. Knowledge of the circumstances of both the *shinden* villages and the amalgamation of those villages as "Kodaira" contributes to the anthropology of Japan, but this knowledge also has been used by natives and by Kodaira City Hall.[1] The natives have used it for the purpose of revanchism, and city hall has used it to promote a "living history" within Kodaira.

The name Kodaira 小平, or "small plain," was coined in 1889 for the new "administrative village" created when seven *shinden* villages were amalgamated. They are Ogawa-*mura*—the oldest, founded in 1656— and Ogawa-*shinden*, Ōnumata-*shinden*, Suzuki-*shinden*, Nonaka-*shinden* (two villages), and Megurita-*shinden*, all founded in the mid-1700s (map 3). Nonaka-*shinden* was composed of three divisions (*kumi*). Two of them, Zenzaemon-*gumi* and Yoemon-*gumi*, were

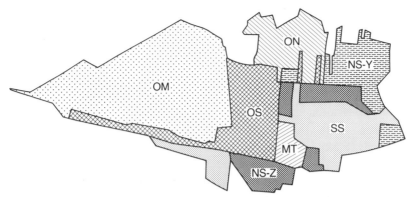

Map 3. The "Kodaira Seven" *shinden*. OM = Ogawa-*mura*; OS = Ogawa-*shinden*; ON = Ōnumata-*shinden*; NS-Y = Nonaka-*shinden* (Yoemon-*gumi*); NS-Z = Nonaka-*shinden* (Zenzaemon-*gumi*); SS = Suzuki-*shinden*; MT = Megurita-*shinden*. (Adapted from *KK* 1983, 80)

located within the boundaries of present-day Kodaira and were developed as independent villages. Delegates from each of these seven villages met to decide on an appropriate name for the new administrative village. They first considered the obvious name Shichiri, literally "seven villages," but eventually settled on Kodaira. *Ko* (the alternative Japanese-style reading for *o*) means "small" and was derived from the "o" in Ogawa(-*mura*). *Taira*, or "plain," was chosen in view of the Musashino area's flat topography (*KC* 1959, 403).

The very act of choosing and assigning place-names is a cogent means of generating "imagined communities" and particular solidarities. The term *imagined communities* was proposed in an "anthropological spirit" by Anderson (1983) to define nation-ness, nationality, and nationalism, which he further referred to as "cultural artefacts of a particular kind,"—lexicological, for example (ibid., 13–14, 101–2). To understand these and other such artifacts adequately, "we need to consider carefully how they have come into historical being, in what ways their meanings have changed over time and why, today, they command such profound emotional legitimacy" (ibid., 13–14).

"Imagined communities" characterizes both *shinden* village–making in the Edo period and the episodic making of Kodaira City, from the naming of the new administrative village in 1889 to Furusato Kodaira today. The name Kodaira has a peculiar kind of self-referentiality, because it enters into the very constitution of the community (cf. Searle

1984, 16). That is, a place-name is suggested by certain features and historical conditions just as it reconstitutes them under a systematizing rubric. What are the implications of the toponym Kodaira?

Ko was the prefix chosen in deference to the historical primacy of Ogawa-*mura*, which remains the city's most socially and geographically intact district. The integrity of this district also inheres in the fact that, of the seven amalgamated villages, its name alone was incorporated into the place-name Kodaira. By the same token, the administrative village of Kodaira acquired, through nomenclatural fiat, a historicity—Ogawa-*mura's*—that belied its newness and artifice. It is no wonder that Ogawa Kurobei (d. 1669), who first set about reclaiming the village he then named after himself, has since been proclaimed the civic ancestor of all Kodaira residents. As noted above, the suffix *taira* was selected in view of the area's flat topography, and much symbolic value subsequently was invested in this flatness. The area's undistinguished landscape corresponds to its desolation prior to Kurobei's reclamation project. There is a confluence of signification between *ko* and *taira* insofar as they both allude in a specific sense to the historical personage of Ogawa Kurobei and in a general sense to the *shinden* pioneers as a hardy breed of settler in a virtual wasteland.[2]

The implications of the name Kodaira are also evident in the preamble to the Kodaira citizens' charter, promulgated in 1972. Three years later, in 1975, the wording of this preamble was contested by one of the six, at the time, Clean Government Party (CGP) assemblypersons. The assemblyperson pointed out that, although it provided the "spiritual structure" for citizen participation, the preamble nevertheless was inaccurate and misleading. He charged that the area was neither uninhabitable nor uninhabited prior to Kurobei, inasmuch as paleolithic settlements were present up to 20,000 years before any *shinden* villages were reclaimed in the Edo period. Mayor Ōshima countered with the argument that the "modern historical development" of the area began with the reclamation of Ogawa-*mura*, which today is a source of spiritual inspiration for cooperative citizen participation. Therefore, "the wording of the preamble is suitable as is" (Ōshima in *KGR*, September 1975, 166, 168).

Ōshima's concern for historical accuracy was superseded by contemporary needs, the acknowledgment of paleolithic settlements not being among them. However, even efforts to publicize and popularize prereclamation history have served effectively to augment the imagination of a unique Kodaira. For example, in his various public lectures, Katō

Y., a Kodaira native and professor of archaeology at Kokugakuin University, draws attention to the uniqueness of "the city's" paleohistory. He emphasizes that nowhere in the world but Kodaira have so many "barbecued rocks" been found, his playful reference to the heated ferrous stones that the ancients had used for cooking purposes. Also, in one of the lectures making up the nine-week "*furusato* seminar" I attended, Katō referred to the paleohistorical inhabitants of the area as "'Kodaira Man,' a species of Cro-Magnon just like the one in Europe." This is not the occasion to challenge Katō's terminology; rather, his neologism illustrates the manner in which the area's ancient and more recent pasts alike have been assimilated under the rubric "Kodaira."

"Slogans and epithets are the materials out of which territorial sensitizing concepts are made" (Erickson 1980, 33). The place-name Kodaira, with its geohistorical reverberations, itself prompts these sloganized tributes to the *shinden* pioneers and the rigors of village-making. The citizens' charter (1977) of the neighboring city of Higashiyamato contains no reference to its sociohistorical legacy, apart from a reminder that it behooves citizens to learn about local history. Whereas both Kodaira charters refer to the city's historical "cultural landscape," the Higashiyamato charter dwells only on the physical environment: "Higashiyamato City is fortunate in being blessed with the natural beauty of Tama Lake and the forested hills of Sayama."[3]

A comparison of citizens' charters suggests that—among the twenty-six cities, five towns, and one village making up the Santama district—Kodaira is unique in drawing parallels and posing metaphorical links between the *shinden* village–making of the past and the *furusato-zukuri* of today.[4] The salient features of this *shinden*-based mythopoeia include pioneers and the intrepid pioneer spirit, the notion of social salvation through wasteland reclamation, local autonomy, and a hybrid philosophy of self-help and mutual aid.

Further explorations of the connections between yesterday's *shinden* village and today's Furusato Kodaira show that the analogies are reciprocal, for it is under the auspices of native place–making that village-making has become an absorbing subject of local historical study. The findings of these studies, moreover, have been appropriated in recent efforts to reclaim the "authentic" community presumed to have characterized the Edo-period *shinden* villages. Not only is the present-day city represented as a "natural" transformation of those villages, but the emphasis on authenticity has more to do with present-day needs than past realities.

The formation of Kodaira-*mura* itself has remained uncelebrated from the start. I offer the following explanation why. Through nomenclature, essentially two coexistent entities—two Kodairas—were created, one an amalgamation of seven villages, the other a symbiosis of Kodaira and Ogawa-*mura*. The name Kodaira effectively assimilated the historicity of Ogawa-*mura*: to commemorate Ogawa-*mura*'s reclamation is to be mindful of Kodaira's beginnings, and vice versa. Thus, one constantly encounters in city publications such anachronistic statements as "Kodaira's origins in 1656" and "Kodaira's pioneering ancestor, Kurobei" (*KGR* 1982, 16–17). By the same token, *Kyōdo Kodaira*, an abridged local history used as a city school text, devotes a quarter of the 120-page chapter on local history to Ogawa-*mura* (*Kyōdo Kodaira* henshū iinkai [1967] 1983). Kurobei's biography and the genealogy of the Ogawa household alone span eight pages. Moreover, Ogawa-*mura* features prominently in the sections dealing with *shinden*-village life and work. Neither the founders nor the beginnings of the other *shinden* villages similarly are observed as civic *causes célèbres*.

The lopsided relationship between Kodaira and its constituent *shinden* villages highlights and reinforces a palpable microlocal patriotism on the part of Ogawa-*mura* natives. To be sure, Kodaira natives as a whole comprise an integral, self-conscious society vis-à-vis the fractionated newcomer sector, but within the natives' society Ogawa indigenes perceive of themselves, and are perceived by others, as Kodaira's "really real" natives. The implications of this civic favoritism, as it were, ramify in a number of domains, from the geohistorical to the religious and politicoeconomic. Since religious creeds and consociations are the subject of chapter 4, and forms of neighborhood organization and association are discussed in chapter 5, my focus in this chapter is on the sociohistorical making and remaking of Kodaira, beginning with the reclamation in 1656 of Ogawa-*mura*.

Ogawa-*mura* and the Musashino *Shinden*

Kurobei, who initiated the reclamation of Ogawa-*mura*, hailed from Kishi-*mura* (Musashimurayama City). According to the 1668 and 1669 cadastral registers (*kenchichō*), Kishi-*mura* consisted of sixty-one households. The Ogawas were one of the eight households owning more than a hectare (about 3.5 hectares altogether) of dry field.

Fifty-three households owned less than one hectare of dry field, and thirty-five owned less than half that amount. Kurobei's *shinden* project was not included in the area surveyed. The relative affluence of the Ogawa household has been linked to its former status as a vassal of the (Odawara) Hōjō clan. The clan settled in the Kishi-*mura* area following its defeat in the protracted wars that culminated in the establishment of the Tokugawa *bakufu* in 1603. Local historians surmise that the Ogawas served the Hōjō until its downfall, whereupon they turned to agriculture. It remains unclear, however, whether the Ogawas were in fact bona fide samurai based in Kishi-*mura* and, if samurai, whether they later relinquished this status to pursue an agrarian livelihood (*KC* 1959, 36–38; *KK* 1983, 44–47; Onuki and Ōtani 1964).

Current members of the Ogawa *ie* (household),[5] as well as other Ogawa-*mura* natives, favor the prestigious samurai-origins thesis. For the Ogawas, samurai status differentiates their ancestors from the motley lot of destitute settlers who typified the *shinden* pioneers; for Kodaira natives, the samurai status of the Ogawas distinguishes Ogawa-*mura* from *shinden* founded by ordinary farmers and/or merchants. Kurobei nevertheless shared with his fellow pioneers the undistinguished status of younger sibling. The vast majority of male settlers were second and third sons, for whom land reclamation provided an opportunity to establish a branch household.

Ogawa-*mura* was originally conceived not as a farming village but as a post station (*shuku*). Located along Oume Road, a major east-west thoroughfare widened and repaired in 1596, Ogawa-*juku*—as the village was named in woodblock prints of the "famous views of Edo" genre—serviced the needs of travelers and traders. Kurobei himself reputedly was involved in the lime trade, the transport of lime and kaolin to Edo being a major reason for the repair of Oume Road. Vast quantities of these natural resources were needed for the construction and maintenance of Edo castle and the city residences of the military elite. They were transported by a post-horse relay system developed by the *bakufu* (Yamamoto 1984, 18–20). It was an efficient operation save for one drawback: the absence of an intermediate post station along a desolate stretch of Oume Road. In 1656—after the completion of the Tamagawa and Nobidome canals, which provided potable water—Kurobei petitioned the local magistrate (*daikan*) for permission to reclaim the barren stretch of grassland. His ostensible purpose was to establish an intermediate post station; agriculture was, at the outset at least, a secondary objective. The following year, the elder councilor (*rōjū*) granted Kurobei official permission to reclaim a swath of land, bisected by Oume Road, extending from the Tamagawa and Nobi-dome watersheds in the west to Tanashi in the east. The eventual eastern border of the new village, however, was much shorter.

Geography assumed a major role in the reclamation of Ogawa-*mura*; for, apart from the need for a post station, the aridity of the land prompted the *bakufu*'s favorable response to Kurobei's petition, since his development project would not exacerbate the chronic depletion of the flora necessary to make compost, the primary fertilizer used at the time. An overview of the *bakufu*'s *shinden* policy provides some necessary background about the beginnings of Kodaira's native sector.

Apart from the truism that virtually all fields and paddies begin as reclaimed land, *shinden* is used here in a narrower sociohistorical sense to refer to paddies and dry fields reclaimed during the Edo period, often in conjunction with village-making, as was the case in the Musashino region (Furushima 1975, 213).[6] The *bakufu* pursued an active *shinden* policy from the start, and by the 1660s much of the most accessible land (i.e., upland, riverbeds, coastland) in the Kansai and Kanto regions had been reclaimed. The less accessible Musashino area remained untouched. One counterproductive consequence of this program was the depletion of wild grasses and foliage utilized as a natural fertilizer, for until the eventual shift to commercial fertilizers (oil cakes, dried sardines) and cash crops (cotton, tobacco) in the early nineteenth century, compost was widely used. To offset the existing damage, the *bakufu* discontinued its *shinden* policy and instead encouraged the reclamation of fallow paddies. At the same time, projects such as the reforestation of denuded riverbanks and the construction of dikes were initiated to prevent silting and flooding. Between 1600 and 1867, 997 farms were reclaimed, although the percentage of those that included the establishment of a village is not known (Kimura 1964, 5). However, since the presence of a village increased the tax base, it is likely that most *shinden* projects included, eventually if not at the outset, a village-making component.

By the early eighteenth century, land reclamation, perceived as an expedient means of increasing the tax base, once again was actively encouraged. This time, the least accessible land was targeted for reclamation. An advertisement for *shinden* investors and settlers was drawn up in 1722 and posted in Nihonbashi, in the heart of Edo. The response apparently was enthusiastic. Within twelve years, seventy-eight new villages were established in Musashino alone—the proverbial Musashino *shinden*—including the villages that eventually were merged to form Kodaira.[7] This was twice the number of Musashino villages that were reclaimed during the entire seventeenth century (Kimura and Itō 1972, 31). According to a 1739 cadastral register (based on a 1736 survey), roughly 1,327 households were established in these villages, 407 of them in "Kodaira," which also boasted the *shinden* village with the largest number of households: Suzuki-*shinden*, with its 123 settler families, followed by Ogawa-*shinden*, with 89. Twenty-eight of the new villages contained five or fewer households (*KC* 1959, 101).

The Musashino *shinden* project represents a major reorientation of the *bakufu*'s agrarian policy, for the object of this second reclamation campaign was not the usual paddy land but, rather, dry fields, which became an important source of taxes from approximately the eighteenth century onward.[8] Until this time, taxation was virtually synonymous with paddy (Furushima 1975, 238–72; Kimura 1964, 6; Kimura and Itō 1972, 14–15). In 1726 the government drew up a proviso for subsequent land registration surveys (in the Kanto region), in which the following categories of arable land were defined: *honden*, or old paddies/fields (land reclaimed prior to 1687); *koshinden*, or old *shinden* (land reclaimed between 1688 and 1716); and *shinden* (land reclaimed after 1716). According to this scheme, Ogawa-*mura* belonged to the second category, and the other "Kodaira" villages to the third. The suffix *shinden* eventually was dropped from the names of villages belonging to the second category, in order to distinguish them from those established after 1716 (Matsuyoshi [1933] 1955, 2, 10–20). Thus, the Ogawa-*shinden* reclaimed in 1656 came to be called Ogawa-*mura*.

In further contrast to *shinden* and *koshinden*, *honden* referred to land taxed on the basis of an estimated yield (*kokudaka*), which in turn was assessed through land registration surveys (*kenchi*) conducted on a countrywide scale between 1596 and 1673 (Kimura 1964, 2). *Shinden* similarly were assessed as their reclamation proceeded, although they generally were taxed at lower rates. Furthermore, *shinden* settlers were guaranteed a tax holiday known as *kuwashita nenki*, or "period under plow," for a period of several years.

Although Ogawa-*mura* was not one of the seventy-eight proverbial Musashino *shinden* (its offshoot, Ogawa-*shinden*, was), it nonetheless was a *shinden* village in Musashino and, like the others, was characterized by an absence of paddies. It was also a meticulously planned village, one imprinted with Kurobei's signature. The following account of the making of Ogawa-*mura* dwells primarily on recruitment and settlement procedures, and household and community composition and organization.

Making Ogawa-*mura*

Even before receiving *bakufu* consent, Kurobei set about recruiting personnel to the site. Would-be homesteaders had to petition him for permission to stake a claim in the new settlement. The petition was to be submitted by the aspiring homesteader's guarantor, usually a village head. It seems that Ogawa-*mura* was exceptional in requiring petitions; in most instances, would-be settlers simply purchased or rented *shinden*—a procedure "not unlike a real estate venture" (Katayama 1959, 188). Petitions served as a means of screening settlers. Kurobei also reserved the right to evict troublemakers, although whether he did so for the sake of the nascent community or with his own interests in mind is debatable.

Many of these petitions are extant, and my abridged translation of one of them, submitted in 1656 by the head of a village in the Oume region, illustrates the selective and strictly supervised nature of Kurobei's recruitment procedures.

> Point: These two men who wish to immigrate to Ogawa-*shinden* [i.e., Ogawa-*mura*] are upright and honest. However, should they break the law or misbehave, this guarantor will assume all responsibility.
> Point: These conscientious men are not given to complaining, but in the unlikely event that they should enter a protest, this guarantor will assume all responsibility.
> Point: Once granted a site, these men will immigrate upon notification from you. Should they by chance renege, this guarantor will force them to immigrate and assume the responsibility of building their house.
> Point: In view of the fact that this is a post station, these men are horse owners and surely will agree to work on behalf of *bakufu* or village officials. Should they refuse, you are entitled to evict them from the village.
> Point: These men are not Christians.[9] (*KC* 1959, 49–51)

Forty-seven aspiring settlers, all males, submitted petitions in 1656. Within a decade, their number had more than doubled, after which the number of petitions submitted slowed to an annual average of one homesteader. Settlement petitions were discontinued after 1680, ostensibly because the village's demographic profile and social structure had stabilized, although the number of settlers continued to fluctuate (*KC* 1959, 55).

Kurobei was not alone in selectively recruiting settlers. In a *shinden* village—making manifesto written in 1795, the author recommends the recruitment of "honest and diligent workers, for if the first settlers are disreputable, then the others who follow will be adversely affected" (Yoshida [1795] 1979, 128). In *shinden* where petition-based recruitment was not practiced, other means of social engineering were employed. Shingaku (Heart Learning) colleges, for example, were established in several *shinden* villages, such as Arakawa-*mura* in Kai province and Higashitsuge-*mura* in Iga province.[10] Village life was organized around the colleges. During the tedious months of land reclamation, Shingaku teachers would continuously recite humorous but edifying parables to foster in settlers a positive attitude toward the grueling labor (Ishikawa 1964, 132; Robertson 1979, 1984b, 1991).

Since Ogawa-*mura* was in an unattractive location, Kurobei solicited settlers by negotiating, on their behalf, post-horse relay contracts with seven nearby villages. He also guaranteed them a share of the nearly six hectares of tax-exempt land reserved for homesteads (*KC* 1959, 47). Many of the petitioners were from lime- and kaolin-producing villages in the Oume area, although there were also immigrants from the Kishi-*mura* area and a significant number from Iruma district in the north (ibid., 49). The immigration of male settlers proceeded eastward and southward from villages in the western and northern reaches of Musashino. None of the petitioners were from the south, and only two immigrated from the east (ibid.).

The same pattern of demographic mobility pertained to the females of settler couples. Most were from villages in the west and north. The sexist rationale given by male settlers for preferring northern brides was that, coming from poorer, non-paddy-farm villages, these women were less likely to complain about a coarse diet and more likely to be hard workers. The voices of female settlers are conspicuously absent from the historical and contemporary literature on *shinden*. Paddy-producing villages were regarded as higher in social status, and paddy farmers, predictably, were unwilling to relocate to dry-field *shinden* (Katayama 1959, 170–71; *KC* 1959, 1187–89; *TKSS* 1969, 1244). The male and female immigrants to Ogawa-*mura* thus tended to be from lower-status villages in west and north Kanto.

It is not clear how many of those who petitioned to immigrate actually did so. According to the existing data, a little over half of the

Table 1. *Ogawa*-mura *Settlers*

Year	No. of Petitions (Totals to Date)		No. of Households	No. of Persons
1656	47			
1657	11			
1658	10	(68)	76	266*
1661	4			
1662	11			
1663	2			
1664	10	(95)	104	364*
1665	7			
1666	1			
1669		(103)	96	336*
1670	4			
1671	1			
1673	1			
1674	1			
1675	3			
1677	1			
1680	1	(115)		
1700			214*	983
1713			205	908
1720			200	888
1734			192	923

NOTE: Figures with an asterisk are my estimates. Other figures are taken from land registers and various primary sources. Figures for extant petitions are from *Kodaira chōshi* 1959, 48. Population figures are from *Kodaira chōshi* 1959, 50, 53–54, 68, 204. The estimated average number of persons per household up to, roughly, the eighteenth century is 3.5, increasing to 4.5 by 1713 through 1845, when the average increases to 5.5, and again to 6.5 by 1857 (ibid., 177), which was also the average for 1980 (*Sekai nōringyō sensasu: Kodaira* 1980, 63).

would-be homesteaders for the period 1656–1680 submitted their petitions within the first two years of Kurobei's recruitment drive (table 1). Since the number of petitioners does not correlate with the corresponding population figures, I surmise that not all the petitioners immigrated or that not all the petitions and petitioners are accounted for. Settlers from Kishi-*mura* probably were exempt from petitioning, since their backgrounds would have been known, although it is not clear how many homesteaders came from there.

The actual number of both applicants and settlers probably was significantly higher. Apart from the recorded figures, this likelihood is indicated by a 1662 petition, submitted to the local magistrate by disgruntled farmers in defiance of their *shinden* contract, in which is mentioned the ruination of 64 settler households: "the wives and children were sold as slaves in Edo and its environs, while the husbands took to vagrancy" (*KC* 1959, 58). It is not clear from this document whether these settlers absconded or were evicted by Kurobei. Given the existing data, their departure translates as a 78 percent population loss, which seems far too extensive under the circumstances. On the basis of the 1658 and 1664 figures, I estimated that the extant petitions amount to about 90 percent of the total submitted. Population estimates for 1658 derive from a petition of protest signed by 76 Ogawa-*mura* households at that time (*KC* 1959, 50). The 1664 land register accounts for 104 homesteads (ibid., 53), although only 95 petitions (90 percent) are extant. Perhaps the remaining 10 percent were immigrants from Kishi-*mura*. Finally, the gap between petitioners and homesteaders may also be explained in part by a significant number of settlers who either absconded or were evicted from the village soon after their arrival, as suggested by the 1662 petition cited above. The population of Ogawa-*mura* grew incrementally from 1713 to 1802, when it leveled off at 220 households (1,018 persons), which is the same number of households accounted for in 1857 (ibid., 177, 205). What the data show clearly is that Ogawa-*mura* attracted a relatively large number of settlers from the outset.

Ogawa-*mura* was reclaimed only after the completion of the Tamagawa canal, which ensured a dependable supply of potable water. Kurobei also secured a supplementary livelihood for the settlers: posthorse contracts with seven villages for the transportation of lime and kaolin to Edo. In addition, by relying on his own funds and network of contacts, he began selectively recruiting settlers before he received official permission to start his reclamation project. Indeed, it was Kurobei's consequent sense of proprietorship of land and settler alike that triggered the 1662 disturbance. It is also important to note that Kurobei himself had established a branch household on the *shinden* at the time of its reclamation. As village head, Kurobei was able to comprehensively engineer and supervise the making of Ogawa-*mura*.

The style in which Kurobei imagined the new community was autocratic. Ogawa-*mura*—apart from being his private domain, "bequeathed by the *bakufu*," as he maintained—was also his "gift" to the sorry lot of destitute farmers and younger sons (Kimura and Itō 1972, 69–70; *Sunagawa no rekishi* 1963, 23). In return, Kurobei expected certain "favors" from the homesteaders: compulsory "thank-money" of three *mon* per *tan* (about ten ares) of dry field and an additional charge of three *shō* (5.4 liters) of rice, to be paid through the settlers' grand-children's generation (*KC* 1959, 50–52). The imposition of these fees, neither of which was a standard practice, demonstrates Kurobei's autocratic tendencies. As early as 1658, seventy-six settlers submitted a signed statement to Kurobei protesting these fees. And in 1662, just five years after the village was founded, nine persons representing the settlers as a whole submitted to him a petition in which they listed their complaints about his actions as village head.

The contents of the 1662 petition, my abridged translation of which appears below, partially reveal the extent of Kurobei's despotic exercise of authority.

> Point: Since 1659, the settlers have not received even one *mon* from Kurobei [of the hundreds owed them] in payment for their post-horse ser-vices.
>
> Point: Money from the local magistrate intended for the settlers in re-muneration for post-horse services rendered him has been entirely con-fiscated by Kurobei.
>
> Point: In 1656, the *bakufu* granted the settlers an emergency fund of 100 *ryō*, of which Kurobei distributed only 54 *ryō*. The remaining 46 *ryō* he claimed as his own funds, which he then lent to the settlers at interest. Since the money originally was intended for the settlers, they deserve repayment of a total sum of 48 *ryō*.
>
> Point: Whenever Kurobei makes a round trip to Edo, eight farmers are obliged to transport him by palanquin all the way to Tanashi, regardless of whether it is raining and the roads are muddy. This is unforgivable!
>
> Point: Daily for the past five years, four farmers have been forced like slaves to perform odd jobs for Kurobei, such as cleaning the stalls and cut-ting the grass at his residence.
>
> Point: Sixty-four households have fallen into ruination—wives and chil-dren have been sold as slaves and the husbands have taken to vagrancy. Their abandoned houses have been sold at a profit by Kurobei.
>
> Point: Kurobei has divided unfairly the profits accrued from the sale of melons to Edo. (*KC* 1959, 57–58)

Although the specific details of the case are not available, the dispute was mediated by two temples, Shōsen-*ji* and Myōhō-*ji*, established in Ogawa-*mura* at the time of its reclamation. The corvée seems to have been discontinued, for it is not among the complaints listed in a 1677 petition protesting actions by the village head. However, the disgruntled settlers had to submit a statement to the effect that they would not cause any further disturbances (Kimura 1964, 121–23). By installing these two temples (which are discussed more specifically in chapter 4), along with two shrines at the outset of village-making, Kurobei effectively extended his control over the internal affairs of the new village. Long after the Ogawa household's politicoeconomic monopoly had loosened, temples and shrines retained their social centrality and today form the core of the native sector.

Whereas Kurobei's despotic style was not appreciated by the pioneering settlers, today he is honored as the civic ancestor of all Kodaira residents. The very character traits that so enraged the Edo-period farmers are now lauded in local-history texts as those of a self-made man. Nostalgic reappraisals of Kodaira's *shinden* past have cast the notorious Kurobei in a heroic light, while the immigrants are relegated to the shadows. In an article titled "The Peculiar Characteristics of the Ogawas," a local historian writes that Kurobei was widely known for his savoir faire throughout the Musashino region and that the Ogawas consistently have been paid the highest respect accorded to village heads. Evidence for the latter claim is based on the scale of their entranceway (*genkan*) alone, "which may be compared to that of a samurai lord" (Itō 1961, 46). Entranceways were key symbols of authority and conceit among the Edo-period elite. Thus, in 1710 an Ogawa-*mura* villager was punished for having erected an entranceway much too fancy for his lowly kind (*KC* 1959, 77). The Ogawa entranceway was declared an "invaluable cultural property" and restored by the city in 1976, the year the citizens' festival was inaugurated. By glamorizing the Ogawa entranceway, the local historian and city hall have further contributed to *shinden* mythopoeia.

Despite their professed desire to "detail as accurately as possible the circumstances and particulars of the making of Ogawa-*mura*, since the village marks the beginning of what is today Kodaira," the editors of the *Kodaira chōshi* (Local history of Kodaira, 1959) nevertheless have glossed over incidents of antinomy between the farmers and the village head. Perhaps to compensate, they occasionally remind the reader that "it was the sweat and toil of the farmers that made Ogawa-*mura* into such an outstanding village" (*KC* 1959, 63, 67). Although I use the *Kodaira chōshi* in constructing my portrait of early "Kodaira," I also make problematic this text and its designs. Plans to create a local-history book were formalized soon after the town-merger campaign failed on account of farm householders' local patriotism. The explicit objective of the planners was to consolidate a Kodaira-specific identity and to nurture a local-place consciousness, although the implicit objective was to rectify the image of Kodaira natives. Significantly, the project was hatched when Ogawa A., a descendant of Kurobei, provided a historian with Ogawa household documents (*KC* 1959, 1373–79).[11]

The editors of the *Kodaira chōshi* claim that the comparatively rapid development of Ogawa-*mura* and the anti-village-head protests that occurred soon after its founding were related to the *honbyakushō*, or titled-farmer, system inaugurated by the *bakufu* in the seventeenth century. The idea was to expand the tax base by reducing the number of untitled, small-scale landholders and the landless and, concomitantly, increasing the numbers of self-sufficient landholders through such means as *shinden* reclamation. The titled-farmer system was in fact more evident in *shinden* villages proper than in old villages whose arable land was increased through reclamation (*KC* 1959, 31, 53–54, 176).

Settling Ogawa-*mura*

A feature of the nascent Ogawa-*mura* that, according to local historians and Kodaira natives, accounts for the configuration and integrity of the natives' society today was the allegedly equal distribution of *shinden* parcels. Kurobei is said to have distributed the parcels in an "egalitarian" fashion; the width of a homestead had nothing to do with a settler's relative status, for a broad frontage indicated a shallow parcel and a narrow frontage a deep parcel. Consequently, Ogawa-*mura* is trumpeted in the local literature as having been a promised land of equal opportunity. However, the following cadastral register figures all but erode this claim, making it difficult to believe that the homesteads actually were distributed equally from the outset.

As I noted earlier, Kurobei purportedly offered prospective immigrants a parcel of tax-exempt land. This was the *yashikichi*, or homestead, the size of which averaged 18 meters across and 45 meters deep. The parcels were aligned along either side of Oume Road, on which they fronted. Each homestead came with a house and several auxiliary buildings, a small service canal (i.e., the Ogawa branch canal, completed in 1657), and a windbreak. Behind each homestead, and just as wide, stretched a long plot of farmland divided into several sections according to arability. These generally included a swath of *gebata*, or low-grade field, 90.5 meters deep, and, behind that, two successive 181-meter

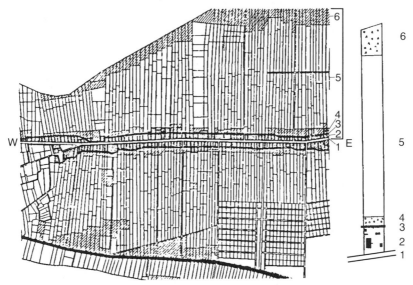

Fig. 9. The ideal-type *shinden* parcel. 1 = Oume Road; 2 = homestead and house; 3 = Ogawa branch canal; 4 = windbreak; 5 = fields; 6 = forest. The Ogawa branch canal encircles the Ogawa-*mura* homesteads. (Adapted from Yamamoto 1984, 35)

strips of *gegebata*, or low-low-grade field, ending in a stand of shrubs and trees. The entire parcel amounted to nearly one hectare (*KC* 1959, 64–65). Such a parcel constituted an ideal-type homestead and its attached farmland in the nascent Ogawa-*mura* (fig. 9). According to the 1669 cadastral register, the village comprised 106 *shinden* parcels, the smallest measuring about 14 meters across and the largest about 127 meters; the majority (59 parcels) measured 18 meters across.[12]

The number of homesteads owned by individual villagers similarly varied. According to the 1669 land register, seventy-eight settlers each owned one homestead; thirteen settlers owned two or more homesteads (Kurobei alone owned six); and five settlers had no homestead of their own. Virtually nothing is known about the situation of these "homeless" homesteaders. One possibility is that they were among the *shinden* landholders known as *mochizoe*, or holders of detached land. Some *shinden*, such as Megurita originally, were known as *mochizoe shinden*, since they were worked not by resident farmers but by commuters from, usually, the "parent" village. Ogawa-*mura*, however, was not within commuting distance from Kishi-*mura*. Another possibility is that they may have been agricultural servants (*genin*). From 1650 to 1700, ten such servants were contracted to work in Ogawa-*mura* for a period ranging from one to ten years, and the Ogawa household alone consistently employed from three to five servants (*KC* 1959, 178).

A plot of residential land is not the same as a residence, and thus the question of dwellings arises. Among the Ogawa household documents is a letter from Kurobei to the local magistrate, detailing the types of houses scheduled for construction on each homestead. Plans were submitted for houses for two, four to five, and six persons, with floor plans measuring 6.4 by 3.6 meters, 8.2 by 4.6 meters, and 9 by 5.5 meters. All three types were bordered on the south and east sides by a meter-wide veranda, and all three consisted of, basically, two rooms: one floored in either bamboo slats or rice husks covered with straw matting, and the other in stamped earth. Walls were fashioned of straw, and material for the supporting poles was limited to chestnut. The roof was thatched with miscanthus (*kaya*) (*KC* 1989, 87–89; Yamamoto 1984, 35–36). Kurobei's comparatively palatial residence stood in marked contrast to these minuscule huts—his entranceway alone was 3.6 by 1.5 meters (Ishihara 1964, 9). Precise details about the original house are not available, but it probably was at least nine times larger than the settlers' huts (Ishihara 1964, 6).

Since the huts were designed for two, four to five, or six persons, we may assume that these figures reflect the composition of settler households, although in what proportion is not known. The average size of a newly settled household is estimated to have been between three and four persons, two of whom presumably were a married couple. A newly established branch household probably consisted of a married couple without children (cf. Ogawa 1983).

Generally speaking, immigration to a *shinden* village offered younger sons from households of limited means an opportunity to strike out on their own, free from the encumbrances of an intra-*ie* hierarchy. This was especially true of *shinden*, such as Ogawa-*mura*, that were not off-shoots of a parent village but were founded as villages in their own right. At the same time, however, the immigration of a branch household, despite its economic independence, constituted a means by which an *ie* could perpetuate itself, for the continuity of the *ie* transcended the constraints of an intra-*ie* hierarchy (cf. Kimura and Itō 1972, 120).

Within Ogawa-*mura*, homesteaders were organized as *chien shūdan*, or place-linked groups. The peculiar conditions of Ogawa-*mura* in particular, and the Musashino *shinden* in general, either discouraged or made unnecessary the so-called *kyōdōtai* system of communal landholding and labor (Itō 1966, 77, 81–82; Kimura and Itō 1972, 219). Although the term literally means "common body," *kyōdōtai* is a chameleonic sociological term, for its meaning depends on the persuasion of the user. Localists such as social historian Daikichi Irokawa regard *kyōdōtai* as "the historical basis of Japanese culture and society" and see in it the operation of democratic procedures and horizontal social relations (Irokawa 1973). Others, such as political scientist Masao Maruyama, insist that the operations of *kyōdōtai* preclude democratic procedures and circumvent horizontal relations (Maruyama 1969, 25–83). *Shinden* scholars tend not to treat *kyōdōtai* as a synonym for village community, and suggest instead that it denotes a type of agriculture characterized by communal property and water regulation, together with compulsory cooperation for their maintenance. According to this view, the prototypical *kyōdōtai*, or communal corps, is the wet-rice-cultivating village, although the term has been used more diffusely to describe communal relations in fishing and forestry villages as well.

Kyōdōtai most commonly is used in reference to, and conjures up the image of, paddy fields, the complicated irrigation and labor-intensive cultivation of which has allegedly "created a very special form of rural, human organization" (Irokawa 1973, 80). As a popular term, *kyōdōtai* is fetishistic, for it is invoked, often nostalgically, as the "authentic" Japanese rural community, the implication being that farm villages inherently are cooperative. It thus connotes a pristine moral society, the resurrection and revalorization of which is the ultimate objective of *furusato-zukuri* campaigns today. An official at Kodaira City Hall remarked that *kyōdōtai*, "as a feature of wet-rice agricultural life," was purposely selected and adapted as a cogent *furusato-zukuri* motif. The irony is that such rural imagery was stimulated not by the historical reality of Kodaira's agrarian past but by the recent imagination of a community of paddy farmers.

What were some of the features of Ogawa-*mura* in particular, and the Musashino *shinden* in general? Itō (1966) has described three main features.

First, these *shinden* contained "relatively large" landholdings, each managed by a single household. The large size of landholdings in Ogawa-*mura* is attributed to the poor quality of soil and consequent low productivity; quantity, in other words, took the place of quality (*KC* 1959, 54) (table 2).

Second, there was a "rational" distribution of arable land. In Ogawa-

Table 2. *Reclaimed Land in Ogawa*-mura

	Low Grade	Low-Low Grade	Homestead
1664			
total	23 ha	59 ha	9 ha
tilled	20 (87%)	36 (61%)	8.1 (90%)
fallow	3 (13%)	23 (39%)	0.9 (10%)
1669			
total	27 ha	142 ha	13 ha
tilled	25 (93%)	85 (60%)	13 (100%)
fallow	2 (7%)	57 (40%)	0

NOTE: The data show that the majority of reclaimed land was low-low grade, a status determined by its relative arability (Kimura and Itō 1972, 330, 332). Low-grade land, however, was tilled more intensively.

mura, land distribution was rational insofar as the rectangular parcels were contiguously aligned along Oume Road, each with direct access to potable water. Kishi-*mura*, in contrast, was a cluster of farmhouses sandwiched between the Sayama Hills and a wide swath of tilled fields (map 4). Ogawa-*mura*, in short, did not conform to the ideal-type portrait of Edo-period villages comprised of scattered landholdings.

Third, the unfertile, loamy soil of the Musashino region necessitated the liberal use of commercial fertilizers. In addition to the rice chaff, ash, and night soil that they purchased, Ogawa-*mura* villagers utilized barnyard manure and compost made from herbage. Commercial fertilizers, especially rice chaff, increasingly were relied on as the advancing reclamation work reduced the amount of grassland. By the late eighteenth century, the high price of rice chaff created serious and perennial problems that remained unresolved through the end of the Edo period (*KC* 1959, 71, 182, 269–70, 278–84).

In Ogawa-*mura*, as in the Musashino *shinden* at large, there was no "common property" (*iriaichi*) on which the villagers foraged for compost material. Forage land, formally referred to as "forest field" (*hayashibata*), was individually owned, comprising as it did the lower portion of each homestead (Itō 1966, 81–82; Kimura and Itō 1972, 133, 140–42).

Itō does not include water use and control among his conditions, but the topic is relevant to this discussion. As noted earlier, *kyōdōtai* (communal corps) connotes a style of social organization based on the

Kishi-*mura*

Sayama Hills

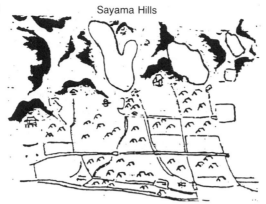

Ogawa-*mura*

Hie-*jinja*

Tamagawa Canal

Nobidome Canal

Oume Road

Shōsen-*ji*

Shinmei-*gū*

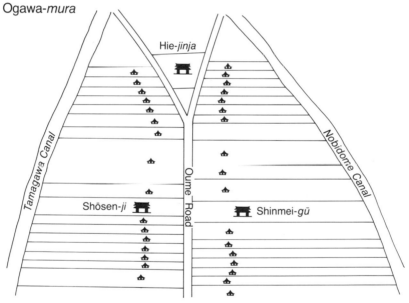

Map 4. Kishi-*mura* (1660s) and Ogawa-*mura* (1690s). Kishi-*mura* (*top*) was characterized by a cluster arrangement of farm households, while in Ogawa-*mura* (*bottom*), homesteads were aligned along Oume Road. (The map of Kishi is adapted from Kimura and Itō 1972, 258; the map of Ogawa is adapted from *Ogawa-mura chiwari zu* [Map of Ogawa-*mura* landholdings] n.d.)

requirements of wet-rice cultivation, paddy irrigation procedures in particular.[13] Modes of paddy irrigation varied considerably from region to region, but as a whole the meticulous complexity of paddy farming—the success of which hinged on a strategy of alternating periods of standing water, running water, and draining—contrasts starkly with dry-field farming in Ogawa-*mura*, where irrigation was synonymous with rainfall. Since Ogawa-*mura* was a dry-field *shinden* village, the mode of social organization associated with water use was different from that of paddy-cultivating villages.

Whereas the Tamagawa main canal made the reclamation of Ogawa-*mura* feasible, it was the Ogawa branch canal that directly served the water needs of individual homesteads. The branch canal, dug at the same time that reclamation work was commenced, took the form of twin channels paralleling either side of Oume Road. Figuratively speaking, the long, narrow *shinden* parcels were the warp and the Ogawa branch canal the woof of, in the words of the "Kodaira Song," "an endless brocade of green." While many *shinden* in the Musashino area shared with Ogawa-*mura* a linear layout, it alone featured a symmetrically arranged set of service canals threading together the otherwise autonomous parcels.

Kodaira Song

The land, an endless brocade of green,
Ripe and fruitful Musashino, where hopes are sown.
Always progressing, Kodaira,
Carrying out ideals. Proud of
our pioneer past—the heart's native place.

Flowers blooming; pure the water flows,
Dreams too, onward, toward a distant future.
A bell tolls loud and clear. Kodaira
Bubbles with youthful vigor;
Academy town, fountain of culture.

Gentle breezes gather the fragrance of tea petals,
Pristine Fuji, glistening Mitake—
Radiant light pours down, in Kodaira
People gather, a new
Peace is their aim, joyfully marching ahead.

Music: Shimōsa Kan'ichi
Lyrics: Katsu Nobuo

Each household was responsible for the upkeep of its segment of the Ogawa branch canal. Part of the village code, compiled in 1715, included the following rules and regulations pertaining to this waterway.

Point: It is forbidden to dump trash and garbage into the canal.
Point: It is forbidden to play, launder clothes, or wash any soiled articles in the canal.
Point: Since the canal provides drinking water for the entire village, each homestead must keep its segment free of debris.
Point: Once or twice a year, each household is to dredge its segment of the Ogawa branch canal.
Point: It is strictly forbidden to tap the service canal by digging auxiliary ditches, however narrow they may be. (Itō 1984, 46)

The net effect of these rules and regulations, although they were carried out on an individual-household basis, was the regular maintenance of the entire village's potable water supply. This arrangement may have nurtured the development among Ogawa settlers of a "communal consciousness" (*kyōdō no ishiki*), which arguably is not the same as a "communal corps" (*kyōdōtai*) (Itō 1984, 48). The rules and regulations pertaining to the Ogawa branch canal were mediated and enacted not by a collectivity but by individual households made conscious of the collective benefits of their individual role in canal maintenance. To interpret communal consciousness as the equivalent of a communal corps is an act of reification on the part of local historians.

Kyodotai is presented in the Kodaira literature as a collectivity limited to a single village, of and for which it is a metaphor. Significantly, the *Kodaira chōshi*, in its diagram of the Tamagawa main canal as utilized during the Edo period, places the canal along the borders of the present-day city. The editors effectively have conflated what was, in effect, a multivillage, multilevel water delivery network to a geographic entity— Kodaira—created in 1889. What is imputed here is that the seven *shinden* villages were organically united before their arbitary merger in the late nineteenth century. The contemporary search for "authentic" community has taken precedence over historical accuracy.

Kumi (Divisions)

The Ogawa branch canal was maintained by individual households; the upkeep of the Tamagawa main canal was undertaken on a *kumi* basis. In its most general sense, *kumi* signifies an intravillage division, of which three basic types were operative in Ogawa-*mura*: *nengugumi*, or tax division; *goningumi*, or five-household division; and *kinjogumi*, or neighborhood division. The upkeep of the Tamagawa main canal was the province of this last division. Each of these types of *kumi* in turn was further subdivided. Membership in all the divisions and subdivisions was largely compulsory and limited to titled farmers (*honbyakushō*). The village head and the clergy, as privileged villagers, were exempt from having to participate in these organizations. Regardless of whether these intravillage divisions were "the brainchild of Kurobei," as one local historian has insisted, or instituted by *bakufu* decree, or both, they nevertheless were key elements in the making of Ogawa-*mura*.

NENGUGUMI

Functioning as units of tax collection and payment, *nengugumi* (fig. 10) were present in villages throughout the Kanto region. In some small villages, *nengugumi* either were absent or a single *nengugumi* coincided with the village proper (Kimura and Itō 1972, 213, 238). As a rule, *nengugumi* were supervised by a *kumigashira*, or division leader, after whom, in the case of Ogawa-*mura*, they were named. Generally speaking, this position, like that of the village head, was hereditary and, in the Kodaira *shinden* at least, limited to males. The "artificial, planned aspect" of the Ogawa *nengugumi* is evident in the fact that they were organized on the basis of "place links" (*chien*), instead of "blood" and/or fictive kin ties, as allegedly was common in unplanned, "natural" villages (Kimura and Itō 1972, 213).

The Ogawa *nengugumi* passed through three phases of development. In Phase I, probably following the 1669 land registration, the homesteads were divided into ten tax divisions proceeding from west to east. Prior to the inauguration of the *kumi* system in general, Kurobei had designated his residence as the boundary separating the nascent village's two temple parishes, each of which originally functioned in a *kumi*-like capacity. In Phase II, another tax division, comprising land reclaimed since the 1669 survey, appeared in the 1674 cadastral register, bringing to eleven the total number of *nengugumi*. In Phase III, which took place during the 1720s, the existing eleven tax divisions were reorganized as eight larger units, which were retained as the official administrative divisions through the end of the Edo period (Kimura and Itō 1972, 213–14). These new units, moreover, were referred to as *ichibangumi*, *ni-bangumi* (first division, second division), and so forth. (Hereafter they are referred to as 1-*bangumi*, 2-*bangumi*, etc.)

The *nengugumi*, in short, were absorbed into a more comprehensive

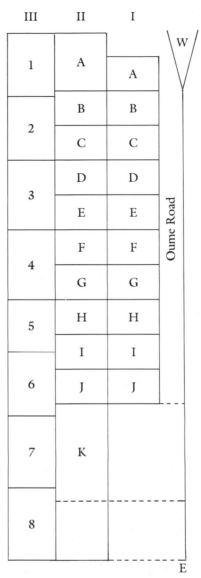

Fig. 10. Ogawa-*mura nengugumi*. I, II, and III signify the three successive stages of development. A–K are the *kumi* units, which preceded the *bangumi*, 1–8. (Adapted from Kimura and Itō 1972, 214)

system of village administration. At the same time, the jurisdiction of each division leader likely shifted to the *bangumi*. That the two temple parishes served as prototypical *kumi* during the decade after the village's founding is suggested by the fact that parish-related activities—memorial services, funerals, sutra-chanting coteries, exorcisms—eventually were organized on a *bangumi* basis. Today the *bangumi* remain intact as the system by which the native sector of Ogawa, now a district (*chō*) of Kodaira, is organized both affectively and administratively. I refer to these *bangumi* collectively as the "Ogawa Eight."

The number of *kumigashira* did not necessarily coincide with the number of *kumi*. There were eleven division leaders in 1679, ten in 1700, nine in 1713, eight in 1733, and six in 1754 (*KC* 1959, 75). The decrease may be related to the practice of not appointing a substitute to complete the tenure of a division leader who either died or retired prematurely. Attrition probably resulted initially from the lack of a suitable heir and later from the decision that the post was dispensable.[14] The data suggest that some of the division leaders were among the original petitioners. Given the paucity of primary data, it is unclear whether some of the Ogawa-*mura* division leaders were appointed by Kurobei, although the probability is very high (Kimura and Itō 1972, 219, 228). In any case, the elite households that emerged during Ogawa-*mura*'s formative years have remained influential to the present day.

Ogawa-*mura* division leaders did not necessarily live in the tax division under their jurisdiction; neither did ordinary farmers. This arrangement seems to have been designed to circumvent the potential buildup of *kumi* loyalties. Even so, a given tax division was named after the current division leader. The *nengugumi* remained fixed geographic units until their comprehensive reorganization in the 1720s. A given tax division did not amount to a *kyōdōtai*, or communal corps. The tax divisions, rather, were arbitrarily determined geographic units, which in several instances were supervised by settlers lacking outstanding residential or kin connections. Furthermore, neither leadership nor membership was contingent upon *kumi* residence (Kimura and Itō 1972, 218–19).

GONINGUMI

The *goningumi* (fig. 11), or five-household division, was introduced by the *bakufu* in the 1620s as a means of more thoroughly articulating its authority at the local level. Within a village, the *gonin-*

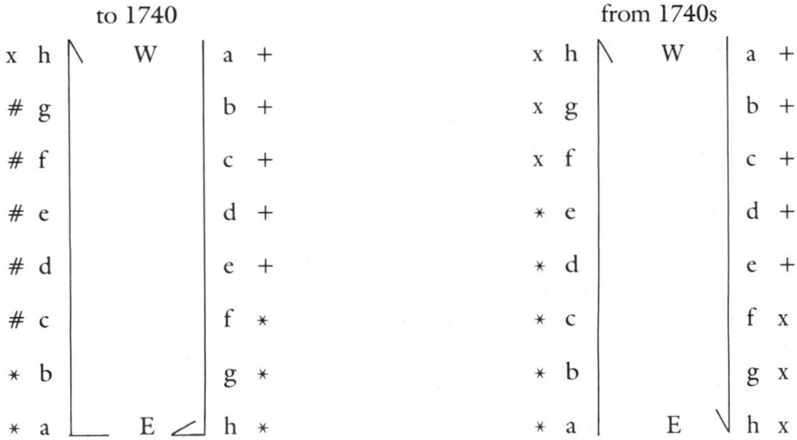

```
        to 1740                              from 1740s

 x  h  \    W    | a  +              x  h  \    W    | a  +
 #  g           | b  +              x  g           | b  +
 #  f           | c  +              x  f           | c  +
 #  e           | d  +              *  e           | d  +
 #  d           | e  +              *  d           | e  +
 #  c           | f  *              *  c           | f  x
 *  b           | g  *              *  b           | g  x
 *  a  ⌞   E ⦨   h  *              *  a      E  \   h  x
```

Fig. 11. *Goningumi* registration. +, *, and # indicate *goningumi* groups, and x signifies unaffiliated households. The *goningumi* households are aligned along the north and south sides of Oume Road.

gumi functioned as a system of interhousehold surveillance and constraint, for the transgressions of one member would make the remaining four subject to castigation. The *goningumi* may be described as a janus-faced system of collective culpability and collective responsibility.

Aspects of the organization of this division are gleaned from the *goningumi-chō*, or register. Until roughly 1740, households were registered in groups of five, beginning with the westernmost and proceeding to the easternmost household on the north side of Oume Road, and continuing without a break from the easternmost to the westernmost household on the south side. From the 1740s onward, however, north- and south-side households were registered separately, from west to east and east to west, respectively (Kimura and Itō 1972, 151). Register entries clearly establish that in Ogawa-*mura* *exactly* five households comprised a *goningumi*, which was not always the case in other villages (ibid.; cf. Befu 1968, 304). Several households, consequently, were not incorporated into a *goningumi*. Perhaps their inclusion within the tax and neighborhood divisions was sufficient from an administrative point of view, a possibility I broach again in the context of the neighborhood divisions. Or perhaps only the households of titled farmers were incorporated. Also, the Shinto and Buddhist clergy, along with the village head, were exempt from this and other divisions. In Ogawa-*mura*, the *goningumi* did not coincide with the tax division, although there may have been some overlap. It is also clear that the composition of each five-household division changed in accord with the rise and fall of the village's population. Thus, previously unincorporated households may have been included in the *goningumi* at a later time.

Ostracism was one of the most severe punishments meted out during the Edo period (see Smith 1961). The equivalent of *murahachibu*, or ostracism from the village(rs), was known as *goningumi hazushi*, or ostracism from the five-household division. *Murahachibu* seems to have been typical in "old" and "parent" villages, whereas *goningumi hazushi* characterized the system of sanctions in "new" or *shinden* villages (Kimura and Itō 1972, 157). The existence of *goningumi hazushi* is further evidence that Ogawa-*mura* as a whole did not operate as a *kyōdōtai*, or communal corps, from which errant households were ostracized.

KINJOGUMI

Documentary evidence suggests that the *kinjogumi*, or neighborhood divisions (fig. 12), were in existence in Ogawa-*mura* by 1690, as were the *goningumi*. The neighborhood divisions were partly a local-level manifestation of *bakufu* authority and partly a local-level approach to the making of the nascent village. The *kinjogumi* were formed prior to the other two divisions, and in Ogawa they constituted the fundamental social matrix onto which the tax and five-household divisions were superimposed.

Today the Ogawa *kinjogumi* comprise five subdivisions, which I have categorized as either "fluid" or "fixed" with respect to their constituency. In the Edo period, the fluid subdivisions represented local-level approaches to the making of the *shinden* village, whereas the fixed subdivisions represented *bakufu*-dictated village structures. The "fluid" category includes the following units:

A. The *ryōdonari mukō*, the smallest neighborhood unit, centering on a single household and including the two households on its left and right and the one directly across from it. The terms *ryōdonari* and *mukō* first appear in documents dating to the 1750s. The *ryōdonari mukō* are not to be confused with a similar style of *kinjogumi* referred to as *mukō sangen ryōdonari*, a six-household unit made up of a central household, the two households on its left

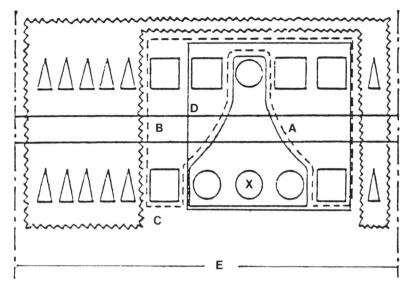

Fig. 12. Ogawa-*mura kinjogumi*. X = central household; A = *ryōdonari mukō*; B = *sashiba*; C = *ōgumi*; D = *kumiai*; E = *bangumi*. (Adapted from *KK* 1983, 138)

and right, and the three households across (usually a thorough-fare) from them.[15]

B. The *sashiba*, two three-household clusters on either side of the *ryōdonari mukō* unit.

C. The *ōgumi*, which encompasses within a single *bangumi* those households not incorporated into either *A* or *B*. The term *ōgumi* first appears in a 1708 document, which may suggest indirectly that *A* was present at that time or that *C* preceded *A* as the primary unit of neighborhood organization.

The "fluid" category of neighborhood division was the basis for the organization and execution of ceremonial activities, particularly weddings and funerals. This is so to a limited extent in the Ogawa Eight today. The *ryōdonari mukō* were and remain especially important and operative on such occasions. Several Ogawa Eight natives believe that postwar social and politicoeconomic changes, together with the recent proliferation of commercial wedding halls, have reduced the ceremonial function of these neighborhood units.

The "fixed" category of neighborhood division includes the following:

D. The *kumiai*, or cooperative group, which encompasses eight households.[16] The cooperative group includes households on both sides of Oume Road, whereas the *goningumi* was limited to clusters of five households on either the north or the south side of that thoroughfare.
E. The eight *bangumi*, discussed earlier in reference to the tax division.

The "fixed" category of neighborhood divisions was the basis for the administrative, as opposed to ceremonial, organization of Ogawa-*mura*, although parish-related activities today are organized on a *bangumi* basis.

All of these fluid and fixed divisions were created by either the village head or the *bakufu* within a half-century or so after the initial reclamation of Ogawa-*mura*. By the eighteenth century, Ogawa-*mura* was a complex weave of interhousehold ties that bound households to both the village and the *bakufu*. These same neighborhood divisions, moreover, are operative in Ogawa-*chō* today. A review of several key morphological features of the *kinjogumi* system concludes the discussion on *kumi*.

First is its striking linear arrangement. The diapered *ryōdonari mukō* network was absent in Kishi-*mura*, very likely because of that village's cluster formation. Also, the preponderance of mutual strangers in the nascent Ogawa-*mura* meant that parishes and other place-linked units, such as the *kumi* thus far described, either took the place of or took precedence over "blood" and/or fictive kin ties as the basis of village-making. With the exception of the village head and clergy—both of whom were exempt from the tax, five-household, and neighborhood divisions—Ogawa-*mura* settlers were incorporated into a system of interlocking geographic units.

That the clergy constituted another order of villager entirely is illustrated by the following anecdote. On the occasion of our first interview, Miyazaki H., the chief priest of Shinmei-*gū*, insisted that Ogawa-*mura* originally was settled by "same-name groups" (*shizoku*) and therefore was a "clannish" village. Although this may have been an accurate portrayal of the Miyazakis, as privileged Shinto clergy, it is not an accurate portrayal of the *shinden*'s initial residents. Since the vast majority of settlers hailed from rather distant villages, ties between them and their relatives "back home" were attenuated, if not severed altogether. Only the Ogawas are acknowledged in the local literature as having maintained close relations with their Kishi line ever since the reclamation period (*KC* 1959, 900).

Much of the tenacity of the natives' society in Kodaira today, however, has to do with the gradual metamorphosis of the original place-links into a network of kindred (*shinrui*) relations as the original settler households established branches, which in turn produced branches. The operation of this network of main and branch households is especially evident in the yard shrine oblations discussed in the next chapter. Finally, the present-day descendants of both elite and ordinary settlers have in common a "nativeness" that now transcends historical status inequities and has been reified as a type of primordial solidarity.

Making Ogawa-*shinden*

Ogawa-*shinden*, reclaimed in 1725, is a representative example of a village-initiated *shinden*; that is, a *shinden* reclaimed by the residents of one village, who each contributed capital and labor. (For a discussion of other *shinden* typologies, see the Appendix.) Ogawa-*shinden* essentially was a nomenclatural extension of Ogawa-*mura*, established as it was on land originally granted to Kurobei as part of his *shinden* package. This land had remained untouched until 1725, twenty-three years after the first petition to reclaim the eastern segment was submitted. The rationale for the new *shinden* project was to increase the amount of arable land, since, as the Ogawa-*mura* head wrote in his petition to the *bakufu*, population was outgrowing productivity (*KC* 1959, 116). Permission was denied, and denied again in 1708, for the reason that reclamation work would deplete natural fertilizer resources and hamper the cultivation of existing fields. By the 1720s, however, the tax-minded *bakufu* once more was encouraging land reclamation, and the conditions proposed by the Ogawa-*mura* head in 1722 doubtless facilitated matters.

The village head agreed to complete the reclamation of about 700 hectares within three years, and acquiesced to an annual auxiliary tax of twenty *ryō*, although the annual tax proper was to be suspended for three years. Permission to reclaim 237 hectares was granted midway through 1724. About 60 hectares, called the detached-land portion (*mochizoebun*), were divided equally among the Ogawa-*mura* households. This worked out to about .33 hectare for each of the approximately 195 households. The remainder, referred to as the independent portion (*dokuritsubun*), was sold to several types of buyers: those villagers who wished to establish a branch household on the new *shinden*; those among the more affluent who wished to increase their landholdings; and those who immigrated from other villages. The holders of independent portions represent the Ogawa-*shinden* settlers proper. They numbered eleven by 1726, seventeen by 1727, and seventy-one by 1730 (*KC* 1959, 115–19). However, those villagers for whom an independent portion was an investment tended not to resettle but, rather, contracted their portion to caretakers (*yamori*), who comprised a low-status group of settlers. As extant contracts reveal, all of the contracts were issued for a maximum of five years, but the terms of the contracted labor varied (*KC* 1959, 125). During the period 1720–1730, caretakers were the subject of much new legislation, indicating the prevalence of the caretaker system by that time, perhaps in connection with *shinden* reclamation (Futagawa 1980, 279).

Within five years of the new *shinden*'s establishment, about 85 (of the approximately 195) Ogawa-*mura* householders had sold their *shinden* shares to other villagers and/or outsiders (*KC* 1959, 118–19). Unlike Ogawa-*mura*'s, the population of Ogawa-*shinden* rapidly became a heterogeneous mix of immigrants. Like Ogawa-*mura* settlers, however, farmers in the new *shinden* were immigrants from northern and western areas, as indicated by their "certificates of identity," which are included among the Ogawa household documents. The majority were younger sons and their wives and, in some cases, children.

As was typical of village-initiated reclamation, the new *shinden* remained under the administrative control of its parent village, Ogawa-*mura*, until approximately 1740. At this time Yaichi, the head of Ogawa-*mura*, turned the position over to his son and established a branch household on the nascent *shinden*, just as Kurobei had done nearly a century earlier. Prior to that time, the headship of both Ogawa-*mura* and Ogawa-*shinden* had been served concurrently by Yaichi. For the Ogawas, *shinden* village–making apparently was tantamount to the process of *inkyo-bunke*, or the establishment of a branch household upon the retirement of the househead. Other Ogawa-*mura* households also tended to combine *shinden* settlement with the formation of *inkyo-bunke* (Katayama 1959, 268), implying a correspondence between the contiguity and continuity of settler households and the process of *shin-den* village–making.

Yaichi's move to the *shinden* took place after the 1736 cadastral survey, which suggests that by that time the *shinden* was sufficiently stable to warrant having its own leadership. However, Ogawa-*shinden* remained under the administration of parent-village leaders. Not only did Yaichi serve in the supervisory post of elder (*toshiyori*) in Ogawa-*mura*, but the annual tax (i.e., the detached-land portion) was collected by the parent village (Kimura and Itō 1972, 79; *KC* 1959, 122).

Ogawa-*mura* was a parent village in a way that Kishi-*mura* had never been, even though the *Kyōdo Kodaira* (Local Kodaira) refers to Kishi-*mura*, Ogawa-*mura*, and Ogawa-*shinden* as "grandparent, parent, and grandchild" villages, respectively—familistic allusions that pertain only to the Ogawas (*Kyōdo Kodaira* henshū iinkai [1967] 1983, 53). Whereas Ogawa Kurobei had initiated and funded the reclamation of a *shinden* village, which he then named after himself, Ogawa-*shinden*, although named after the parent village, was initiated and partly funded by Ogawa-*mura* villagers.

The *bakufu* encouraged immigration to Ogawa-*shinden* by offering subsidies for housing (two *ryō*, two *mon* in gold). It also granted, as funds for agricultural implements, a reward of 624 *mon* for every ten ares reclaimed (*KC* 1959, 100). However, the entire *shinden*—even the unreclaimed sections—was declared taxable, for the taxation rate was based upon a projected reclamation schedule. Settlers thereby were compelled to reclaim land in order to meet their taxes (ibid., 102). In Ogawa-*mura* the settlers had protested the autocratic antics of Kurobei; in Ogawa-*shinden* the primary target of disgruntled immigrants was the exploitative *bakufu* (ibid., 109).

Conclusion: Ogawa-*mura* and Kodaira Nativism

Today the Ogawa Eight are imagined by natives and newcomers alike as the historical and authenticating core of Furusato Kodaira. Local media—including the "Kodaira Song," "Kodaira Citizens' Festival Song," "Kodaira *Ondo*," and the "local-place playing cards" (*kyōdo karuta*) sold at city hall—follow the local-history texts in eulogizing Kurobei and Ogawa-*mura*. Kurobei represents the subjective human agent and personifies the sociohistorical process of village-making. Eulogized as the civic ancestor of all Kodaira residents, Pioneer Kurobei is presented by local historians and city administrators alike as an exemplar for residents to emulate in the quest to reclaim a "new *furusato*." Their point is that *furusato-zukuri* ultimately is a crescive process calling for local, self-initiated action. Likewise, the citizens' festival, conceived as a populist expression of "old village"–making, is promoted by its planners as a "spontaneous event." Kurobei, the name, has become a Kodaira-specific metaphor for "a process in which communities were more nearly the products of personal and human nature than the contrivances of planners, bureaucracies, and depersonalized institutions" (Suttles 1972, 9).

The irony, of course, is that Kurobei was an autocrat and that *furusato-zukuri* was initiated by city hall. Nevertheless, the paternalistic style of Kurobei and the Ogawa household has been evoked to spice up Kodaira history. Even the Ogawas' wholly autocratic practice of exacting tribute from the villagers is dramatized unproblematically in local-history texts, as the following example illustrates. Until the amalgamation of Kodaira-*mura* in 1889, New Year's Day in Ogawa-*mura* was a time for villagers to pay tribute to the village head. Early in the morning, villagers appeared at the Ogawa entranceway with a New Year's gift of sacks of rice, millet, and wheat. A division leader was assigned to record the gifts and the names of their donors. Later, the head, outfitted in ceremonial garb, was paraded along Oume Road in a palanquin. As his entourage passed by, the villagers lining either side of the thoroughfare were obliged to kneel, bow their heads, and call out the auspicious greeting "omedetō gozaimasu" (Itō 1961, 46–47).

Ogawa-*mura* is the only *shinden* of the Kodaira Seven whose founder and founding have been commemorated on a citywide basis. In view of its historical primacy and geographic scope alone, the civic favoritism accorded Ogawa-*mura* is not altogether surprising. The village was founded about seventy-five years before the others were reclaimed, although in the mid-seventeenth century the Suzukis had attempted to reclaim land in the eastern and southern sectors of Kodaira. Their failure only underscores the alleged engineering genius of Kurobei, thereby enhancing the mythic aura about Ogawa-*mura*.

Geographically, the former Ogawa-*mura* monopolizes the eastern half of Kodaira and, with the former Ogawa-*shinden*, constitutes nearly half of the entire city. Moreover, the eight Ogawa *bangumi* remain intact as administrative and social units, and they are further integrated by virtue of their encirclement by the Ogawa branch canal. That the canal remains functional owes much to the efforts of Kodaira natives to preserve it and other branch canals for posterity and as a rainwater runoff. In 1981 city hall, with the cooperation of the agricultural cooperative, declared the last two Tuesdays of May "Clean the City's Branch Canals Day" (*KSH*, 20 May 1981). Mobilizing the nonfarming newcomer population to clean the canals purportedly sensitizes them to the historical presence and boundaries of the native sector.[17]

Newcomers are also brought into closer contact with the natives' society through the activities of the Kodaira Association for Tourist Agriculture, founded by about fifty farm households in 1979, and also through the "home vegetable garden" (*katei saien*) program inaugurated by city hall in 1983. The association seeks to secure a stable local market and expose newcomers to "agricultural culture." Farmers grow only those vegetables—cucumber, Japanese radish, Chinese cabbage, eggplant, carrots, lettuce, green pepper, leek, burdock—ordered in advance by consumers, who then collect their custom-grown produce at harvest time. The association also sponsors "pear-apple" (*nashi*)–picking, sweet potato–digging, and chestnut-gathering events every fall. These events are promoted as "a way of bringing Kodaira's nonfarming population [i.e., newcomers] closer to the soil" and introducing them to "the joys of toiling and sweating and chatting with [their] neighbors" (*KSH*, 20 June 1979, 20 June 1984).

A poll conducted in 1984 by the city hall's Public Relations Department showed that 21 percent of the residents have made use of the home gardens and that 58 percent have purchased produce, eggs, and/or plants directly from farm householders (*KSH*, 5 May 1984). Finally, the annual agricultural fair, cosponsored by the agricultural cooperative and city hall and first held in 1977, is billed as a means of introducing to newcomers "the actual conditions of inner-city farming and husbandry" and "cultivating harmony" between the city's farming and nonfarming sectors (*KSH*, 5 October 1983).

What are the contemporary circumstances and situation of Kodaira's natives? A key factor contributing to the civic favoritism accorded Ogawa natives today is the sociogeographic integrity of the Ogawa Eight despite potentially divisive developments. A brief review of twentieth-century landholding patterns in the former Ogawa-*mura* adds more texture to the portrait of the Ogawa Eight today (1985) and in the Edo period.

This area began to undergo unprecedented internal changes beginning in the 1920s. In 1923 about 200 hectares of dry-field and forested land in the southern reaches of Ogawa-*mura* and Ogawa-*shinden* were sold to the Hakone Realty Company. There were approximately 115 farm households in the Ogawa Eight at that time, and about 23 in Ogawa-*shinden*, as compared to about 225 and 88, respectively, in 1857–58. In the immediate postwar period, the same company was also responsible for developing Kodaira Gakuen (now Gakuen Higashi-*chō*) in the mold of the German "academy town" (*KC* 1959, 205–7, 398, 402, 430, 436, 557). The overall decline in the number of farm households is attributed to several factors, two of the major ones being the Matsukata deflation of the 1880s and the advent of land developers, such as the Hakone Realty Company. Named after the finance minister at the time, the Matsukata taxation and deflationary policies, while beneficial to the government, had an adverse effect on farmers. Crop and food prices went down, but the land tax remained the same, forcing farmers to double the percentage of agricultural production for tax payments (Hane 1986, 100).

During the period 1946–1963, about 1,185 hectares of arable land were sold, the majority of which were converted to residential property. Since then, there has been a decline in the number of households owning 2 or more hectares and an increase in those holding from between 50 ares to 1.5 hectares. The turnover peaked from the late 1950s through the early 1960s, as did the postwar population growth, which ballooned from a total of 15,595 residents (1,895 households) in 1944, to 32,520 (5,967) in 1957, and 72,156 (22,944) in 1963. The population has stabilized since 1985 at around 153,000 persons (about 57,000 households) (*KC* 1959, 430; *KCH*, 5 July 1961; *KSH*, 5 December 1965, 1 January 1985; Kodaira-*shi* sōmubu shomuka 1983, 11).

The Kodaira Seven apparently had none of the large-scale absentee landlords typical of paddy-farming villages, although the presence of a "landlord-tenant system" was clearly evident by the 1870s, as revealed by land registers (*tochi daichō*) compiled at that time. There were no absentee landlords at all in Ogawa-*mura* and Ogawa-*shinden* (*KC* 1959, 547). The Ogawa Eight were exceptional because, unlike the turn-of-the-century situation in the other Kodaira *shinden*, most of the land sales or exchanges occurred among resident (as opposed to outside) investors. In other words, although land changed hands—and farm households folded—it did so among residents of the Ogawa

Eight, effectively maintaining the sociogeographic integrity of the area (*KC* 1959, 440).

In 1928 farm households comprised 83 percent of the population, or 807 of a total 971 households; and 43.5 percent Kodaira (about 1,226 of a total 2,815 hectares) comprised cultivated land in 1929. By the 1950s these percentages had decreased to 18.5 percent, or 1,020 of 5,517 households, and to 32 percent (898 hectares). The increase of 213 farm households in the early 1950s, even though the number of farm households in the total Japanese population decreased drastically, can be attributed to the sale of farmland to postwar immigrants who were obliged to farm as part of a central-government-engineered effort to replenish the food supply in the decade following World War II. Recent (1984) statistics show that 12.5 percent (353 hectares) of Kodaira is devoted to agriculture and that farm households comprise 1 percent of the population, or 577 of approximately 57,000 households (*KC* 1959, 468, 560; *KK* 1983, 205, 224; *KSH*, 1 January 1985).[18]

Prior to the 1946 land reforms initiated by the United States government, 43–49 percent of the total arable land in Kodaira was tenanted, although—in the former Ogawa-*mura* especially—the tenanted land was owned by resident landlords. By 1955 the average rate of tenancy had fallen to 6.7 percent, nearly 2 percent lower than the national average. The number of owner-cultivators, in contrast, rose from 23 percent prior to the land reform to about 70 percent in 1955 (*KC* 1959, 589, 591, 596). The consequences of the land reforms were reported in a 1949 survey. According to that survey, 26.5 percent (or 265) of the 998 farm households at the time had their landholdings increased (59 percent by thirty ares or less, and only 2.6 percent by one hectare or more); 14.5 percent (145) had their holdings reduced (73 percent by thirty ares or less, and 2.1 percent by one hectare or more); and 59 percent (588) neither gained nor lost land. The relatively uneventful land reform is attributed to the fact that the largest landholdings in Kodaira amounted to less than thirty hectares, far less than the one thousand hectares owned by some paddy landlords in Niigata and Yamagata prefectures (*KK* 1983, 216–17).

The Ogawa Eight presently boasts the largest concentration of farmers in Kodaira, as well as the distinction of having retained its *shinden*-village configuration, although almost all of the thatched-roof houses have been replaced by concrete ones. In 1958–59, for example, about 50 percent of the households in the Ogawa Eight declared agri-

Table 3. *Ogawa Farm Households (1975)*

	Total Households	Farm Households	% of Farm Households
KC	52,907	634	1.2
OG1	3,953	155	3.92
OG2	1,145	72	6.29
NM	482	59	2.38

NOTE: KC = Kodaira City; OG1 = Ogawa-*chō* 1-*chōme*; OG2 = Ogawa-*chō* 2-*chōme*; NM = Naka-*machi*. Data are from *Kodaira-shi no nyōgyō* (Kodaira-*shi* sōmubu shomuka 1975).

OG1 and OG2 encompass the Ogawa Eight and contain 36 percent of all the farm households in Kodaira. Moreover, 67 percent (30 households) of all the full-time farm households in Kodaira (45) are located in the Ogawa Eight and almost exclusively in OG1. Of all the part-time farm households (589), 33 percent (197) are based in the Ogawa Eight. Only 7 percent of all farm households in Kodaira in 1975 and 1980 were full-time agriculturists; 93 percent were part-time agriculturists. Data for 1980 are from *Sekai nōringyō sensasu: Kodaira* 1980, 1.

culture their livelihood. This is more than twice the citywide average for 1955, in which 19 percent of the working population was engaged in agriculture, down from 35 percent in 1950 and 79 percent in 1920. Kodaira agriculture as a whole remains an overwhelmingly inner-city occupation. In 1958–59, 98.5 percent of Kodaira farmers worked on local land, in contrast to the 94 percent of office workers (newcomers) who commuted to offices outside Kodaira. These same percentages hold for the 1980s as well.

The Ogawa Eight is unique in possessing the highest concentration of farmers: over 10 percent in 1975, as opposed to 1 percent citywide (table 3). A significant percentage are young, indicating a degree of generational succession and continuity. A survey conducted by city hall in 1978 indicated that 56 percent of the total number of farm householders intended to remain in agriculture for at least another decade, and 35 percent for at least another five years (Kodaira-*shi* keikaku zaiseibu keikakuka 1980, 72). Although statistics are unavailable, these percentages doubtless were and are much higher among Ogawa-*chō* farm households. The presence of farmers, in turn, facilitates the preservation of both historical institutions, notably shrine and temple parishes, and the vaunted "atmosphere of olden Musashino." Because of its geographic integrity, visual antiquity, and large concentration of farmers, the Ogawa Eight constitutes the most intact sector of the natives' society.

In this chapter, I have traced the progress of Kodaira from the making of Ogawa-*mura* to the circumstances of the native sector today, and specifically the Ogawa Eight. Present efforts to unite the native and newcomer sectors through such productions as the citizens' festival and "tourist agriculture" amount to affective city-planning strategies. However, in seeking to instill in newcomers a sense of belonging and commitment to Kodaira, city hall also has spurred an increasingly palpable microlocal patriotism on the part of natives, epitomized by the Ogawa Eight. The paradox here is that the consciousness among both natives and newcomers of having Kodaira residency in common has had the effect of putting a special emphasis on that which differentiates them (Erickson 1980, 101). How differences between natives and newcomers are constructed, perceived, and deployed by each sector informs the following chapters.

CHAPTER FOUR

Religious Revanche

Shinmei-*gū*: Kodaira's Premier Shrine

Religious activity is perhaps the most explicit means Kodaira's natives have for reclaiming their place within the suburban city. Shrine and temple events provide natives with a focus for communal activities and newcomers with a display of "living history." This chapter continues the project of chapter 3 by providing an account of the making of Kodaira, focusing in particular on religious institutions in the former Ogawa-*mura*. The past and present conditions of these shrines, temples, and yard shrines underscore the differences between natives and newcomers.

Shinmei-*gū*, the largest and most prosperous shrine in Kodaira today, was one of the first two shrines established in Ogawa-*mura* along Oume Road, the other being the modest and relatively inactive Hie-*jinja*. The Shinmei-*gū* office distributes free of charge a leaflet printed on glittery handmade paper in which is outlined the shrine's origins, the names of the various *kami* enshrined there, and the festivals, events, and sundry activities organized by the shrine. The numerous large signboards placed here and there throughout the compound provide the same information and more. In one entitled "Myself and exquisite Japan, where divine virtues are revered," the chief priest, Miyazaki H., expounds at length on the central position and function of *kami* in Japanese culture and society. On a small table set in front of the main hall are stacked copies of *Shinmeisama*,[1] the shrine's monthly news-letter, and a flier, issued monthly by the Tokyo Bureau of Shrines, featuring a moralistic proverb. While the other Kodaira shrines and temples post a brief history, their precincts are not studded with the large numbers of signs found here. This penchant for explanation and instruction reflects the personality and temperament of the current chief priest, who is the eleventh-generation descendant of Shinmei-*gū*'s first priest, Miyazaki Shūme. Because of his important role in the religious revanche of the native sector, I dwell on the chief priest at some length; later, for the same reason, I discuss in detail his Buddhist counterpart, the incumbent priest of Shōsen-*ji*.

I arranged to interview Miyazaki one morning. While waiting for him in the Shinmei-*gū* office, I was given the leaflet by his two sons, both of whom are lower-ranking priests. Their mother, a slight, stooped woman, appeared with a cup of green tea, and I, in turn, presented my gift of Japanese confections. We struck up a conversation. I asked about the large expanse of farmland behind the shrine, and, suddenly pensive, she replied that "before the Pacific War" (i.e., prior to the postwar land reforms), all that land belonged to her natal household, the Miyazakis. Her family? Yes, her husband is an adopted son-in-law, for the Shin-mei-*gū* Miyazaki line historically had few sons and many daughters. Shortly, the chief priest himself bustled in, a slight, wiry man with a raspy voice, clad in slacks and a polo shirt. He suggested that we talk in the sitting room of his house, a spacious two-story building tucked between the office and the nursery school managed by the shrine. His wife disappeared.

The small, parquet-floored sitting room was jammed with furniture and a hodgepodge of objects set on every available surface: a garish porcelain horse, a sea-green ceramic "fish couple" set on a pseudo-marble pillar, an outdated globe, knobby glass ashtrays with felt bot-toms, and a meter-long wooden crocodile. The sliding glass doors at one end of the room looked out on the giant zelkova trees lining the stone path to the shrine. We sat across from each other on upholstered couches separated by a long, low table.

I had come prepared with specific questions, but Miyazaki right away plunged into the history of Kodaira, beginning with a paleo-geography lesson, for which he brought out a long rectangular box filled with vials of soil samples. He pointed out the sandy clay found at 120 meters, the conglomerate at 10 meters, and the dusty topsoil that is sent swirling with every breeze. There were vials of fossils, too, since much of the Kanto Plain was under seawater an estimated 240,000–400,000 years ago (*KC* 1959, 1101–2). Miyazaki quickly worked up to Ogawa-*mura*'s reclamation, at which juncture I steered him toward a discussion of Shinmei-*gū*'s role in the newly founded village, since there is a dearth of information on this subject.

He obliged me in part by proceeding to recount a questionable genealogy of the Miyazaki *ie*, which includes such illustrious antecedents as the fourteenth-century moralist Yoshida Kaneyoshi (Kenkō) and the fiftieth emperor, Kanmu. He then added that of course there was no recorded genealogy or definitive documentation of the Miyazaki line. The "main-main household" (*honhonke*) is still in Kyoto, from where branch households eventually migrated east to settle in the Musashino area. In a later interview, he remarked that the main household of the Shinmei-*gū* Miyazaki line was based in West Tama. Within Kodaira his is the main household to the branch that administers Kumano-*miya*, a shrine established in Ogawa-*shinden* by Shūme's son in the early 1700s. From the turn of the century to the present time, the Miyazakis have carefully maintained the "purity" of their line through marriages with near relatives. This is a somewhat typical strategy favored by elites for several reasons. Such marriages are safer and more economical, since they do not bring in an additional set of kin; existing kindred relations are thereby reinforced, and familiarity simplifies the process of finding and selecting suitable spouses (Nakane 1967, 164–66). How far back this particular marriage strategy was practiced could not be ascertained.

The background of the Miyazaki *ie* in Kodaira since the time of Ogawa-*mura*'s reclamation is less obscure. According to the shrine's leaflet, Shūme assisted Kurobei in his *shinden* project and, in 1661, moved Shinmei-*gū* from Kishi-*mura* to a nearly one-hectare site granted by the *bakufu* for this purpose. The so-called Kishi-*mura* Shinmei-*gū* is described as one of the prestigious *Engishikinai-sha*, or shrines listed in the *Engishiki* (Procedures of the Engi period, published in 927), and is said to have a history dating from before the seventh century. Another account notes, more specifically, that Shūme was the younger brother of the chief priest of a shrine in a village near Kishi-*mura*. Upon Kurobei's petition to the elder brother, Shūme was provided with a "share" (*bunrei*, also *wakemitama*) of the shrine's *kami* to enshrine in Ogawa-*mura* (*KCH*, 20 July 1962; *KK* 1983, 102–3). The process of petitioning for and receiving a share of a given shrine's *kami* was referred to as *kanjō*, originally a Buddhist term. The majority of *shinden*-village shrines apparently were established in this way (Chiba 1970, 61–63).

The enshrinement of a *kami*-share is somewhat analogous to the establishment of a branch household, and in the present case this process coincided with the founding of a Miyazaki branch household (i.e., Shūme's) in Ogawa-*mura*. The *kami*-share in question was an *ubusunagami*, which, however, was enshrined in Ogawa-*mura* as a *chinjugami* (*KK* 1983, 102; Ashida 1977, 265). Although the distinctions between these two types of *kami*—in addition to a third, *ujigami* (also known as *shizokugami*)—have since been conflated, they are significant in the *shinden* context.

Briefly, *ujigami* (also *shizokugami*) refers to the tutelary *kami* of a single *ie*—its ancestors, descendants, and fictive kin. An *ubusunagami* also is recognized as a tutelary *kami*, but one to which no kinship ("blood" and/or fictive) is claimed. Instead, the object of protection is farmland and the cooperative labor group that works it. An *ubusunagami*, then, is recognized as a *kami* of production and productivity. Finally, *chinjugami* denotes the guardian *kami* of a given territory or place without any overt connection to either kinship or (agricultural) production. It is best conceptualized as the guardian of both a given social order and those who are members of that society (Chiba 1970, 294).

Most Japanese scholars of religion recognize a linear progression from *ujigami* through *ubusunagami* to *chinjugami*. The actual *kami* do not change; rather, it is the purposeful function of a given *kami* that evolves over time. Paralleling this transformation was a gradual change from kinship ties to place ties, the latter generally predominating in a *shinden* context. Since the reclamation period, however, there has been a reverse trend among native households from place ties to kinship ties, as I discuss later. The establishment of Shinmei-*gū* traces a progression from an *ubusunagami* to the enshrinement of its *kami*-share as a *chinjugami*. A formerly more exclusive tutelary *kami* thereby was made available for worship by persons of diverse and humble backgrounds, although the priesthood of Shinmei-*gū* was assumed as the hereditary prerogative of the Miyazakis, a position they continue to occupy.

This transformation is further illustrated, albeit indirectly, by a legend recounted in the shrine's leaflet (but nowhere else). According to it, Shinmei-*gū* was established by Shūme in 1657 under *bakufu* orders on a site between the Tamagawa and Nobidome canals (in present-day Nakashima-*chō*). At that stage in its development, the shrine was referred to as a *yama-no-kami*, or, literally, "mountain kami."

"Mountain" (*yama*) in this context signifies any uninhabited, forested area. Since it also refers to an *ie*'s private cemetery, *yama-no-kami* also signifies an ancestral spirit (Chiba 1970, 296). The Shinmei-*gū* legend, then, portrays the shrine as initially an *ujigami* (qua *yama-no-kami*) that was later installed as the village's *chinjugami*. The leaflet goes on to remark that this mountain/ancestral *kami* presently is Shinmei-*gū*'s outer shrine, Ichino-*miya*, a somewhat grandiose designation belied by the unkempt condition of the tiny building. The Nakashima-*chō* woman who directed me to the shrine, hidden in the middle of a low-income housing tract, mentioned that nobody worships there. The only ornamentation was a weather-beaten poster urging residents to make their New Year's pilgrimage to Shinmei-*gū*. It was here, the legend continues, that Shūme beseeched the *kami* for rain to fill the dry canals. On the fifteenth evening, a cloudburst so filled the canals that they flowed all the way to the Arakawa, a river that empties into Tokyo Bay. The Miyazakis use this fable, which glorifies their ancestors' role in re-claiming Ogawa-*mura*, to help secure a prominent role for Shinmei-*gū* in the making of Furusato Kodaira today.

In 1681, twenty years after its initial establishment, Shinmei-*gū* was rebuilt on its present, more central site, for which purpose a little over 1.5 hectares were officially granted. According to the leaflet, the main reason for the move was to make commuting to the shrine more conve-nient for the settlers. It is equally likely that relocating Shinmei-*gū* was one of several steps taken by the village head to further unify the grow-ing village, which, by the time of the 1664 cadastral survey, consisted of over 104 households (*KC* 1959, 53, 68). The move coincided with a protracted period of antagonism between Kurobei and the villagers, who resented his autocratic measures. Therefore, Kurobei probably sought the assistance of the shrine in tempering dissent.

By the same token, the move may have been prompted by *bakufu* efforts to control religious activities and observances. From around the mid-seventeenth century onward, the *bakufu* began issuing edicts for-bidding arbitrarily scheduled festivals, and it called for the dismantling of "shrines of evil *kami*."[2] These measures, however, were moderated by concern that a crackdown would precipitate popular dissent (Miyata 1976, 300–303). Festivals had to be cleared with a government official before they could be staged, as outlined in an 1827 edict circulated in the Kanto region (Itō 1981, 350). Given the heavy hand wielded by the *bakufu* in *shinden* affairs, together with the fact that a special land grant facilitated Shinmei-*gū*'s relocation, the move may be interpreted as part of a design to regulate villager activities through the offices of a sanc-tioned shrine. It is also telling that the shrine's new site was directly across from Shōsen-*ji*, the village's premier temple. Buddhist temples, as extensions of *bakufu* authority, maintained close surveillance over village life, including shrine activities, through a strictly organized and compulsory *danka*, or parishioner, system, as I discuss later.

The Meiji Restoration effectively reversed the political fortunes of Shinto shrines and Buddhist temples. Shinmei-*gū* was designated a *son-sha*, or village shrine, in 1873; and in 1884 it was promoted to the status of *gōsha*, or district shrine, the only such shrine in Kodaira. Then in 1907 it was awarded the status of *heihaku gūshin jinja*, which denotes a shrine—usually one per village—selected by the regional governor to receive ritual offerings of *heihaku* (cloth or paper strips) and *shinsen* (the term for the rice, *sake*, fish, fowl, fruit, vegetables, salt, and water offered up to the *kami*). The criteria for selection included the require-ment that the compound and buildings be in good order and that the shrine fall into one of several categories, which for Shinmei-*gū* was probably that a shrine be related to one listed in the *Engishiki* (Fridell 1973, 13).

The offerings were made on the occasion of several "new" festivals scheduled by the Meiji government. These festivals, which continue to be observed at Shinmei-*gū*, include the "ordinary grand festivals" of *kinensai*, *niinamesai*, and *reisai*, and also such "extraordinary grand fes-tivals" as *honden senzasai*. The *kinensai*—also known as *haru matsuri*, or spring festival—is conducted during the planting season to ensure a bumper harvest and general prosperity. The *niinamesai* also is referred to by the generic *aki matsuri*, or fall festival, an occasion for celebrating the annual fall harvest. During the festival of *reisai*, generally held on days deemed auspicious by a shrine, the celebrants offer thanks to the *kami* for their protection. *Honden senzasai* are held to celebrate the re-construction or relocation of a shrine. Participation in these festive rites was legally required of the mayor or village head, who, dressed in priestly garments, served as the government's representative on such occasions (Chiba 1970, 244–45; *KK* 1983, 102–3). As Fridell has noted, this "fusion of governmental and priestly roles is a striking in-stance, at the grass roots level of Japanese society, of the ancient Jap-anese principle of. . . the 'unity of (Shinto) rites and government'" (1973, 14).

These conferred shrine statuses reflect the Meiji government's preferential treatment of shrines over temples, particularly after the promulgation of the Meiji Constitution in 1889. In 1906 the government inaugurated its national shrine-merger program. The plan was to have a single, central shrine serve as the exclusive focus of communal consciousness and solidarity—a plan that Miyazaki is keen on reviving today. Accordingly, three ungraded shrines in east Ogawa were merged with Shinmei-*gū* in 1909.

Preceding the shrine-merger program by almost two decades was a village-merger campaign, activated in full between 1888 and 1889, to broaden centralized control prior to the promulgation of the new constitution. In 1889 the seven *shinden* villages were amalgamated to form Kodaira-*mura*. But Shinmei-*gū* did not automatically become the new village's representative shrine; rather, the appellation Kodaira Shinmei-*gū* is a relatively recent invention, reflecting Miyazaki's aspirations for the shrine to be recognized as the affective core of Furusato Kodaira. According to the Shinmei-*gū* leaflet, the name Kodaira Shinmei-*gū* was bestowed in 1975 by the Grand Shrine, Ise *jingū*, which donated the sacred lumber used in the Kodaira shrine's 1976 renovation. Each of the amalgamated *shinden* villages maintained its own tutelary shrine, although the administration of those shrines eventually was assumed by Shinmei-*gū* and Kumano-*miya* (*KC* 1959, 1285).

Kumano-*miya*: Fraternal Differences

The Shinmei-*gū* priest was born into the Kumano-*miya* Miyazaki household and later adopted as a son-in-law by the main household, the Shinmei-*gū* Miyazakis. His account of his relations with Kumano-*miya* offers some insights into the relationship between the two shrines and between the Shinmei-*gū* priest and his older brother. The brother is the eighth chief priest of Kumano-*miya* and occupies the awkward—for an elder brother—subordinate position of head of the branch household. The Shinmei-*gū* Miyazaki confided to me that, although he would rather fraternize as equals, his older brother insists on the strict maintenance of the main household–branch household relationship. As the main household, he complained, Shinmei-*gū* must assume two to three times the financial burden of ceremonies and other ritual functions: "three gifts to Kumano-*miya*'s one," as he put it. Given the historical tenacity of kin relations punctiliously maintained by Shinmei-*gū*, the chief priest's professed desire for liberation from main household–branch household ties is ironic and unlikely to be realized.

As a result of a city library's (Naka-*machi* branch) recent project to index the historical documents stored for generations by certain native households, the circumstances for the establishment of Kumano-*miya* in Ogawa-*shinden* have become clearer. Whereas the usual accounts indicate that Kumano-*miya* was founded at its present site in 1704 (*KK* 1983, 109–10), new findings suggest a more likely date of around 1727, when formal permission to establish the shrine was granted by the magistrate in charge of temple and shrine affairs. The 1704 date is now thought to correspond to Shūme's founding of a small "nature shrine" in a hackberry (*enoki*) orchard, the eventual site of Kumano-*miya* (Kodaira-*shi* kyōiku iinkai 1981, 97–110).

It seems that Kumano-*miya* was brought to Ogawa-*mura* from Kishi-*mura* along with Shinmei-*gū*. But whereas Shinmei-*gū* was erected soon thereafter, Kumano-*miya* temporarily was installed within Kurobei's homestead until the reclamation of Ogawa-*shinden* in 1724. At that time, the village head arranged with Shūme to establish the shrine as the junior village's guardian deity (*chinjugami*). The collusion between the village head and the priest reflects, in retrospect, the special stature of Shinmei-*gū* within Ogawa-*mura* (*KC* 1959, 853). Shūme's second son—his eldest succeeded him at Shinmei-*gū*—was among the group of farmers that set about reclaiming the new *shinden*. Like him, many of the settlers were the second and third sons of Ogawa-*mura* households. The Miyazakis went on to distinguish themselves as skillful agriculturists and were later successful in sericulture and in tea and indigo production.

Kumano-*miya* was promoted to the rank of "village shrine" in 1873 and in 1907 was selected to receive ceremonial offerings from the Meiji government. A smaller and, visually at least, less prosperous shrine than Shinmei-*gū*, it presently sits tucked behind a housing tract. Both shrines, however, outdistance the other Kodaira shrines in prestige, patronage, size, and financial solvency; and both signify the historicity of Furusato Kodaira.

They also represent Kodaira's outward-facing creed by virtue of their public, official character. Their unofficial counterparts are the private yard shrines maintained by native households. Yard shrines are the focus of a variety of coteries and communal activities among natives; collectively, they represent the native sector exclusively. In view of their private, unofficial, and exclusive character, they constitute an inward-facing creed.

Yard Shrines

There are well over one hundred small, private shrines maintained by native Ogawa-*chō* households, most of whom are in some way involved with farming and husbandry. The shrines are known as *teinaisha*, or "yard shrines," and more popularly as *yashiki-gami*, or "homestead *kami*." Since shrines and *kami* tend to be conflated (with the exception of the "adult" shrines in the citizens' festival), *yashikigami* refers to both the shrine building itself and the enshrined *kami*.

Without trespassing, one can get a fairly good idea of the prevalence of yard shrines among native householders, since their red *torii* peek above the dense hedge or stone wall around most natives' homes. Sometimes the shrines themselves are visible. Most are the size of a large dollhouse, although a few are as big as a large toolshed. Not all yard shrines have *torii*; some, having rotted away, remain unreplaced, even though prayers and oblations continue to be performed at the shrine itself. The casual looker will conclude that the Katō *ie* maintains the best-preserved, and some of the most elaborate, yard shrines. Most are outfitted with a shiny red *torii*, crisp paper decorations, and polished offering vessels set out on the tiny porches alongside a pair of sparkling white ceramic foxes (fig. 13).

According to Miyazaki of Shinmei-*gū*, about one hundred of these Ogawa-*chō* household shrines are registered with his shrine. Every year he provides the owners with *gohei*, the white or red zigzag paper strips embodying the *kami*. One yard shrine owner and Shinmei-*gū* parishioner, Koyama K., mentioned that he purchased the strips from Miyazaki when the latter made his priestly rounds several days prior to the *hatsuuma* festival in February (described below). Koyama offers between 400 and 1,000 yen in return for the ritual papers.

As the following anecdote shows, the overwhelming majority of the yard shrines are dedicated to Inari—a *kami* of agricultural productivity and material wealth whose messenger is a fox. I asked Ogawa Z., a descendant of Kurobei and chair of the Gakuen Nishi-*chōkai* (neighborhood association), whether he knew anything about *yashikigami*. He promptly replied that there were extremely few in Kodaira, which is

Fig. 13. A yard shrine owned by an Ogawa Eight farm household.
    (Photo by author)

simply not true. Thinking that he might have misunderstood me, I described a typical yard shrine, adding that there were over a hundred in
Ogawa-*chō* alone. He brightened and exclaimed, "Oh! You mean Inari-
san!" Other *yashikigami* include Benten, Suijin, Konpira, Kōjin, and
Hōsōjin, who are known, respectively, as the *kami* of culture and protector of women; water *kami*; ocean *kami* and protector of sailors and
fishers; kitchen *kami*; and smallpox *kami*.

These various household *kami* have the attributes of *chijin*, or earth-
place *kami*. Inari, for example, is said to have territorial rights to and
spiritual authority over a given place. The territorial aspect of Inari has
been explained in reference to the homonym *inari*, which means "to
become settled in a place." Symbolically, Inari/*inari* represents the con-
tingencies of the reclamation and settlement of *shinden* and the ensuing
process of village-making (Namiki and Tachikawa 1964, 31).[3] Should a

family move, its yard shrine is often left behind and can fall into disrepair if the new residents do not worship or care for it. The departing family may hand over the shrine's *gohei*—the paper strips that embody the *kami*—to a neighbor who agrees to worship on their behalf. The assumption is that, left unattended, the *kami* (Inari) will be thrown into confusion and start a fire or bring ill fortune (*HMSS* 1971, 984–85).

Yoshino notes that, according to the theory of *gogyō* (the five agents: wood, fire, earth, metal, water), Inari is endowed with an "earth" nature, which means that it is activated or animated by fire (1981, 97–98). Uegaki, a sericulturist and farm manual writer active in the late 1700s, explains that *hatsuuma*, the lunar calendrical day on which Inari is paid special homage, marks a period during which yang forces, such as sunlight, are at their peak ([1803] 1981, 69).[4] Since the earth is made productive by sunlight, Inari thus is associated with agricultural productivity. For Inari to start a fire implies a topsy-turvy state of affairs; and since Inari is a *kami* of wealth and fortune, the further implication is that a confused and unattended yard shrine will bring poverty and bad luck.

Many native Ogawa-*chō* households have legends to relate about their yard shrines. Collectively, these stories illustrate the place-*kami* aspect of Inari and also describe the circumstances that lead to the installation of yard shrines in general. For example, the story told by the Tachikawa household is part of a repertoire of Kodaira folktales. Their property formerly belonged to the Arai household, also Kodaira natives. One year, "a long time ago," an elderly member of the Tachikawa household fell ill, and a fortune-teller advised the family members to pay homage to their *yashikigami*. They were surprised, for they were unaware that an Inari inhabited their property. A deep hole dug at the base of a zelkova tree yielded a stone fox, which they began to worship on that spot. Needless to say, the ailing family member subsequently recovered (Namiki and Tachikawa 1964, 33).

My Kodaira landlord, Ōto S., told a similar story. About twenty years ago, he and his family had "found" and thus "inherited," as he put it, a stone shrine on their property near the outhouse. The Shinmei-*gū* priest—the Ōtos are parishioners—advised them to move the shrine to a more auspicious site and, since the old one had crumbled, to buy a new one as well. The roof of the found shrine, which now lies behind the new shrine, is supposed to have a name and date carved on it, but we could find no inscriptions. Like its predecessor, the new shrine is made of stone. Ōto mentioned that he had bought it at a "bargain price"

(150,000 yen) from Ogawa Y., a stonemason and descendant of Kurobei. (Stone shrines require less upkeep and are generally crude versions of the more intricate wooden structures.) The elevated base of my landlord's shrine was incised to resemble a castle wall, and a bamboo leaf design was carved on both sides of the miniature shrine proper. Its makeshift plywood door was jammed shut. As Ōto fiddled with it, his wife wondered aloud if there was really an image inside. "Nah, the kids probably took it out," but he never did manage to get the door open for us to see for sure. My impression was that the Ōtos, unlike the Katōs, were neither knowledgeable about nor assiduous in their treatment of the household Inari.

The installation and upkeep of yard shrines are related to the establishment of branch households and the tenor of their relations with main households. Collective oblations at a yard shrine may help to cement relations between main and branch households (cf. Nakane 1967; Sekiguchi 1972). By the same token, close relations between main and branch households may facilitate the initial installation of a share of the main household's *yashikigami* in the yard of a branch household. However, not all native households who claim to maintain tenacious intra-*ie* ties possess yard shrines, and not all native households with *yashikigami* maintain close main household–branch household relations.

A study of yard shrines in neighboring Higashikurume City revealed that old branch households tended to possess a yard shrine when the main household did; if the main household had never possessed or no longer possessed a shrine, then, usually, neither did the branches (*HKSS* 1979, 1048). This tendency seems to hold for Kodaira's native households as well, although the situation is complicated by a branch household's dependence or nondependence on the main household, as I discuss below. In the Ōto family, the main household had gone bankrupt and moved to Tachikawa "some years ago." It was at that time, it seems, that the Ōto yard shrine fell into disrepair. To give another example, neither the Asami main household nor any of its branches possess yard shrines. The househead of one rather recently established branch explained to me that the Asamis were not wealthy landowners on a scale large enough to warrant a household shrine. He also admitted that relations between main and branch households have been loose and informal.

Since Asami is a native *ie* of means, we might wonder how large is "large enough." While exact landholding figures are not publicly available, it is clear that Kodaira households with yard shrines, such as Katō, Koyama, Kobayashi, Ogawa, Hosoda, and Miyadera, were and are still—despite the postwar land reform—affluent and influential landowners who are well respected, particularly within the native sector. However, the extent of a household's landholdings alone does not constitute a necessary condition for having a yard shrine. Nor does an agricultural livelihood, although most *yashikigami* owners presently pursue or at one time pursued farming as a full-time or part-time occupation. It was also common in the Edo period, when the majority of yard shrines were established, for merchant and artisan households to have yard shrines (Miyamoto 1981, 282).

In Kodaira, among the main-branch relationships that affect and are affected by yard shrines, two of the most typical are (1) main households with dependent branches and (2) main households with nondependent branches. When the branches were, at the time of fission, economically dependent on the main household, they made their oblations at the main household's yard shrine. Since the majority of dependent branches were established within the main household's residence compound, it was a virtually foregone conclusion that they would share the same shrine. The same is true of branch households today that occupy the upstairs in a two-story house—I learned of two such situations in the Ogawa Eight. Whether or not these branch households will install a yard shrine of their own when and if they move somewhere else seemed to be a wholly subjective and negotiable matter.

Old branch households that were not economically dependent on the main household tended to have their own yard shrines. In the Ogawa Eight, dependent branches usually were established within the main household's homestead and were not incorporated within the system of neighborhood divisions described in chapter 3. Moreover, during the Edo period, they were entered in the religious sect and population registers under the main household. Nondependent branch households were the overall norm among those formed in Ogawamura, probably because of the possibilities for independence in a *shinden* situation (*KC* 1959, 913–14), where land was available for acquisition in the following ways: (1) a branch could establish itself in another *shinden* village; (2) in the same village, a branch could take over the land of a settler who could not perform the rigorous labor of reclamation; or (3) a branch could start a commercial operation, such as milling or oil pressing.

In Kodaira the greatest amount of household fissioning occurred after the Meiji Restoration (*KC* 1959, 852–53, 868), although a number of native branch households were established on *shinden* in and around the Kodaira Seven before that time. Between 1680 and 1804, the Shimizus, who were among the original settlers in Ogawa-*mura*, established eight branch households in that village and also in Nonaka-*shinden* and Tokura-*shinden* (Kokubunji City). Similarly, the Katōs established branch households in Tokura-*shinden* in the 1750s (Itō 1961, 87; Katayama 1959, 267–68). In Ogawa-*mura* the decision to establish a branch household was made by the househead in consultation with the eldest son, and the majority of branches were established at the time of a younger son's marriage.

The explanation given for the comparatively low rate of fissioning during the Edo period is that the infertile *shinden* were not productive enough to warrant partitioning (*KC* 1959, 912–14). In the Meiji period, on the other hand, the burgeoning of sericulture and tea and indigo production, which individual households could manage sufficiently, facilitated the emergence of nondependent branch households. Sericulture especially predominated during the late nineteenth and early twentieth centuries. In 1874 nearly 52 percent of all Ogawa-*mura* farm households were engaged in sericulture, rising to 74 percent in 1886. Corresponding percentages for Ogawa-*shinden* are 55 percent and 83 percent. When the worldwide demand for silk plummeted in the 1930s, many of these farm households collapsed and turned instead to shop-keeping (*KC* 1959, 376–77, 576–78).

Although precise data for Kodaira are not available, a 1983–84 survey of yard shrines in neighboring Higashiyamato City offers comparable supporting evidence for the second pattern of branch household formation in conjunction with *yashikigami* possession. The survey revealed that, of the twenty-eight yard shrines whose origins could be substantiated, nine were established during the Edo period and the rest between 1868 and 1940. Moreover, only two of the fifty-nine shrines surveyed were "found objects," while about seventeen were said by the present owners to have been "brought along" by the household in question when it was set up as a branch (Higashiyamato-*shi* jishū gurūpu 1984).

That a main household and its nondependent branch or branches have their own yard shrines does not preclude a close relationship between them. In the first place, a branch's shrine was usually installed as a share of the main household's shrine, signifying the extension of a transcendent, affective bond between the households. Moreover, given the place-*kami* aspect of Inari, this "sharing" of a *yashikigami* may have, at one time, signified the consolidation of an *ie*'s spatial domain, both in the sense of actual landholdings and in the sense of affective enclosure. And although each branch household still celebrates its own *yashiki-gami*, every year on *hatsuuma*, it also offers up to the main household's shrine rice steamed with red beans (*sekihan*), *sake*, fried tofu (*aburage*), dried sardines (*mezashi*), and tapers (*tōmyō*). On this date, the branches also assist in cleaning the shrine and help erect colored banners, usually inscribed with the phrase "shōichi-i Inari daimyōjin" and their names.[5] These joint activities demonstrate symbolically the relative tenacity of intra-*ie* ties, although, as some natives have remarked, the fact that their main and branch households no longer feast together on that day indicates the gradual thinning of those ties.

A given household's shrine may also serve as the focal point for a voluntary but exclusive consociation (*kō*) based on faith (*shinkō*) and heartfulness (*kokoro*). The yard shrine of Koyama K. offers an exemplary case in point. It also illustrates the manner in which a yard shrine may become a place of public worship. Popularly known as Kasamori Inari, or "pox-warding Inari,"[6] the shrine was installed about 135 years ago. Although no one quite knows why, Kasamori Inari was the focus of rowdy pilgrimages at the turn of this century. Tea shops, snack stalls, and bonsai vendors lined the path to the shrine, where Shinto dances (*kagura*) were performed and young couples danced until midnight. The shrine's prosperity sparked quarrels among its custodians over the disposition of donations and offerings. In the ensuing squabble, Kasa-mori Inari was forgotten—at least until 1961, when the Koyamas and their neighbors in the same *bangumi* formed an Inari-*kō* and rebuilt the shrine on a smaller scale. The shrine's revival was prompted by a spate of traffic accidents and other misfortunes in the neighborhood, which the native residents interpreted as signs of Inari's anger at having been neglected for so long (Namiki and Tachikawa 1964, 32). The inauguration in 1960 of the native-run Kodaira Local History Study Society, which campaigned for the renovation of historical structures, also may have influenced the decision to rebuild the shrine.

There are about thirty wooden slats nailed to the outside walls of Kasamori Inari shrine, and on each one an Inari-*kō* member's name and donation are recorded in descending order of the amount given. Koyama's recently deceased father leads the list with a donation of 40,000 yen. Six tall *torii*, offered upon the fulfillment of a prayer, strad-dle a short stone path in front of the shrine. Inside the toolshed-sized structure are hundreds of locally produced terra cotta and ceramic foxes stacked from floor to ceiling on either side of the altar, which is decorated with two red and one white *heisoku*, or sacred zigzag papers mounted on sticks. And on shelves fitted to an outer wall are stacked hundreds of dusty votive tablets (*ema*). Koyama's mother and several Inari-*kō* members offer daily prayers at the shrine, and on *hatsuuma* both the Inari-*kō* and members of the Koyama *ie* (including the main household) congregate to perform oblations.

Kasamori Inari also demonstrates how a yard shrine can provide a focus for intra-*ie* relations of a nonhierarchical nature, insofar as the shrine belongs to a branch household and is also worshiped by the Koyama main household. Although this branch, established in the 1850s by Koyama Umazō, prospered in the sesame oil trade, its economic rise did not correspond to a decline in the main household's fortunes, in which case a branch often assumes the role of a main household (Nakane 1967, 115). The intra-*ie* worship of Kasamori Inari represents not a change in the internal hierarchy between the main and branch households but, rather, an affirmation of the affective aspect of their relationship.

The Inari-*kō* is one of the consociations linking neighboring native households—nonnatives are not welcome—in a voluntary and horizontal manner, irrespective of other fixed or fluid forms of neighborhood divisions within a given *bangumi*. The Inari-*kō*, in short, is based on and revolves around faith and camaraderie—subjective qualities which, as the Kasamori Inari legend suggests, may yield to avarice should a shrine lose its exclusivity and become popular among the public at large. (This potential for avarice, in fact, is the rationale given for excluding newcomers from native consociations.) The Inari-*kō* intersects with Shinmei-*gū*: *kō* members are also parishioners, and Kasamori Inari is registered with the premier shrine, from which it receives ceremonial paraphernalia. There is, then, a degree of spatial articulation between the Koyama yard shrine and its Inari-*kō* and between Shinmei-*gū* and its parish; and this articulation further integrates the Ogawa Eight.

The Kasamori Inari-*kō* is one of several such consociations in the Ogawa Eight. There are also pilgrimage *kō*, organized on a *bangumi* basis, such as the Mitake-*kō* and the Mitsumine-*kō*, named after mountains in Saitama prefecture. Each year the members designate several representatives to make a mountain pilgrimage on their behalf. When the pilgrims return, a party is given for them. At this party, the pilgrims recount their adventures and distribute talismans, which are then plastered on the fences, mailboxes, and doors of native homes, distinguishing them from newcomer households. The talismans feature a wood-block print of a terrifying dog, seated and teeth barred, above which appears the name of the mountain shrine (*KC* 1959, 1210; *KK* 1983, 134–35; *Asahi shinbun*, 25 April 1984).

Yard shrines not only symbolize a household's (or *ie*'s) nativeness, but the mere obeisance to *yashikigami* indicates a recognition on the part of native households of their collective role as the custodians of "tradition." Apart from the actual exclusion of newcomers from membership in coteries such as the Inari-*kō*, the yard shrines visually distinguish native from newcomer homes, as do the "wolf-dog" talismans. Yard shrines and their owners also are the subject of legends and folktales that help to mystify the nativeness of native households. The Koyamas, who own Kasamori Inari, are perhaps the most notorious in this respect.

Even among natives, the Koyamas are referred to, without a trace of malice, as "kind of different" (*chotto kawatta*). The household is popularly known as *oni no yado*, or "house of demons." The name stems from their practice of entertaining demons during the end-of-winter (*setsubun*) festival in February, when all other households seek to purge evil from the premises by throwing beans and shouting, "Demons outside, fortune inside!" It is thought that this unusual practice was started by Umazō, who established the branch household to which Kasamori Inari belongs. *Sekihan*, or rice steamed with red beans, is prepared and heaped onto a square of paper that has been placed upon a round straw mat, the cover of a cylindrical straw bag used to store grains. (The paper has been creased twice to symbolize a crossroad.) *Sake* is sprinkled liberally over the festive rice; tapers are then lit, and the demons who have been expelled from neighboring households are invited to the feast. At midnight the househead escorts them to a crossroad, ostensibly to confuse the demons and keep them from returning to cause mischief; deposits there the straw round heaped with rice; and returns home, taking special care neither to look back nor to be discovered by anyone (Namiki and Tachikawa 1964, 31). According to the present househead, the demons are now escorted to an isolated corner of the homestead, since the increase in late-hour traffic on Oume Road precludes conducting the ritual along this historic thoroughfare.

The standard explanation for the Koyamas' demon-feasting ritual is that Umazō felt sorry for the expelled demons and hit upon the idea of feasting them in order to forestall any revengeful notions on their part. He was also keen on cajoling them into working their magic on behalf of his household, which was making a start in the oil-pressing business. It was cautiously volunteered by several natives that the "differentness" of the Koyamas extends to their being fox-spirit holders. Accompanying the belief in possession by human and animal spirits is the belief that certain households "hold" animal spirits, which usually work to enrich their owners, although the spirits may also abandon or turn against their holders. The Katōs, who maintain the most elaborate yard shrines, have also been implicated, albeit through innuendo, as fox-spirit holders. It is significant that both households are among the largest landowners in Kodaira; Koyama and Katō also are the most numerous names in the Ogawa Eight.

Yoshida has noted that animal-spirit holding is most common and that spirit possession occurs most frequently among unrelated neighbors and among families whose farmlands are in close proximity. He cites the relative autonomy of such neighboring households and the relative weakness of kinship ties as predictors of conflict, manifested in the form of spirit possession and accusations of animal-spirit holding. Unstable economic activities such as sericulture also facilitate these phenomena (Yoshida 1984, 86, 96, 102–3). The conditions for spirit holding and spirit possession enumerated by Yoshida fit the *shinden* context described in chapter 3, particularly the predominance of place (over "blood" and/or fictive kinship) ties and the striated arrangement of homesteads. Although one local historian, Oda T., mentioned to me that pilgrims to Kasamori Inari during its heyday were sometimes possessed by the resident spirit, it is not clear whether these incidents were attributed to the Koyama household as a fox-spirit holder. Although animal-spirit holding is a sensitive issue not easily broached by outsiders such as myself, an in-depth study of the Musashino *shinden* villages should yield much insight into this practice in the Kanto region.

It is no secret that the Koyamas are "different," for the story of Umazo feasting the demons is included among the folktales and research reports published by the Kodaira Local History Study Society. The unusual custom of the Koyamas is even mentioned in publications such as the Kodaira Women's Association newsletter (*Fujin no tsudoi nyūzu*, March 1984). Like the despotic antics of Ogawa Kurobei, the "kind of different" practices of the Koyamas add a dash of spice to Kodaira local history. Moreover, the fact that the Koyamas still feast the demons every February makes their custom a "living history."

Customs such as this one not only distinguish the native sector in Kodaira but imbue the city with an "authenticity" that vitalizes the image of Furusato Kodaira. In this connection, Koyama K.'s wife remarked half seriously and half facetiously that since their demon-feasting custom is so well known in Kodaira—"and your work will make us famous in the United States, too"—perhaps they should stop the practice. She claimed to be uninterested in the household's lore, since she does not view their lifestyle as "marvelously strange" (*fushigi*). However, she continued, her daughter does find it strange and has made researching the Koyama *ie*'s history her hobby. Perhaps other members of the new generation of *tochikko* will also be self-conscious enough about their household's nativeness to make it an object of research, quite apart from the question of whether they will actively perpetuate these customs on their own.

Shinmei-*gū*: Native Parishioners, New Worshipers

A discussion of the Shinmei-*gū* parish (*ujiko*) and related consociations will complement my review of the more exclusive neighborhood coteries associated with yard shrines. The Shinmei-*gū* ritual and ceremonial agenda is divided into two broad social categories—native and newcomer—each with activities specific to its residential status. The division exists for practical as well as ideological reasons, despite *furusato* rhetoric to the effect that Shinmei-*gū* is Kodaira's premier shrine and serves each sector of the city equally.

Ogawa S., a onetime sericulturist who now manages a grocery store in the Ogawa Eight, mentioned, with a touch of condescension, that neighborhood relations were "dry" outside the Ogawa Eight because "they" (the outsiders) did not have a parish shrine (*omiya-san*).[7] On the occasion of my unannounced visit, he and his fellow Shinmei-*gū* parishioners were busy assembling and decorating their *bangumi*'s lantern-float (*mandō*),[8] which the younger men would shoulder and bear boisterously in the evening's festive procession—the Yagumo *shinkōsai*—along Oume Road. Yagumo-*jinja*, one of the eight small shrines incorporated into the Shinmei-*gū* complex, is dedicated to Susanoō, the tempestuous younger brother of the sun *kami*, Amaterasu. *Shinkōsai* denotes a procession in which the *kami*-body, temporarily enshrined for the occasion within an elaborate portable shrine, is paraded through the parish, purging it of noxious influences. This festival is but one of the Shinmei-*gū* parishioner-centered events in which the integrity of Ogawa Eight natives in particular stands out in high relief against the "dry" land inhabited by the newcomers.

A prior word about the significance of *ujiko*, both the parish and the parishioners, is in order. The term literally means "children or subordinates of the *uji*," which originally referred to a clan chieftain who, as an ancestral spirit, evidently was worshiped as an *ujigami* (or *shizoku-gami*). As explained earlier, when the *ujigami* gradually lost its lineal exclusivity, the *ujiko* came to comprise patron households of diverse backgrounds located within a specifically demarcated area. In 1871, soon after the Meiji Restoration, the government decreed that parishes (particularly of a district shrine, such as Shinmei-*gū*) were to double as census tracts and that the possession of a shrine's talisman was evidence of a household's parish registration. Although this system—which recalls the Edo-period temple parish system discussed below—was discontinued two years later, shrine parishes continue to retain their place-centeredness (Chiba 1970, 241–42). The Shinmei-*gū* parish encompasses the native households of Ogawa-*chō* and secures the boundaries of the natives' society.

The Shinmei-*gū* parish is subdivided into ten constituencies: the Ogawa Eight plus the peripheral Ogawa Hon-*chō* and Ogawa Sakakita. The last two formerly were autonomous extensions (*aza*, or small [village] sections), which in 1962 were incorporated into Ogawa Nishi-*machi* and Ogawa Higashi-*chō*, respectively. Only the parish constituency representing the Ogawa Eight, however, entered lantern-floats in the Yagumo procession. As one woman watching the procession with me remarked: native households (like hers) farther back from Oume Road formed a less integrated alliance, even though, nominally at least, they were equally represented in the parish (refer to map 6).

According to Miyazaki of Shinmei-*gū*, there were about six hundred registered parish households as of 1984. He also noted that there are many others who call themselves *ujiko* but who are not registered. That these unregistered households regard themselves as parishioners is not entirely unwarranted; after all, the shrine advertises itself—in posters for the New Year's pilgrimage, for instance—as the city's tutelary *kami* (i.e., *ujigami*), implying that all Ogawa-*chō* residents, native and newcomer alike, are *ujiko*. Similarly, one of the set of local playing cards (*kyōdo karuta*) distributed by city hall to newcomers, as a means of introducing them to historical institutions and customs in Kodaira, defines an *ujiko* as, simply, a group of residents ("villagers") who worship at the same shrine. There is, in short, a glaring discrepancy between the popular (*furusato*) rhetoric dealing with the Shinmei-*gū* parish and the actual constituency of the *ujiko*, which is limited to Ogawa natives.

Each parish household has a membership card, filed in one of Miyazaki's several folders, on which is printed an address, the name of the househead, and the name of the head's successor if one already has been selected. The predictability of the succession and continuity of a household within the same setting continues to ensure the integrity of the Ogawa Eight. As Miyazaki paged through the folders, I could see that the vast majority of names belonged to native households, and in fact the *ujiko* essentially is limited to select native households.[9] The criteria for membership, apart from house ownership, include permanent residence within Kodaira, local seniority and stature, and the guarantee of a successor to assume responsibility for the household's religious (i.e., parish) obligations.

Historically, the parish was a less exclusive organization in that a pilgrimage to the shrine and the payment of certain fees, in addition to house ownership and financial solvency, were sufficient grounds for membership. Presently, at Shinmei-*gū*, there is a token membership fee of 100 yen, which is separate from the donations for festival-related and other expenses throughout the year. In addition, the wealthier parishioners foot the cost of shrine repairs (*Shinmeisama*, 1 June 1984).

Miyazaki also pointed out that there is no longer an *ujiko* handbook; the parishioners prefer a less formal, word-of-mouth style of administration. This practice alone reveals the select clientele that parishioners now represent, for the disregard of a standardized protocol suggests that they are familiar enough with one another to make informal agreements and tacit understanding feasible modes of administration. Actually, it was not until our second interview that Miyazaki acknowledged the exclusivity of the Shinmei-*gū* parish. At our initial meeting, he had casually remarked that it was relatively easy for a household to join. The househead merely had to ask the *ujiko* delegate of his area; "it was as simple as that." I interpreted this implausible statement as a sign of his initial desire to cater to what he presumed to be my "democratic American" sensibility; his long digressions on Shinto as a universalistic, peace-loving religion may have been delivered for the same reason. Only later did he admit to the existence of strict criteria for parish membership noted earlier.

In addition to those criteria, Miyazaki has added neighborhood stability, regardless of a given household's native status. Thus, native households in Sakae-*chō*, despite their eagerness to do so, have not been permitted to join the Shinmei-*gū* parish. The area, says Miyazaki, is simply not stable enough to guarantee a succession of *ujiko* custodians, of whom there must be three for each constituency: the parish subdivision delegate, the neighborhood association chair, and the chair of the agricultural association. As a rule, the *ujiko* custodians are elected to serve a three-year term, although some have served for over thirty years. Two or even all three of the posts are sometimes held concurrently by the same individual, and, moreover, the nepotism often characterizing these posts recalls their hereditary nature during the Edo period.

The Sakae-*chō* area remained mostly forested and unpopulated through the 1950s. Between 1963 and 1970, however, it experienced the largest percentage of population growth of all the city's districts: from 50 to 898 persons (14 to 248 households). By 1983 more newcomers had moved to Sakae-*chō*, bringing the population of this higgledy-piggledy sector to 1,394 persons (469 households) (Kodaira-*shi* shiminbu shiminka 1983b, 22; *KSH*, 20 May 1959, 1 October 1970). Although parish membership is not available to them, natives from Sakae-*chō* have been recruited instead for the Shinmei-*gū* worshipers' association (*sūkeikai*). This group, as a rule, is composed not of households but of individuals recruited by a shrine to participate in certain activities (see Chiba 1970, 36–37).[10] New branches of Ogawa Eight households are also considered prime worshipers' association candidates and often graduate to parishioner status after they have established themselves—a state that, according to Miyazaki, takes about ten years to achieve. The shrine's *sūkeikai* recruitment campaign, which includes advertisements in its newsletter, is conducted each year in June. Presently there are about ninety worshipers from Nakashima-*chō* and a dozen or more each from Sakae-*chō*, Tsuda-*machi*, and Gakuen Nishi-*machi*. All these areas lie within the domain of the former Ogawa-*mura* and—again according to Miyazaki—are unable to maintain a stable parish (refer to map 6). In short, the constituency of the Shinmei-*gū ujiko* and *sūkeikai* is contingent upon both the original settlement pattern of Ogawa-*mura* and the subsequent (and projected) population growth and development of Kodaira as a whole.

In contrast to the general trend, Shinmei-*gū* parishioners far exceed the number of worshipers' association members, largely because of the strict membership criteria demanded by Miyazaki. He is able to be so selective because Shinmei-*gū* can rely on the steadfast support of Ogawa Eight natives. Native households in turn provide this support as a means of controlling the circumstances of their existence, in the wake of rapid population growth and internal transformations, and to demonstrate, increasingly self-consciously, their enduring local stature and influence.

Generally speaking, the only condition for membership in worshipers' associations is said to be the "subjective will" or "faith" of individuals.[11] As a group, however, they may be bound by similar occupations or common interests, which in turn may presuppose regional or residential factors (Chiba 1970, 51–53). Thus, although the *sūkeikai* domain is not explicitly limited to a particular region, residence and, by extension, place identity can serve to regulate membership. Also, although individuals generally are recruited, households are often the actual units of membership.

Miyazaki explained that, although they are segregated by membership criteria, Shinmei-*gū* parishioners and worshipers participate as equals in most of the shrine's festivals and ceremonies. Still, the Yagumo lantern-float procession largely is the undertaking of Ogawa Eight parishioners, although some members of the worshipers' association join in shouldering the floats. The status disparity between the two organizations may be summarized as follows: whereas parishioners support ceremonial activities as a duty (*gimu*), worshipers do so as a privilege or a right (*kenri*).

The chief priest rationalized his shrine's prominence and integrity by noting that, unlike Kumano-*miya*, Shinmei-*gū* enjoys a stable and supportive parish. That is, whereas the Ogawa Eight have retained much of their historical texture and composition, dramatic social and topographical changes, such as high-rise projects and tract homes, have disturbed the contiguity of the Kumano-*miya* parish, which is spread out over most of the area of the former Ogawa-*shinden* (namely, Naka-*machi*, Kihei-*chō*, and Gakuen Higashi-*chō*) (refer to map 6). Nor does Kumano-*miya* enjoy the luxury of clear-cut, aligned, and coinciding parish, neighborhood association, and *bangumi* territories. Its parish region is peppered with manifold autonomous neighborhood associations reflecting the diversity of the area, which is popularly regarded as the domain of *sararīman*. The Ogawa Eight, on the other hand, is recognized as the domain of native (farm) households.

A somewhat different fate has befallen the 220 (as of 1962) parishioners of the modest Hie-*jinja*. Its parish covers the first to fourth *bangumi* in Ogawa-*chō*, apparently a vestige of an earlier division of parishioners between it and another small shrine on the east side that later merged with Shinmei-*gū*. The premier shrine, however, has all but monopolized the membership of these 220 households. Hie-*jinja* is now looked after by a *sūkeikai*-like parish that lacks the strength of commitment and obligation accorded Shinmei-*gū*. Nevertheless, its priesthood has remained the hereditary prerogative of the Yamaguchi household.

The influence- and territory-consolidating tendency of Shinmei-*gū* is further demonstrated by Miyazaki's relatively recent appointment as priest of Musashino-*jinja* in Tenjin-*chō*. (Miyazaki is also the priest of Kumano-*jinja* in Higashiyamato City.) Since the position of priest of this and all other smaller Kodaira shrines (with the exception of Hie-*jinja*) formerly was held concurrently by the Kumano-*miya* Miyazaki, this situation indicates a recent redistribution of power between the two brothers who represent Kodaira's two largest shrines.

As another means of increasing Shinmei-*gū*'s affective reach, Miyazaki has inaugurated several innovative "small festivals," such as the children's festival immediately following the rather perfunctory annual thanksgiving ceremony in September. Miyazaki pointed out that small festivals, although they are nominally less significant than grand festivals, can be staged on a grand scale, whereas a grand festival might actually amount to no more than a truncated, mechanical ritual attended by key parish officials. The children who participate in the children's festival are pupils of the kindergarten opened in 1963 with the parishioners' permission within the shrine compound. Not all of the 150 or so pupils are from native households, and quite a few are bused to and from their homes in neighboring cities.

One attraction of this kindergarten, as Miyazaki's wife, the vice-principal, noted, is that it offers a "comprehensive religious education." By the same token, these small festivals also guarantee a steady "outsider" clientele, since parents (mostly mothers) invariably come to watch their daughters and sons shoulder miniature portable shrines, several of which are made during art class. The children often end up partaking in other school cum shrine events as well, such as the annual outdoor exorcism (*oharai*) held at the end of June. By linking the school's curriculum with the shrine's ritual and ceremonial calendar, Miyazaki has expanded both the "outsider" clientele and, by association, the affective reach of the shrine. Other festivals at which outsiders are welcome include *setsubun* in February, *shichigosan* in November, and the New Year's pilgrimage. *Setsubun* has already been described in connection with the Koyamas' yard shrine. *Shichigosan*, literally "seven-five-three," is a ritual performed to ensure the healthy development of three-, five-, and seven-year-old children. All these events are openly acknowledged as fund-raising events. The basic fee for the *shichigosan* ritual at Shinmei-*gū* was 10,000 yen in 1984. As with the "child" shrines paraded in the citizens' festival, reference to shrine ceremonials as "*children's* festivals" implies that the event is intended not only for children but also for nonnatives and outsiders, for whom the prefix "child(ren)" is a euphemism.

Attendance at Shinmei-*gū* functions is treated as a form of obligatory and privileged participation, and the "upcoming events" column in the shrine's newsletter indicates as much. In the 1 July 1983 edition, parishioners and worshipers were urged to attend the ancestors' festival (*obon*) and associated summer exorcisms.[12] Festival and other events explicitly open to outsiders are announced as such, and the fact that outsiders are welcome to participate is emphasized. Both the Yagumo lantern-float procession and the New Year's pilgrimage are widely advertised by posters and ads placed in the local edition of the major newspapers.

The territory within which the Shinmei-*gū* parish and worshipers' association are organized lies within the former Ogawa-*mura*, and membership in the parish especially has remained more or less limited to native Ogawa-*mura* households. A hard-and-fast distinction is drawn between "us" and "them," despite the numerical predominance of newcomers. A major factor facilitating this distinction is the coincidence of the *bangumi*, neighborhood association, and parish boundaries, a factor in turn facilitated by the continuity and contiguity of native households over the course of centuries, in some cases. At least 600 (90 percent) of the 668 households who are members of neighborhood associations (*jichikai*) in the Ogawa Eight are also Shinmei-*gū* parishioners (table 4).

Parish households typically are also members of their *bangumi*'s neighborhood association. Not only do association chairs serve concurrently as parish custodians, but neighborhood association meeting places double as sites for late-night festivities following Shinmei-*gū* festivals. Directly after the Yagumo lantern-float procession, for example, each of the eight *ujiko* groups retired to its *bangumi*'s meeting place to drink (and drink and drink), dance, and gossip the night away. Unlike most neighborhood associations, none of the Ogawa Eight interdict religious activity. As I discuss in the next chapter, the tenacious integrity of the natives' society (among other factors) has prompted certain

Table 4. *Ogawa* Bangumi *and Neighborhood Associations*

Bangumi	Neighborhood Association
1	92
2	45
3	60
4	57
5	140
6	69
7	50
8	155
H	197
S	244

NOTE: Listed above are the ten Shinmei-*gū* parish subdivisions: the eight *bangumi* plus Hon-*chō* (H) and Sakakita (S). There are 668 neighborhood association member households in the Ogawa Eight, and 441 in Hon-*chō* and Sakakita, which together constitute a demographically more diverse area. Therefore, most of the 600 registered parish households are probably accounted for among the 668 Ogawa Eight neighborhood association member households. Data are from the Neighborhood Association Registry (1983–84) provided by the Civic Life Department, Kodaira City Hall.

newcomer households to form their own neighborhood associations as enclaves within the Ogawa Eight. That the Ogawa Eight parish and neighborhood associations overlap to a singularly high degree is illustrated, in contrast, by similar figures for the Megurita-*chōkai*. The Megurita neighborhood association, like its Ogawa Eight counterparts, forms an integral domain and is considered a native enclave. But of the 729 member households, only 26 (3.5 percent) are parishioners of Hikawa-*jinja*.[13]

Shinmei-*gū* is a public institution, although it also maintains a private aspect manifest in the form of an exclusive parish and a selectively recruited worshipers' association. Visitors who are not parishioners or members of the worshipers' association are not denied entry to the shrine, but they may participate only in those festivals to which they have been invited, such as the summer exorcism, various children's festivals, and the New Year's pilgrimage. Distinctions between natives and newcomers, insiders and outsiders, are also maintained by Kodaira's historical temples.

Original Temples and Temple Origins

During the Edo period, temples were far more en-
meshed in politics than shrines were, and they intervened more overtly
in community affairs than shrines did. Temples were an instrument and
extension of the *bakufu*, which (in accordance with its anti-Christian
policy) required all Japanese to register as members of a Buddhist parish to "prove" their orthodoxy. Shrine patronage, in contrast, generally
was not as systematized and was informed by custom, as opposed to
law—although these distinctions tended to coalesce over time, as the
term *customary law* suggests (Maruyama 1975, 629).

Shōsen-*ji* presently is the sole temple in the area formerly known as
Ogawa-*mura*, although two temples were established there in 1656 at
the outset of the village's reclamation. The other was Myōhō-*ji*, which
was transferred to Enoto-*shinden* (Kokubunji City) in 1909. By the
middle of the eighteenth century, however, its parish—which consisted
of all but a section of Enoto-*shinden*—had already been subsumed by
Shōsen-*ji*. Shōsen-*ji* was established in Ogawa-*mura* as a branch of
Gekkei-*ji* in Edo, which was affiliated with Enkaku-*ji*, the famous Rinzai Zen temple in Kamakura.[14] Shōsen-*ji*'s principal image is Yakushi
Nyorai, the Buddha of medicine and healing. Kurobei probably commissioned a Rinzai temple for the *shinden* village because his parent
village's parish temple was of that sect. The eventually relocated
Myōhō-*ji*, however, belonged to the Sōtō Zen sect,[15] and its principal
image is Shaka Nyorai, the historical Buddha (Ashida 1977, 265;
Harada 1964, 42; *KK* 1983, 111–12).

Both Shōsen-*ji* and Myōhō-*ji* were established by "special petition"
(*kanjō*) as *hikidera*, or "commissioned temples." A commissioned temple symbolized the relative autonomy of a *shinden* village and its independence from the parent village, for its establishment meant that a
given *shinden*'s residential population was sufficiently stable to form and
support a temple parish. The stability of such temples was directly contingent upon the number of parishioner households (*danka*) in their
charge. Because the loss of even one parishioner household could pre-
sage collapse, temples were sometimes ferociously competitive in their
efforts to secure a parish.

The emergence of the *hikidera* system accompanied the widespread
reclamation of *shinden* in the 1720s and reflected the *bakufu*'s "one village, one temple" policy, implemented at the outset of the Tokugawa

regime. In tandem with this measure was a measure aimed at restoring and preserving "historical temples" (*koseki-ji*). The criterion for "historical" and thus tax-exempt status was included in a 1688 edict: temples constructed prior to 1631 were classified as "historical temples," and those after that date were classified as "new site temples" (*shinchi-ji*). Not a few temples fabricated an illustrious history and a sectarian genealogy in order to qualify for the tax exemption. Priests were forbidden from holding concurrent posts, and temples lacking a resident clergy were categorized as foundered temples. The policy forbade both the construction of temples representing new sects and the establishment of "private" temples (Andō 1977, 111; Sakamoto 1966, 81, 86, 91). A similar policy to abolish temples with neither a parish nor a resident clergy was implemented in the Meiji period, and in the 1870s the number of temples countrywide was reduced from 94,000 to 72,600 (Andō 1977, 150, 164).

Commissioned temples were not considered "new," since they were mainly foundering or foundered temples transferred (in name) to another locale and thereby revitalized. These insolvent temples often were branches of "historical temples," a main-branch relationship that was resumed and perpetuated through the *hikidera* system (Sakamoto 1966, 83, 97). Tax-exempt land (*jochi*) was especially designated by the *bakufu* for temple or shrine use only.[16] This official land grant occasionally was augmented by a gift of land from the head of a *shinden* village, in an attempt to induce a "historical temple" to reestablish an impoverished branch in that *shinden*. Since the *bakufu* effectively had limited the number of viable temples, branches available for revitalization were sometimes in short supply, making for competition among *shinden* villages in quest of commissioned temples. The annual tax levied on the donated land, which was not tax exempt, was borne by village officials (Sakamoto 1966, 100).

The choice of one sect's temple over another usually was based on demographic factors. If the majority of a *shinden*'s initial settlers hailed from the same village and parish, then they had the right to choose a commissioned temple of the same sect as the parent village's (Sakamoto 1966, 98–100).[17]

Once a commissioned temple was established, the village head, in the capacity of *kaiki* (the term for a temple's pioneer founder—the founding priest was called *kaizan*), was responsible for ensuring the stability of the parish and often wielded authority over the temple itself (Kimura and Itō 1972, 201). Ogawa Kurobei was among the more autocratic *shinden* heads in this respect. One of his preconditions for settlement was that all settlers convert to the Rinzai sect (Harada 1964). Authoritarian measures such as this made establishing branch temples in *shinden* villages an attractive proposition for the Buddhist sects. The Ōbaku Zen sect,[18] founded in 1659, made rapid inroads mainly because its priests were encouraged by the *bakufu* to establish temples in *shinden* villages. The single Ōbaku temple in Kodaira is Enjō-*in*, whose founding priest was also a *shinden* financier.

Although Kurobei's control over Buddhism surely aroused the indignation of the *shinden* settlers, no records survive of any disputes between them and the head on the matter of sect conversion and parish registration. However, temple-related disputes that erupted in the other "Kodaira" *shinden* are better documented and serve to illustrate what may have transpired in Ogawa-*mura* as well. Prospective settlers in Nonaka-*shinden*, for instance, were forced to pledge allegiance to Enjō-*in*. It was not long before the immigrant farmers reneged on their initial agreement; they belong to different Buddhist sects and in the end were unwilling to convert to the Ōbaku sect. Instead, in 1728 a group of eight farmers registered with a temple in Fuchū, a village several kilometers to the south. Just as there were settlers who were reluctant to convert, there were also those who wished to but were restrained from doing so by their parish temples, as demonstrated by disputes involving Ōnumata-*shinden* settlers. The immigrant farmers, who at first had remained parishioners of their respective parent-village temples, petitioned for a commissioned temple in 1743, about seventeen years after their arrival. The reason given was that the parent-village temples were too far away to serve the parishioners' immediate needs. The Ōnumata-*shinden* head thereupon negotiated with a certain priest, who suggested revitalizing Senzō-*in*, a foundered Tendai temple in a neighboring village.[19] The priest of the main temple readily agreed to the scheme, and permission for the transfer was granted in 1744 by the magistrate of temples and shrines. The settlers then appealed to their respective parent-village temples for permission to switch parishes. Not surprisingly, the temples refused, for the loss of parishioners would adversely affect them; and in 1745 the temples appealed to *bakufu* officials. The officials ruled in the settlers' favor, ordering each parent-village temple to surrender part of its parish to Senzō-*in* (Kimura 1964, 226–27; *KC* 1959, 134–36).

Although records are unavailable, the prevalence of parish-related disputes in the Kodaira *shinden* villages suggests that Ogawa-*mura* was similarly affected to some degree. Ogawa-*mura*, however, was unusual in that Kurobei established two temples from the start. One, Shōsen-*ji*, he named after himself (*shōsen* is the Chinese-style reading for *ogawa*). He established this temple as his household's *bodai-ji*, the term for a temple, dependent upon parishioners, that is primarily concerned with funerals and memorial services (Ashida 1977, 265; Kimura and Itō 1972, 200–201). Shōsen-*ji* was the larger and more prestigious of the two temples, as demonstrated by the three hectares of tax-exempt land (*jochi*) reserved for its construction. The second temple, Myōhō-*ji*, was built on a two-hectare site (*jochi*) a little over one kilometer east of the other temple.

In a blatant demonstration of autocracy, Kurobei designated his residence as the boundary dividing the two parishes, and until Myōhō-*ji*'s eventual displacement, efforts were made to equalize the number of parishioners belonging to each. In 1665, for example, two households from the Shōsen-*ji* parish were transferred to that of Myōhō-*ji*, whose parish had decreased by that number. The two households were to be transferred back to their original parish once the smaller temple's parish increased in number. By the time the village divisions (*kumi*) were formed, Shōsen-*ji*'s was the sole parish in the village (Kimura and Itō 1972, 203). It appears, then, that the two parishes initially functioned in the capacity of *kumi* to organize the growing village; but once the actual *kumi* system was inaugurated, one parish evidently was not only sufficient but also desirable from an administrative point of view. By initially dividing the village into two equal parishes, Kurobei was able to mediate both the authority of each temple and the loyalty of its parishioners. Similarly, the relocation of Shinmei-*gū* across from Shōsen-*ji*, in 1680, effectively unified and made spatially isomorphic the temple and shrine parish territories, a situation that has contributed to the integrity of the Ogawa Eight (cf. Kimura and Itō 1972, 183–84).

"Commissioned temple" is the generic term for two fundamental types of Buddhist institutions: *bodai-ji* and *kitō-ji*. *Bodai-ji*, among which the Zen and Jōdō[20] sects are most common, are temples "specializing" in funerals and memorial services; they do not, in principle (as opposed to practice), earn additional income through supplicant-centered services, such as exorcisms and devotionals. Generally speaking, those activities are the prerogative of temples classified as *kitō-ji* (*kitō* means "devotions"), among which the Shingon, Tendai, and Nichiren[21] sects predominate (Miyata 1972, 123; Tarumi 1983, 43–

Table 5. *"Kodaira Seven" Temple Parishes (1959)*

Type	Name (Sect)	Parishioners	
bodai-ji	Shōsen-*ji* (Rinzai)	600	All OM
	Heian-*in* (Rinzai)	200	All OS
	Enjō-*in* (Ōbaku)	250	NS (part Z & Y); part SS
	Kaigan-*ji* (Rinzai)	165	Part SS, Z, & MT
	Total	1,215	
kitō-ji	Senzō-*in* (Tendai)	120	All ON
	Enmei-*ji* (Shingon)	51	NS (part Z & Y)
	Hōjū-*in* (Shingon)	83	Part SS & MT
	Total	254	

NOTE: OM = Ogawa-*mura*; OS = Ogawa-*shinden*; NS = Nonaka-*shinden*; Z = Zenzae-mon-*gumi*; Y = Yoemon-*gumi*; SS = Suzuki-*shinden*; MT = Megurita-*shinden*; ON = Ōnumata-*shinden*. *Bodai-ji* refers to funeral temples and *kitō-ji* to devotional temples, although their functions have blurred over time. Data are from *KC* 1959, 1298. According to the incumbent priest of Shōsen-*ji*, the temple's parish numbered over 1,000 households in 1984, and similar increases may be assumed for the others.

The Nichiren temple, Daisen-*ji* (not included above), originally was located in Asakusa, where it was destroyed in the 1945 air raids. It was reestablished three years later in Kodaira. The temple has no Kodaira parish but, rather, continues to serve its former parishioners. Compared to the well-kept native temples which enjoy stable local support, Daisen-*ji* is in decrepit condition and also lacks an attached cemetery.

44). Kodaira's seven temples are roughly divided between these two types of institutions, although the Zen sect temples, as *bodai-ji*, monopolize the vast majority of parishioner households (table 5).

It was not long before Kodaira's *bodai-ji* began selling or bartering posthumous names in addition to installing and managing, either within their compounds or at locations throughout the village, small shrines housing a particular Buddhist deity or Shinto *kami*. During the Edo period, thirteen such shrines were established in Ogawa-*mura* alone, seven of them within Shōsen-*ji*. Competition among temples was not limited to securing a parish but involved attracting supplicants and clients (*shinja*) with an interest in devotionals as well. Presently, in this connection, an annual *daruma* fair, at which images of the Zen patriarch, Bodhidharma, are sold, is held at Shōsen-*ji* in March. Just as funeral temples adopted devotional rites, devotional temples undertook funeral services, although the former have maintained a larger number of parishioners.

Before I proceed to a discussion of Buddhist consocations, a brief word on Heian-*in* is in order. The relationship between Shōsen-*ji* and Heian-*in* is analogous to that between Shinmei-*gū* and Kumano-*miya*. Heian-*in*, a branch of Shōsen-*ji*, was established in 1739 as the parish temple of Ogawa-*shinden* settlers, who represented branches of Ogawa-*mura* households (*KC* 1959, 121). Its name formerly belonged to the pagoda at Gekkei-*ji*, from where the Ogawa-*mura* head summoned a priest to reside at the new *shinden* temple. Its main image is Shaka Nyorai, and its parish coincides with that of Kumano-*miya* (*KK* 1983, 114–15).

Heian-*in* is much smaller (.63 hectare) and lower in rank than Shōsen-*ji*, but it has never been destroyed by fire. (Unfortunately, however, the temple's historical records have yet to be indexed and analyzed.) In addition to funeral services, the small temple, like Shōsen-*ji* and several others in Kodaira, continues to stage an annual *segaki* ceremony in August and a star festival in December. The former is a memorial service to placate restless spirits. Parishioners buy *tōba*—the tall, thin, wooden grave markers that are the objects of the service—from the temple. A marker is sometimes taken home and utilized in a household's ancestor festival rites; afterward it is returned to the gravesite (see Smith 1974, 41–43). The star festival is a predominantly Shingon festival that other Buddhist sects (and Shinto shrines too) have incorporated into their ceremonial repertoire. It is essentially an occasion for celestial augury.

Memorials and auguries aside, both ceremonies continue to serve as fund-raising events. Miura H., the incumbent priest of Shōsen-*ji*, criticizes his colleagues for being businessmen first and priests a distant second, although he himself is an astute entrepreneur. Several years ago, his temple began selling *mizuko* Jizō, small statues of the Bodhisattva of children, offered up to the souls of aborted fetuses (*mizuko*). The high rate of induced abortion among Japanese women, coupled with their desire to mollify the allegedly agitated soul of the fetus, has made this sideline a most profitable one for temples.[22]

Buddhist Consociations

Apart from small shrines, markets, and *mizuko* Jizō, another primary way in which temples have augmented their income is by organizing *kō* (consociations). Temple-centered consociations emerged early in the Edo period as "money-collecting instruments" and soon met with the *bakufu*'s disapproval (Miyata 1976, 280–81). From the early 1700s on, edicts were promulgated forbidding the assembly of the consociations, some of which boasted as many as one hundred members; but the practice continued. It was not only their size that was alarming; the fact that some consociations admitted both men and women disturbed the officials' sense of Confucian sexual propriety (ibid., 280).

One of the seven small shrines established within Shōsen-*ji* consists of a Jizō statue given jointly in 1718 by a certain Ogawa and the custodians of the local *nenbutsu-kō* (*KC* 1959, 1315). Judging from the inscriptions on other donated statuary, the *nenbutsu-kō* appears to have been the only Buddhist consociation of its kind in the Kodaira Seven (see ibid., 1301–14). It remains active today, if greatly reduced in scale, primarily as a friendship coterie organized within each *bangumi* by the women of certain native, parishioner households. The association of *nenbutsu-kō* with Shōsen-*ji*, a Zen temple, is of interest here.

Historically, the *nenbutsu-kō* is a Jōdō sect consociation, its Zen sect counterpart being the Kannon-*kō*.[23] In Kodaira, only *nenbutsu-kō* were active, with the exception of a mysterious Kannon-*nenbutsu-kō* based in Ogawa 8-*bangumi*, as inscribed on a memorial stele gifted to Shōsen-*ji* in 1817 (Kodaira kyōdo kenkyūkai 1983, 20). The name suggests a conflation of the two different consociations.[24] Generally speaking, both types of consociation are explicitly territorial in terms of membership and activities, and both groups assemble at their parish temple for sessions of sutra chanting.

The *nenbutsu-kō* and Kannon-*kō*, with their emphasis on temple-centered functions, effectively helped to unite *shinden* villages comprising people of diverse backgrounds. These consociations assisted in delineating a village's social and geographic boundaries by installing landmarks, in the form of statues, which in turn provided a focus for the collective enactment of ritual activities (Kodama 1976, 235–38). The siting of these statues continues to demarcate and reinforce the boundaries of the natives' society. Miura, Shōsen-*ji*'s incumbent priest, told me that the *nenbutsu-kō* today is organized within each *bangumi* and meets at private homes. He noted that each group has its own peculiar style of sutra chanting. Whereas the members of one *bangumi*'s consociation sit in a circle and rotate a giant rosary among themselves, the members of another finger their own small rosaries. Style, then, also distinguishes the affective and instrumental boundaries of each *bangumi*, which, collectively, delineate the boundaries of the natives' society.

Another consociation, one more peripherally related to temples, is the *zenwan-kō*, or "tray-and-bowl" consociation, which was in existence in Kodaira by the early 1800s. The only extant records dealing with the *zenwan-kō*, however, concern a group in Suzuki- and Nonaka-*shinden*. In the *Wan-kō renmeichō* ([Tray-and-] bowl consociation rollbook, 1821), it is noted that sixteen farmers from Suzuki-*shinden* and five from Nonaka-*shinden* belonged to the consociation, which had two custodians. The membership distribution suggests that it was organized within the Enjō-*in* parish. The purpose of the tray-and-bowl consociation was to rent out banquet paraphernalia for Buddhist memorial services, weddings, and other large-scale events (*KC* 1959, 294–95). This function recently has been assumed by neighborhood associations and commercial wedding halls. The Gakuen Nishi-*chōkai*, for example, lends out gratis to members not only trays and bowls but also cushions, tents, radio-cassette players, tables and chairs, cordless microphones, and even a transceiver. Unlike the paraphernalia rented out by the *zenwan-kō*, these items are mostly hand-me-downs. Although the consociation is now defunct in Kodaira, it remains active in neighboring Higashi-yamato City (Musashino bijutsu daigaku seikatsu bunka kenkyūkai 1983, 427–70).

In its time, the *zenwan-kō*, like the *nenbutsu-kō*, was instrumental in forging and maintaining interhousehold ties between place-linked groups. The existence of this consociation seemed to signify the thinness of "blood" and/or fictive kinship ties, along with the relative absence of interhousehold relations based on economic dependency. *Zenwan-kō* in general are not established in villages or within parishes where wealthy main households provide their subordinate branches with the necessary banquet paraphernalia. In other words, the virtual absence, in the Kodaira Seven, of tenacious main-branch or other interhousehold relations structured around economic dependency, together with the prevalence of place ties over kinship ties, occasioned the viability of the tray-and-bowl consociation. Recently, however, wedding halls and neighborhood associations have absorbed the function of *zenwan-kō* in the native sector as well.

Shōsen-*ji*: Parishioners and Supplicants

In comparison to Shinto shrines, Buddhist temples have been mobile, extraterritorial institutions. These aspects were manifested in *shinden* villages in the form of commissioned temples and temporary parishes. More generally, despite the *bakufu*'s "one village, one temple" policy, the parish of a given temple often included a portion of the population of a neighboring or even distant village. Nevertheless, the majority of parish-dependent commissioned temples did serve to consolidate new villages, both in the sense that they were usually established by collective demand and because their stability was contingent upon securing an entire village's population as parishioners. Perhaps for these reasons, Kodaira's temples have proved very durable since their founding. Temple parish membership today involves a somewhat more formal procedure than shrine parish registration. A seal-impressed contract, in which the applicant pledges never to deviate from the Buddhist law and the sect's doctrine, is *de rigueur*. Membership, furthermore, is contingent upon securing a burial site in the temple's—in this case Shōsen-*ji*'s—cemetery, whereupon the names of a household's deceased members are duly recorded in the temple's death register.

Referring specifically to burial sites, Miura claims that Shōsen-*ji*, of which he is the seventeenth-generation incumbent, is patently concerned with fostering place identity. The following quotation is a synthesis of his remarks on this subject during our conversation in the temple's unpretentiously elegant reception room. The *tatami* room, filled with Zen ink paintings and Chinese antiques, contrasted sharply with the eclectic, Western decor of the Shinmei-*gū* sitting room. The robust, kimono-clad Miura affected an uncultivated manner, professing his belief that the preservation-through-use of an earthy local dialect— which I do not attempt to anglicize here—is the key to both social morality and communal integrity. In further contrast to Miyazaki, Miura did not volunteer any genealogical information or distribute any public relations literature.

> I oversee [as chief priest] four temples: Shōsen-*ji*, Heian-*in*, Gekkei-*ji*,[25] and another in Hakonegasaki, northwest of Kodaira. In my experience, the parishes of inner-city temples, such as Gekkei-*ji*, are rapidly decreasing, while those of suburban temples, like Shōsen-*ji*, are increasing. More people are moving to the suburbs, and inner-city land available for cemeteries is shrinking fast. Just this year alone, the Shōsen-*ji* parish increased by over one hundred households.
>
> But not just anyone can join the parish. Just the other day, I turned down a request from a rich Tokyo businessman. He was interested in buying a rural, but nearby, gravesite and was willing to pay an enormous amount of money for it. But I'm not—that is, Shōsen-*ji* is not—interested in money only. The temple's main responsibility and obligation is toward Kodaira natives. People feel

at ease when their household's gravesite is nearby. Since there's only so much cemetery space at Shōsen-*ji*, I'm obliged to reserve parishioner status for Kodaira people over outsiders.[26]

For example, some newcomers from Kyushu wanted to become parishioners now that they live in Kodaira. But I was only willing to recognize them as *shinja* [supplicants, clients]. "Look," I told them, "your ancestors are in Kyushu. It's your responsibility to make pilgrimages to Kyushu, not move your ancestors to Kodaira!"

Selecting parishioners isn't my personal choice, mind you, but the temple's.[27] The relationship between a household and the temple is what counts. That's why parishioners are and should remain Kodaira folk. I've even allowed about one hundred branches [of native households] located outside of Kodaira to join, because their main households can handle all the necessary parish obligations. Most newcomers, on the other hand, aren't interested in maintaining the temple or contributing to the local community; they're only interested in services that benefit them alone. That's called the "*shinja* mentality": *shinja* are like those who join a shrine's worshipers' association—only interested in their own needs. They're not concerned about Buddhist teachings at all. That's why the stonemasons [described below] are getting so rich!

A temple depends on its parish just as parishioners depend on the temple; and local people with deep roots in Kodaira and a strong sense of commitment to this place are the most responsible parishioners.

Miura, the private citizen, further contributes toward the integrity of the Ogawa Eight as a member of the Shinmei-*gū* parish. Miyazaki, contrarily, does not belong to the Shōsen-*ji* parish, since from the Meiji period onward his ancestors were given Shinto funerals (*KC* 1959, 369–70). Jokingly, Miura noted that, whereas he donates money to the shrine, Miyazaki does not have to make a similar contribution in return. Miura also indicated that the Shinmei-*gū* and Shōsen-*ji* parishes more or less comprise the same households, and thus there is a good deal of cooperation between the two, especially when it comes to participating in seasonal events and footing the cost of renovations. Moreover, a *bangumi*'s temple and shrine delegates are often one and the same person. This probably is precisely the sort of interdependency Ogawa Kurobei had in mind when he located the two institutions across Oume Road from each other three centuries ago.

Conclusion: Religious Revanche

Regardless of the exclusivity today of the Shinmei-*gū* parish and worshipers' association, certain festivals take place beyond the borders of the shrine compound. Such festivals have the effect of retracing the boundaries of the natives' society. The Yagumo lantern-float procession aptly illustrates my point. The procession, on 28 April 1984, set off from the parking lot of the agricultural cooperative, which marks the boundary between the former Ogawa-*mura* and Ogawa-*shinden*, and proceeded up Oume Road to Shinmei-*gū*. One of the bolder (or drunker) young men shouldering a lantern-float was clad only in a skimpy red loincloth. A woman standing next to me on the sidewalk gleefully shouted to her in-laws, "Look, [Ken]-*chan* is doing it naked!"

It is this sort of repartee between the performers and their audience that creates local heroes and memories to be laughed over, elaborated, and incorporated into the stock of native legends and gossip. The lantern-float bearers and the appreciative natives in the audience collectively were performers and their repartee another order of performance. The Yagumo procession not only retraced the geographic boundaries but also reinforced the affective alignment of the Ogawa Eight by generating enough "Did you see so and so do such and such?" material to fuel conversations and camaraderie among native householders for a long time. I was struck, in this respect, by the palpable difference in atmosphere between the Yagumo procession and the citizens' festival. The difference was symptomatic of the relationship between the performers and their respective audience: in the lantern-float procession, natives on their own turf; in the citizens' festival, myriad strangers sharing a public space.

Rivalry on the funeral front has prompted native temples to assert their central position in Kodaira history and social life. The rivals in question are the recently constructed "cemetery temples," as I call them, and stonemasons. The cemetery temples, some of which constitute little more than a prefabricated office building, cater almost exclusively to new residents and/or out-of-town clients who own household plots in the twenty-five-hectare municipal cemetery converted from Kodaira farmland in 1948. Most of these temples are located in the vicinity of the cemetery, along with the many stonemasons and Buddhist paraphernalia shops.

Stonemasons (*ishiya*) deal in gravestones and religious statuary and have assumed such templelike services as providing flowers, water buckets, and incense for pilgrims. Stonemasons invariably are located in the vicinity of temples or cemeteries, and the majority in Kodaira are clustered around the entrance to the municipal cemetery. The manager of one such shop informed me that they provide relatively inexpensive services regardless of a client's religious affiliation. Shops like hers, the manager continued, are less financially demanding on their clients than are temples. It is noteworthy that native stonemasons, such as Ogawa Y., do not compete with native temples in this way; rather, the stonemasons and the temples enjoy a reciprocal relationship.

One of the largest Buddhist paraphernalia shops is the Memorial Art Ōnoya, a virtual supermarket of household altars (*butsudan*) and assorted ritual items. Its distinctive sphinx emblem stands out among the many "memorial art" store advertisements posted in the area. Ōnoya not only publishes a newsletter but boasts a counseling service dedicated to introducing needy clients to temples, none of which are among the native Kodaira temples. The store also sponsors, in collaboration with an out-of-town temple, a crematory memorial service for old Buddhist altars.

In the face of increasing competition from the cemetery temples, stonemasons, and religious supply stores, who blitz the newspapers with glossy inserts, especially around the equinox (*higan*) and ancestors' festival seasons, Kodaira's native temples have increased their efforts to secure and maintain stable parishes. This is a situation somewhat like the competition, during the Edo period, between commissioned temples and parent-village temples over parishioners. Their message is simply that "native is best," and virtually all native and many senior local householders have burial plots within one of the seven Kodaira temple cemeteries. Their posted histories emphasize that the temples were established by and for the *shinden* pioneers in order to enhance the quality of pioneer life. Natives today add that, because their ancestors reclaimed the barren Musashino plain and established temples and shrines as civilizing agents, the legacy of these institutions should remain in their keep, as Shōsen-*ji*'s incumbent priest has argued.

This revanchist stance, however, was not necessarily fostered by a longstanding respect for customs and concrete historical artifacts per se but, rather, was provoked by the tremendous influx of newcomers during the 1950s and 1960s, together with the "salary man–ization" (*sararīmanka*) of farm households. It is as though natives were recommissioning the temples and shrines to service the needs of the native sector within the newly reclaimed Furusato Kodaira. Moreover, various monuments dedicated by native parishioners to temples and shrines effectively demarcate both the affective and the instrumental boundaries of that sector.

The numerous explanatory signs posted throughout the Shinmei-*gū* compound not only reflect Miyazaki's didactic temperament but also remind natives, and inform newcomers and outside clientele, of the shrine's prestigious ancestry, its leading role in the reclamation of Ogawa-*mura*, and its present importance as Kodaira's tutelary shrine. The posted histories of other Kodaira landmarks likewise demarcate the boundaries of the natives' society.

Since 1980 both city hall—as part of its long-term social education and *furusato-zukuri* strategy—and the Kodaira Local History Study Society—whose members include the priests of local temples and shrines—have encouraged efforts to renovate and preserve historical objects, architecture, and customs, especially Kodaira's native temples and shrines. Temple and shrine renovations are mostly financed by donations in money or kind from parishioners. The city assembly allocated forty million yen toward historical restorations over the period 1981–1985. Most of the funds were spent on the restoration of privately owned structures, such as the entranceway to Ogawa Kurobei's residence. One may speculate that the election in 1983 of Mayor Senuma E., the incumbent priest of Enmei-*ji*, influenced the surge in temple and shrine renovations since 1984.

Kodaira's new, postwar residents appreciate the historical temples and shrines not only as social forums but also as "green spaces" or gardens. The preservation of the city's diminishing trees and stretches of open fields apparently was, in 1983, the foremost concern of Kodaira residents at large (*YC* 1983, 61, 63). Although newcomers cannot join certain shrine and temple consociations, they nevertheless can enjoy the historical buildings and gardens of Furusato Kodaira. By the same token, shrine festivals, such as the Yagumo lantern-float procession, are similarly effective displays of Kodaira's "living history."

As the percentage of newcomers who regard themselves as locals continues to grow, the "really real" natives incline increasingly toward a revanchist stance in their efforts to reclaim a special status within Kodaira. This tendency is evident in the exclusivity of religious consociations and temple and shrine parishes, as well as in the recent publication of *Komyunitei Kodaira*, a newsletter by and for natives. Regardless of whether newcomers actually seek to join these groups, they are not even given the opportunity to decline membership. There is a contradiction here. That is, while Shinmei-*gū* posters urge Kodaira residents at large to make their New Year's pilgrimage to "Kodaira's tutelary shrine," Miyazaki strictly limits membership in the parish and worshipers' association to select native households. The exclusivity of temple and shrine parishes makes membership in these consociations all the more meaningful for natives, whose collective identity and claims to Furusato Kodaira are thereby reinforced. The integrity of the native sector today stems in part from an almost adversarial reaction to newcomers, from whom the minority natives seek to differentiate themselves. It is a reaction that has become more pronounced as the majority newcomers are urged to accept and think of Kodaira as their native place. Some of the implications and ramifications of this development are examined in the next chapter.

CHAPTER FIVE

Native Place, New Time

Two of a Kind

The editors of the *Kodaira chōshi* have split the population of Kodaira into two broad sectors: farm households (*nōka*) and nonfarm households (*hinōka*). Farm households are further qualified as natives (*tochikko, jimoto*), while nonfarm households are also referred to as newcomers (*ten'nyūsha*). Newcomer children, and by extension all newcomers, are called *kodairakko*.

As discussed in the preceding chapters, newcomers are systematically excluded from native neighborhood organizations. According to the editors of the *Kodaira chōshi*, the "native neighborhoods have put up various barriers against newcomers," ostensibly because of an exclusivism stemming from the "paternal lineage–like nature" of native neighborhoods, particularly the Ogawa Eight (*KC* 1959, 863, 877). They remind readers that Ogawa-*mura* was made by the "sweat and toil of the *shinden* settlers," but they do not attempt to eulogize the postwar immigrants and their part in the making of Kodaira. Since the promulgation of the citizens' charter in 1972, however, newcomers have been encouraged to regard themselves as pioneers involved in Kodaira's "second reclamation." In this chapter, I trace the background of native-newcomer antinomy in Kodaira, focusing on the geohistorical configuration of these sectors and their respective experience of spatial and temporal displacement.

150

The editors of the *Kodaira chōshi* distinguished the two sectors by the antithetical occupational terms *farm* and *nonfarm households*; the differences posed by city administrators today are both temporal (old and new households) and spatial (native and newcomer). The statement on "community" in the Second Comprehensive Long-Term Plan illustrates this later orientation.

Recently, as a consequence of postwar economic growth, the material life of [Kodaira's] citizens has become affluent. At the same time, however, neighborly love and the spirit of reciprocal communality have thinned. The spiritual side of life, in other words, is beset by anomie and loneliness.

The mixing of old and new citizens; the . . . separation of home and workplace; the proliferation of nuclear families; and demographic fluidity and instability collectively pose pressing social problems. Moreover, these problems are further exacerbated by the indifference and apathy of some residents.

Even so, there are signs among other residents of a strong desire for naturally generated neighborliness and a revival of humanity within regional life. Herein is the germ-seed of a new community configuration with an unlimited, active, creative potential. Harnessing the influx of boundless energy is the first step toward a new age of the local [*kyōdo*].

This achievement is contingent upon infrastructural stability in conjunction with the emergence of a spontaneous populism and subjective activism on the part of an area's residents. The citizens' charter was promulgated in October 1972 to instill residents with pride . . . in their Kodaira citizenship. The charter, a "roadmap of civic life," must be honored and upheld by all citizens collectively. (Kodaira-*shi* keikaku zaiseibu keikakuka 1980, 129–30)

Lofty rhetoric aside, the statement locates certain problem areas requiring resolution if a "new community" is to be, in the language of the above plan, "re-reclaimed" (*saikaihatsu*). The plan claims that the mixing of natives and newcomers has precipitated a host of pressing social problems. As I show, however, the *nonmixing* of natives and newcomers also has occasioned problems.

Passing mention was made in chapter 3 of the Hakone Realty Company and the development of Kodaira Gakuen in the 1920s. In 1923 about two hundred hectares of dry-field and forested land in the southern reaches of Ogawa (-*mura* and -*shinden* combined) were sold to the company. Two years later, the land was divided into lots measuring 331 square meters. The company also constructed the still-operant Tamako Line, which now serves as the boundary between east and west Gakuen. Each plot came with a 20-square-meter bungalow and was put on the market for 500 yen. Since the main appeal of the Gakuen development was its academy-town image, the company negotiated with Meiji University to transfer its campus to Kodaira. However, in the aftermath of the devastating 1923 earthquake, the university was unable to raise enough funds to subsidize the move, whereupon the company approached the Tokyo College of Commerce (renamed Hitotsubashi University in 1949) and successfully negotiated the transfer of its branch college to Kodaira. Even so, the lots did not sell as quickly as expected, and it was not until the late 1930s that farm householders, from whom the property had been procured, were paid in full. The lengthy delay fostered resentment on the part of natives toward the developers and new residents, foreshadowing the subsequent antinomy between farm and nonfarm households (*KC* 1959, 438).

Although the development of Kodaira Gakuen marked the first phase of the spatial displacement of farm households, the construction of large-scale military installations from 1939 to 1945 triggered the initial transformation of Kodaira from an agrarian village into a suburban bedroom town. Altogether, five such installations were constructed on land expropriated by the central government from farm households. Farmers in the southernmost portion of the former Ogawa-*shinden* lost 62 percent of their arable land, and many resigned themselves to a nonagricultural livelihood, renting rooms and houses to military personnel (*KC* 1959, 442). Only a part of the expropriated land was returned to agriculture; most was converted to residential use in the form of low-rent corporation and municipal housing tracts, initially occupied by ex-military personnel, evacuees, and salaried workers. Residential projects for the most part were developed on forested or relatively unproductive dry-field land, whereas military installations were constructed on prime agricultural land, on which mass-housing projects were built after the war. Between 1946 and 1950, however, there was a brief recrudescence of agriculture in order to ease the immediate postwar food shortage. These in fact were the halcyon years of Kodaira farm households, whose number rose from 749 in 1941, to 819 in 1946, and again to 1,118 in 1950, before declining to 1,020 by 1955. The percentages of full-time agriculturists for those dates were 60, 51, 63, and 57, respectively (*KC* 1959, 539; *KK* 1983, 212).

Over 623 mass-housing projects were constructed between 1947 and 1954, representing 869 households (3,803 persons) and 33 percent of the town's overall population growth. The population of Kodaira in 1945 stood at 2,300 households (14,400 persons), doubling to 4,900 households (25,000 persons) by 1947. The other developments facilitating immigration to Kodaira during this period were the belated growth of Kodaira Gakuen and the construction of public and private facilities, including a rehabilitation center for disabled people, Tsuda Women's College, a branch of Hitotsubashi University, an industrial college, Kanto Police Academy, a Self-Defense Force base, and a major medical center (*KK* 1983, 206–7). An additional 4,799 families took up residence in these corporation and municipal mass-housing units during the period 1955–1960. The employers of this second generation of mass-housing occupants included the Bridgestone Company, Hitachi, the Telephone and Telegraph Company, the Defense Agency, the Ministry of Labor, and the Agricultural Chemicals Research Institute. In addition, several high-rise public housing compounds (*danchi*) were constructed (*KK* 1983, 210).

The reasons for selecting Kodaira as the site for these large-scale industrial and residential projects included its relative proximity to central Tokyo, the availability of large tracts of arable and forested land for development purposes, the relatively low cost of real estate, and a convenient transportation network (*KK* 1983, 206). The block- or cluster-like distribution of these new housing units contrasts with the linear arrangement of farm households along historical thoroughfares, such as Oume Road. Just as the Ogawa Eight epitomize the native sector, the corporation and municipal housing units exemplify the newcomer sector.

Neighborhood Associations New and Old

A digression on the fire brigade and the related issue of fire drills will illustrate the nature of native-newcomer antinomy and attempts at its resolution. The fire-fighting division (*shōbō-gumi*) was a distinct organization by the time Kodaira-*mura* was formed in 1889. The exact nature of the fire brigades in the seven *shinden* villages is not known, although the intrepidity of Suzuki-*shinden*'s Su-*gumi* has been memorialized in a local folktale. The newly amalgamated village of Kodaira was served by six fire-fighting divisions—Nonaka was regarded as a single village in this case—which were further subdivided. The Ogawa *shōbō-gumi*, for example, comprised eight sections; namely, the Ogawa Eight. This system was discontinued in 1914 and the Kodaira *shōbō-gumi* installed in its place. The change was a nominal one, for the earlier subdivisions remained intact (*KC* 1959, 987). In 1939, when military mobilization was a pressing national concern, the fire brigade assumed the role of a vigilance corps, and the subdivisions were regrouped as eight branches, which remain the units of organization today. The newcomer's complaint, in the 1960s, about the exclusivity of the fire brigades is not surprising given the confluence of the fire-fighting branches with the former *shinden*-village and intravillage divisions. Moreover, the leadership of the fire brigades has remained the province of Kodaira natives.

Recently, fire drills have been conducted by the neighborhood associations, the subject of the following paragraphs. Neighborhood associations are referred to as *jichikai* or *chōnaikai*, and although the terms are used synonymously, the former literally means "self-governing association." It is the demilitarized, postwar equivalent of the earlier *chōnaikai* (also *chōkai*), or "town-section associations." Some neighborhood associations have retained the older name—Gakuen Nishi-*chōkai*, for example, of which I was a member. On the other hand, the Ogawa Eight have assumed the more modern and "democratic"-sounding *jichikai*—1-*bangumi-jichikai*, for example—although these associations, as their names reveal, essentially are isomorphic with the *bangumi* formally established in the 1720s.

City hall defines *jichikai* (and *chōnaikai*) as follows:

Jichikai are associations spontaneously organized and democratically administered by the local residents. Their purpose is to promote and facilitate neighborliness and mutual aid between members and to raise the quality of their social welfare. *Jichikai*, in short, are nonprofit organizations formed within a specific area of the city and registered with city hall. Excluded from *jichikai* status are organizations formed solely for the management of street lights [etc.]. (Kodaira-*shi* seikatsuka 1973)

In 1967 there were 220 registered neighborhood associations, increasing to 272 by 1969, to 314 by 1971, and to 380 by 1984. According to the staff of the Civic Life Department, which oversees *jichikai* affairs, the greatest number of new registrations coincided with cityhood in 1962, when more subsidies became available to neighborhood associations. The staff suggested a correlation between overall population growth and the number of neighborhood associations formed, but the number of associations has continued to grow since 1976, when the population stabilized at around 153,000 persons. Rather, as I see it, neighborhood associations signify another type of settlement pattern in the episodic making of Kodaira. Their growth correlates with specific local developments, such as a new "my home" tract or an apartment complex in, say, uptown Hanakoganei, where many of the newer associations are located. Neighborhood associations that encompass an entire high-rise project or mass-housing complex tend to be most consistently active as social welfare organizations. The 1,440-household Kodaira Danchi-*jichikai* in Kihei-*chō* is a case in point. The members' manual published by this association is as professional and thorough, in its design and content, as the city's own residents' handbook.

Each neighborhood association is required to submit to the Civic Life Department a membership roster together with a statement of purpose, bylaws, and operating procedures. Only the largest (and wealthiest) associations, however, distribute members' handbooks. There are some exceptions to this rule. The large and wealthy Ogawa Eight *jichikai*, for example, have submitted only brief rosters. These associations are composed primarily of native households and also overlap with other historical consociations, including shrine and temple parishes and fire brigades. Manuals detailing the purpose and function of the *jichikai* are unnecessary, given the familiar informality preferred by natives. Moreover, the intended audience for members' handbooks in general is newcomers, whose membership in Ogawa Eight circles is not altogether welcomed anyway.

The exclusivity of the Ogawa Eight *jichikai* has prompted some newcomers to form their own associational enclaves, such as the twelve-household Jūni-sho Kita-*jichikai*, which lies within the territory encompassed by the Ogawa 1-*bangumi-jichikai* (see map 5). The name Jūni-sho Kita reflects the fact that it is located north (*kita*) of the No. 12 Elementary School (*jūni-sho*). Regarding *jichikai* names in general, native associations invariably are named after a historical, geographic entity, such as a *shinden* village, *ōaza* (large [village] section), *bangumi*, or *aza* (small [village] section). The names of newcomer associations are much more diverse, based as they are on housing projects, landmarks, flowers and trees, calendrical terms, colors, ideals, and even weather patterns.

Neighborhood associations also are formed by budding off of a "parent" association, usually after a period of internal dissension. The rationale for forming a splinter group must be submitted to city hall, and the records show that the most common reason for divisiveness involved the management of sewers and sewage disposal.[1] Generally speaking, internal dissension is most common in newcomer associations formed among tract-home owners. By the same token, the small-

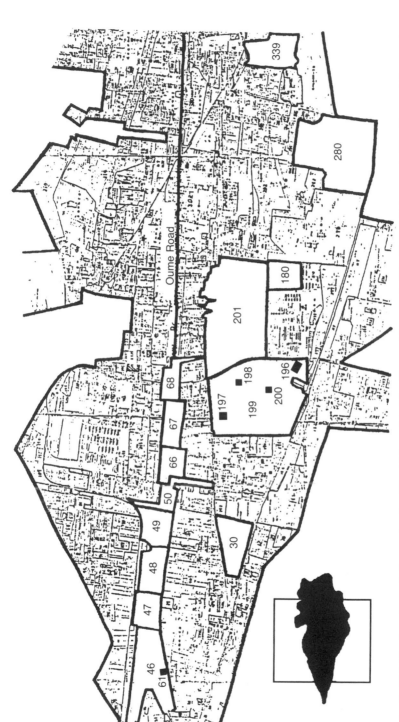

Map 5. Neighborhood association territories. 30 = Takanodai; 46 = Ogawa 1-*bangumi*; 47 = Ogawa 2-*bangumi*; 48 = Ogawa 3-*bangumi*; 49 = Ogawa 4-*bangumi*; 50 = Ogawa 5-*bangumi*; 61 = Jūni-shō Kita; 66 = Ogawa 6-*bangumi*; 67 = Ogawa 7-*bangumi*; 68 = Ogawa 8-*bangumi*; 180 = Kodaira Danchi; 196 = Kodaira Danchi; 197 = Akanedai; 198 = Gakuen Nishi Jūtaku; 199 = Gakuen Nishi-*machi*; 200 = Tōei Danchi; 201 = Gakuen Higashi-*chō*; 280 = Miyuki-*chō*; 339 = Hanakoganei Minami-*chō* 2-*chōme*. Names and numbers as they appear in the neighborhood association registry were kindly provided by the Civic Life Department. The map is a reduced and modified version of the one maintained by the department and represents the situation in 1984. Only key associations mentioned in the text are outlined and identified.

est associations frequently are ephemeral, since their raison d'être often is but a single exigency needing immediate resolution, such as sewage disposal—despite the fact that *jichikai* are not to be premised on single issues. Finally, unlike their native counterparts, newcomer *jichikai* are neither extensions of prewar and interwar associations nor entities superimposed on Edo-period and later neighborhood divisions, and therefore tend to be more prone to fractionation.

Some neighborhood associations divide; others merge to form larger, presumably more efficient (or less redundant), units; and not a few collapse after several years of existence. A staff member of the Civic Life Department pointed out, somewhat sarcastically, that a significant number of these short-lived associations were formed simply to qualify for subsidies from city hall, although in 1984 subsidies amounted to 3,265,800 yen—an average of only 8,550 yen per association. In practice, the actual amount varied according to the size and needs of a *jichikai*. Separate funding for street lights and bulletin boards is also provided by city hall.

As I see it, *jichikai* membership in Kodaira assumes three basic patterns: exclusive, voluntary, and solicited. The first characterizes the natives' neighborhood associations; the second, small scale newcomer *jichikai* formed among a group of like-minded neighbors. The third pattern, solicited membership, is not uncommon among older, nonnative, large-scale organizations, such as Gakuen Nishi-*chōkai*.

One recent newcomer wrote to a citizens' advice column in the local newspaper that immediately after the family's arrival they had been approached by a *jichikai* official who sought to register them in that neighborhood's association. The newcomer noted that never before had they experienced such zealous recruitment efforts. Although they regarded membership as a bothersome responsibility, they were worried about the possible negative repercussions should they decline to register. After praising *jichikai* as "autonomous, democratic organizations," the newspaper's anonymous advisor noted that, although membership is not (legally at least) compulsory, the benefits accruing to those who join probably outweigh the more bothersome aspects. Neighborhood associations, the advisor concluded, are the basis for "solidarity-making" and "cheerful neighborhood–making" (*KSH*, 20 October 1979).

The advisor glossed over the fact that a number of neighborhood associations, such as the unidentified one in question, are keen on increasing their membership in order to broaden both their financial base and their local influence. Since I am most familiar with Gakuen Nishi-*chōkai*, the city's largest and supposedly wealthiest association, a discussion of its operations will serve to contextualize the third pattern (i.e., solicitation) of *jichikai* membership and provide general insights into the operations of neighborhood associations.

Gakuen Nishi-*chōkai*

Gakuen Nishi-*chōkai* (hereafter GNC), established in 1949, was originally known as Mutsumi-*kai* and comprised 267 households. There were 1,826 member households in 1984. Its present territory includes all of Gakuen Nishi-*machi* and part of Tsuda-*machi*, the latter theoretically an illegal addition, since *chōnaikai*, as the term implies, are associations (*kai*) limited to households within (*nai*) a specific *chō*. According to one of the GNC officers, the partial inclusion of Tsuda-*machi* is a throwback to the earlier prewar association of which the present association essentially is a continuation. In contrast to the mammoth GNC, the four other neighborhood associations within Gakuen Nishi-*machi* are much smaller and composed entirely of newcomers. They are enclaves within the larger GNC domain.

The absence of horizontal affiliations between *jichikai* inhibits the overall effectiveness and influence of all but the largest neighborhood associations in mediating relations between residents and city hall and in negotiating for public welfare projects such as sewer systems. The largest associations, including GNC, procure a heftier share of the subsidies offered by city hall and enjoy a substantial income from membership fees and donations, which affords them both financial stability and flexibility.

GNC currently (1985) comprises twelve wards (*ku*), which are further subdivided into 113 squads (*han*), and is administered by thirty-two officers (twenty-five of whom serve concurrent terms): emeritus chair (one person), consultant (one), secretary (one), chair (one), vice-chair (three), accountant (one), and ward managers (twenty-four). In addition, each squad is headed by a ward secretary. Although the thirty-two officers nominally are limited to a two-year term, and the ward secretaries to a one-year term, successive reelections are not prohibited. Among the Ogawa Eight *jichikai*, it is not unusual for an officer to have served in the same capacity for over twenty-five years. The GNC bylaws indicate that the officers are elected from among the ward managers (the ward secretaries are elected from among the members at large), although, as one officer remarked, the GNC posts usually are rotated among "old boys."

As of 1985, both GNC and the old-boy network are headed by Ogawa Z., a descendant of Kurobei. Ogawa and several other officers are also assemblypersons. The overlapping of their duties and interests is noteworthy, inasmuch as, according to the bylaws, "It is inappropriate for this association to collaborate with the municipal administration or to represent or function as a subordinate appendage thereof" (Gakuen Nishi-*chōkai* 1982, 9). A number of GNC members told me that certain assemblypersons tended to view neighborhood associations as similar to *kōenkai*, or politicians' personal support organizations (cf. Allinson 1979, 195–96).

The somewhat "tainted" politicking within GNC also is evident in connection with the construction, in 1984, of a bona fide meeting house. Prior to that time, the officers met once a month at the welfare center, and the ward secretaries convened their three annual meetings at an elementary school, where the annual general meeting was also held. The ground-breaking ceremony was conducted by GNC officers; for, as a ward manager explained, engaging the services of a Shinto priest would have exceeded by several times the 42,218 yen that was spent. The officers were less economically minded about furnishings, however, since a plain, simple shoe shelf (constructed by a GNC member) had cost over 76,500 yen. Similarly, the drains were installed by a native firm, Ogawa Construction, for the tidy sum of 190,000 yen, and the total cost of the meeting house, a prefabricated building, came to 2,115,253 yen (Gakuen Nishi-*chōkai* 1984c). Finally, Chair Ogawa's local stature and the fact that he serves on the city assembly's construction committee doubtless were instrumental in procuring a site for the meeting house, prime real estate on which a regional center is slated for eventual construction by the city.

True to the historical propensities of the Ogawa household, the current GNC chair, who assumed the post in 1982 after serving concurrently as vice-chair and general director, oversees the association in a somewhat autocratic manner. Actually, Ogawa Z. and the officers preside over what appears to be, judging from my experience as both a GNC member and a guest at the officers' meeting, a virtual oligarchy—

a seeming consequence of the members' apathy coupled with the officers' arrogance. A description of the ward secretaries' second meeting on 27 October 1984 contextualizes my overall impressions.

The meeting began at two o'clock in the afternoon at the new meeting house. The fact that I was able to sit in on the proceedings—as the first rank-and-filer, not to mention foreigner, to do so—was the result of several months of circuitous permission seeking. I first approached my squad's manager, who contacted the ward secretary, who put the question to the general director, who approached the chair, who then mulled over my request for many weeks with the other officers before finally giving his consent. In the meantime, I was asked to prepare a short autobiography and statement of my reasons for attending the otherwise exclusive meeting. I was also visited without warning on several occasions by the ward secretary's wife—partly out of her curiosity alone and partly to assess my character and lifestyle. At the meeting, she zealously assumed the role of my caretaker, introducing me to the officers and her female colleagues, after coaching me on how I should thank them for the privilege of attending. The general director ordered me to sit in the far corner of the room and asked that I please refrain from actively participating in the proceedings.

Each officer signed a rollbook immediately upon entering the meeting house—only 96 (66 percent) of the 145 officers and ward secretaries attended. My caretaker explained that attendance was much higher at the first meeting in April. Stretching across the south end of the spacious rectangular *tatami* room was a row of low formica tables, behind which sat, from (their) left to right, the general director (also a Kodaira native), the chair, the public relations section chief, the women's section chief, and the accountant. Seated on cushions along the east wall were, from (their) left to right, the chiefs of the traffic, crime, equipment and facilities, disaster-prevention, public welfare, and youth sections. The ward secretaries filled up the middle of the room. Only 12 of the 96 persons present were men, 9 of them section chiefs. The head of the women's section was the only female of that rank. The other women were attending as proxies for their absentee husbands, who were the nominal ward secretaries. The de jure leadership of GNC, in other words, is virtually all male. Although Kodaira's (married) female residents are extolled by city hall as, collectively, the nucleus of "cheerful neighborhood–making," in addition to being both the target audience for neighborhood association activities and the overwhelming majority of those attending *jichikai* meetings, they have not yet assumed any formal leadership roles in that particular organization, nor have they had access to such roles.

The ward secretaries' meeting proved to be a rather perfunctory affair. The chiefs read their state-of-the-section reports. Longest was the accountant's painstaking reading of the entire budget, despite the fact that copies had been distributed beforehand to everyone in attendance. This is an opportune moment to briefly review the GNC budget for 1984. The annual income and expenditures balanced out to 3,959,300 yen. Seventy-two percent of the association's income came from annual membership fees: 130 yen a month (1,560 yen per year) per single-family dwelling. Apartment buildings are charged a lump monthly sum of 1,000 yen, which is divided equally among member tenants. Nearly 9 percent of the GNC income in 1984 consisted of subsidies from city hall: 346,700 yen, well above the average grant of 8,550 yen cited earlier. The remaining 19 percent derived from additional grants and miscellaneous sources (Gakuen Nishi-*chōkai* 1984a, 1984b).

The chair's report consisted of two announcements made on behalf of the Self-Defense Forces, whose camp actually lies within Gakuen Higashi-*chō*. One concerned a free helicopter ride, and although the offer was open to all present, Ogawa quite arbitrarily gave the nod to a fellow officer who had expressed interest, all the while joking that the chopper might crash whereupon the officer's wife would strike it rich on insurance money. (The morbid humor was prompted by a recent rash of "insurance money murders" sensationalized in the mass media.) The second announcement involved two guest tickets to a military function, which Ogawa doled out in a similarly arbitrary fashion.

The ward secretaries' meeting is not an occasion for dealing with the details of GNC operations. There was virtually no input from the proxy secretaries present, whose main function seemed to be to serve as an audience for the section chiefs' reports. More pressing business, such as preparing the annual budget, is conducted at the monthly ward managers' meetings, at the officers' extraordinary meetings, and through personal communication between certain officers.

The meeting closed with a terse statement by the women's section chief in her only remarks, since she had nothing to report earlier about her section's affairs. Between Ogawa's announcements and her closing remarks, the general director made a speech urging the (proxy) ward secretaries to work harder at increasing the association's membership, which, he lamented, amounted to only 18.2 percent of the Gakuen

Nishi-*machi* population. Ogawa, in turn, criticized newcomers for their "absolute lack of interest in *jichikai* and neighborhood affairs." My calculations indicate that, of the 54 percent of the *chō*'s households registered with one of the five *jichikai* in Gakuen Nishi-*machi*, 47 percent belong to GNC. The general director's numbers differ from mine because he based his percentage on the difference between the total number of GNC households and the total number of people (as opposed to households) living in the area. The result is a low, and therefore rhetorically useful, percentage that is a misleading and inaccurate indicator of GNC membership, since households and not individuals usually register with an association. Nevertheless, although newcomers are excluded from various historical consociations, their reluctance to join a neighborhood association may be interpreted as an expression of their desire for autonomy.

Following the meeting, green tea and several varieties of Japanese confections were served by the women in attendance. Meanwhile, I chatted with Ogawa, who insisted that GNC operated "democratically" but in the same breath shouted "Oi!" for one of the women to serve him more tea. The women congregated around a block of tables in the northwest corner of the room talking loudly, no longer their earlier silent selves. Apart from myself, the only persons sitting at the front row of tables were the male officers. Shortly before I left at four o'clock, when the refreshment period ended, the public relations chief asked me to write a short essay for the GNC newsletter about my impressions of both the meeting and my neighborhood and to make comparisons with equivalent organizations in the United States. (Later, in exchange for my essay, I was presented with a small hand towel.)

Typologically, Gakuen Nishi-*chōkai* is a hybrid organization: partly native (Ogawa Z. and several of the other officers) and partly newcomer (ward secretaries and the rank-and-file members). Unlike the Ogawa Eight *jichikai*, however, GNC natives are not also agriculturists, although their natal households may be or were so in the past. An analysis of the GNC handbook, in which all the members are listed by ward or squad, name, occupation, and address, reveals that the association has no farmer members and that *sarariiman* predominate, followed by military personnel and merchandisers. The GNC natives, in short, are native by virtue of their genealogy in Kodaira, most having become *sarariiman*-ized by the early 1960s, when a poll conducted by city hall revealed that about 79 percent of a typical farm household's annual income derived from nonagricultural sources, particularly land sales and rentals. Although Ogawa Z. remains quite adamant about maintaining distinctions between "blue-blood" Ogawas and the household's fictive kin, most native householders of my acquaintance in Gakuen Nishi-*machi* seemed less concerned about the genealogical "purity" of their *ie* than with its historical seniority.

Varieties of *Jichikai* Experience

One form of spatial displacement is occupational in nature. In the *sarariiman*-ized farm households, this displacement may be manifested as a move out of the fields and into the office. The difference between native office workers and newcomers, however, is that the former have long roots in Kodaira and are, for the most part, locally employed. Certain GNC native leaders, for example, are both business-people and members of the assembly. That Gakuen Nishi-*machi* originally was part of Ogawa-*mura* doubtless has much to do with the fact that natives dominate its leadership.

The largest of the 380 neighborhood associations has 1,826 registrants, and the smallest has 2 registrants. The majority (209, or 55 percent) of the associations consist of 10 to 50 members. Naka-*machi* (formerly Ogawa-*shinden*) in particular abounds in small, autonomous associations and has the double distinction of being the city division with the largest number of *jichikai* (47, or 12.3 percent) and the largest number of associations headed (as of 1984) by women: 5 out of 17 citywide. The 17 neighborhood associations headed by women comprise a mere 4.5 percent of the total number of the city's *jichikai*. They range in size from 7 to 83 households, with most averaging 25. All consist of quintessential newcomer households: new housing tracts, mass-housing units, and high-rise projects. How these gynecocratic *jichikai* operate—whether they differ, self-consciously, from their androcratic, androcentric counterparts, and whether female headship is perpetuated as a matter of principle—is a subject for an independent study proper, particularly in connection with the role (formal and informal) of married women in neighborhood- and community-making. The concentration of publicly active women in Naka-*machi* is manifested by their status as formal neighborhood leaders. Generally speaking, Kodaira's female leaders preside over neighborhood associations that have fewer than 100 members (25 on the average) and are organized among newcomer households. The largest, most bureaucratic, and native neighborhood associations are headed by males.

If Naka-*machi* has the highest concentration of neighborhood associations, three city divisions share the dubious distinction of having but one *jichikai* each: Takanodai, Miyuki-*chō*, and Hanakoganei Minami-*chō* 2-*chōme* (see map 5). To be sure, they are large associations: 464, 322, and 617 member households, which comprise 66 percent, 70 percent, and 82 percent of the total *chō* households, respectively. Both their large size and higher-than-average membership percentage (the average being 60 percent) may be attributed to a variety of factors.

Miyuki-*chō* consists of a small resident population sandwiched between the Kodaira Country Club and Koganei City. In Hanakoganei Minami-*chō*, company housing units predominate. Takanodai is characterized by a dense cluster of houses and a large number of shops. Shopkeepers, generally speaking, are more inclined toward neighborhood-making, in order to secure steady and stable clientele. Although they are *jichikai* members, they also maintain their own special organizations, known as *shōtenkai*, or shopkeepers' associations. Kodaira boasts twenty-four such associations, which are clustered mostly around each of the city's seven train stations. The shopkeepers are organized under the auspices of the Kodaira Chamber of Commerce. In 1984, in response to consumers' opinions, the chamber issued a twelve-point plan for the revitalization of the city's shopping districts. A public opinion survey conducted in 1983, for example, revealed that local consumers favored the installation of parking zones for bicycles and cars; the establishment of larger retail stores, such as supermarkets; and more helpful and polite city clerks (*YC* 1983, 59). Among the twelve points was included one designed to foster *furusatosei*, or *furusato*-ness, by sponsoring spring and autumn festivals, early-morning markets, ancestors' festival dances, local arts and crafts fairs, and songfests (*Kodaira shōkōkai-dayori*, 20 March 1984).[2]

The extenuating circumstances for Naka-*machi*'s double distinctions are geographic and nomenclatural. The place-name Naka-*machi*, literally "relationship-ville," was purposely selected in 1962, when the former intracity divisions were reorganized as *chō*, to signify and encourage "civic harmony and intimacy" (*KCH*, 5 September 1962). The central citizens' hall was constructed there, and the central library was built nearby (both were relocated in 1984–85 to an even more "central" location in the vicinity of city hall). Moreover, in 1969 the city's board of education moved its office to the central citizens' hall, which effectively increased traffic in and out of Naka-*machi*, the fourth-largest *chō*. As I heard mentioned repeatedly at the fourteenth annual Kodaira citizens' hall convention, held on 5 February 1984, the overwhelming majority of those who use the facilities—an art gallery, local-history seminars, arts and crafts classes, language classes, and rental rooms—at citizens' halls are women, and newcomer women in particular. The statistics show a female usership of 70 percent citywide in 1982–83, all of whom have lived in Kodaira for less than ten years. The most frequent users live within two kilometers of a hall (*KSH*, 5 March 1969).

While mass- or high-rise housing projects seem to facilitate *jichikai* membership among newcomers, nativeness is the catalyst for membership in the Ogawa Eight. As explained in chapter 4, nearly 90 percent of the eight Ogawa Eight *jichikai* comprise native households. Nativeness, apart from being a significant factor in its own right, also implies parish (shrine and temple) membership as well as inclusion in historical neighborhood divisions, such as the *bangumi*. Newcomer *jichikai* effectively incorporate propinquitous but otherwise autonomous households, whereas those neighborhood associations composed of native households essentially have been superimposed, like a transparency, upon preexisting, bounded organizations. Moreover, the fact that these historical associations, such as the shrine and temple parishes, have always been headed by male househeads virtually—and unproblematically—sanctions the male leadership of the Ogawa Eight *jichikai*. Also relevant in this connection is that, generally speaking, these native males are locally employed—as farmers or local businessmen—and therefore, unlike newcomer males but like married newcomer females, are part of the city's daytime population. There is, then, a resemblance between native males and married newcomer females in view of their daily presence in Kodaira and participation in local institutions and neighborhood activities. But whereas native males preside over historical organizations, newcomer females are the de facto representatives (and in some cases de jure leaders) of comparatively new neighborhood associations.

It is instructive to note the overall extent of *jichikai* membership and participation in Kodaira, since city administrators regard neighborhood associations as the basis for community-making in general. Public opinion surveys conducted by city hall in 1979 and 1983 reveal that 20 percent and 25 percent, respectively, of the average 1,500 male and female respondents were actively involved in *jichikai* affairs (*YC* 1979, 58; 1983, 49). In 1979, 9.2 percent of the respondents served in a leadership capacity, 11.2 percent were actively participating members, and 31 percent occasionally participated; 3.1 percent considered themselves members in name only, and 45.5 percent were not in any way involved in *jichikai* affairs. Half of those surveyed in 1983 indicated that they had no interest in *jichikai* activities, although the survey did not indicate whether they may have been nominal members of an association at that time.

My own calculations show that in 1984 an average of 40 percent (ranging from 10 to 70 percent) of the city's 54,790 households were not registered with a neighborhood association. Some of these householders regarded PTA membership in particular as sufficient community involvement. Married women tend to become more involved in *jichikai* affairs as they get older, having earlier been active in citizens' hall and subsequently PTA activities. The general trend of female participation illuminates the processual nature of membership. Women in their twenties and early thirties—usually newly married or young mothers—tend to pursue their own interests and thus make use of the citizens' hall facilities; those in their late thirties and forties are concerned primarily with their children's needs and participate in PTA affairs; women in their fifties and sixties develop an interest in their neighborhoods, becoming increasingly active in *jichikai* affairs (Kodaira-*shi* kyōiku iinkai 1980, 16).

The Community Mystique

Ideas and boundaries of "community" are problematic issues for natives and newcomers alike—for the former, because of spatial displacement within their historical setting; for the latter, because of spatial displacement within a new setting. A 1979 public opinion survey conducted by city hall included a question on the respondents' knowledge of the term *community*. In the questionnaire, the term, which was never defined, was rendered in *katakana* as *komyunitei*.[3] Like the postwar term *jichikai* (neighborhood association), *komyunitei* is preferred for its modern, democratic ring, although the more dated *kyōdō-tai* (communal corps) is favored within the affective and nostalgic context of *furusato* rhetoric. *Komyunitei* signifies the city's bureaucratic modernity and progressiveness, while *kyōdōtai* imparts an ambience of "tradition" through its allusion to the communal solidarity presumed to

have characterized Edo-period agricultural villages. Of the 1,569 respondents, 51 percent professed to be very knowledgeable about the
term *community*; 35 percent had heard of the word but were unsure of
its meaning; and 12.5 percent had not heard of the word and did not
know what it means.

The respondents most familiar with the term *komyunitei* (55 percent
of the above 51 percent) hailed from survey areas that collectively encompass the city's university, *sarariiman*, and uptown sectors. The
lowest percentages of knowledgeable persons (15 percent of the 51
percent) were registered in areas that coincided with the most visually
and residentially intact portions of the native sector—namely, the former Ogawa-*mura*, Ogawa-*shinden*, and Ōnumata-*shinden*. The survey
also revealed that those who were most familiar with *komyunitei* were
students, civil servants, and engineers, while those who were least
familiar included farmers, manual laborers, and unemployed persons.
Differences between natives and newcomers thus cleave along linguistic
lines as well. Natives tend to be unfamiliar with trendy, foreign-derived
jargon, but, at the same time, they are protective of their own local
dialect. Miura, the incumbent priest of Shōsen-*ji*, for example, believes
that the preservation-through-use of a local dialect is the key to the
native sector's integrity and continuity. Kodaira natives regularly use
hyakkoi to refer to chilliness or coldness, instead of the more conventional or standard word, *tsumetai*.

Unfamiliarity with the term *komyunitei* does not necessarily imply an
unappreciation or absence of community, in the sense of a bounded and
integral place whose members negotiate its boundaries. Nor is mere
familiarity with the term per se tantamount to its concrete manifestation. Public opinion surveys conducted by city hall define the presence
of *komyunitei* by the degree of *tsukiai*, or interaction, between proxi-
mate households. In a 1979 survey, *tsukiai* was characterized by two
activities: greeting neighbors and, when a family goes on vacation,
asking neighbors to look after the house (*rusuban*).[4] The figures indicate that 73 percent of the respondents regularly greeted their neighbors. Ninety percent of those respondents involved in agriculture (i.e.,
the native sector) and 80 percent of those over thirty-five years of age
exchanged greetings, while students, office workers, and salespersons,
who collectively comprise the most transient population, greeted only
certain persons. Only 28 percent of the respondents always asked their
neighbors to look after their house. *Rusuban* implies a certain level of
intimacy and trustworthiness between households and apparently is less

evident in Kodaira, with its predominantly newcomer population, than is the courtesy of greeting one's neighbors (*YC* 1979, 54–55). Community, however, cannot be determined solely by fixed and measurable criteria; affective and subjective considerations also are involved. The logic of the survey suggests that the mere exchange of greetings is indicative of the existence of *komyunitei*, which is a simplistic and erroneous notion. It is clear that the Ogawa Eight—which has the highest percentage of farmers, the group least familiar with the term—forms an integral group whose like-mindedness is strengthened by history, geography, religion, and, most recently, nativeness.

The integrity of the native sector, epitomized by the Ogawa Eight, is both reflected in and perpetuated by congenial interhousehold relations, which until recently were encouraged by the use of communal wells and jointly owned agricultural equipment.[5] Several natives identified modern plumbing and the private ownership of farm equipment as factors leading to the relatively diminished contact between farm households.

Cognitive maps of *komyunitei*, a social construction, are as varied as the groups bounded by it. Although only 51 percent of the respondents in the 1979 public opinion survey were familiar with the word, about 84 percent nevertheless had a definite idea of its spatial or geographic scope:

immediate neighborhood	16.6%
neighborhood association	44.4
city subdivision (*chōme*)	8.0
elementary school district	6.9
junior high school district	3.1
three to five city divisions (*chō*)	4.5
do not know	11.5
no answer	4.0

Kodaira City planners, for reasons of convenience, regard "community" and the elementary school district as synonymous, but the respondents seemed to favor the neighborhood association as constituting a *komyunitei* in its own right (*YC* 1979, 61).

As I see it, geographic scope is not the crucial factor here, since neighborhood associations assume various sizes and configurations anyway. The Ogawa Eight *jichikai* conform to the historical *bangumi* division, on which they have been superimposed; the Gakuen Nishi-

chōkai encompasses an entire city division; and some neighborhood associations are limited to high-rise projects, while others consist of only two households. The 44.4 percent of the respondents in the 1979 public opinion survey who selected neighborhood association as the spatial unit that most closely conformed to their cognitive map of *komyunitei* were basing their choice not on size, as the survey implies, but on the "official" definition of neighborhood associations as "spontaneously organized and democratically administered by the local residents . . . to promote and facilitate neighborliness and mutual aid" (Kodaira-*shi* seikatsuka 1973). The premise of the city's survey therefore is inadequate, for not only are some of the areal units listed coincident, incorporated, or overlapping but the questionnaire fails to distinguish between territory as administrative unit and territory as cognitive map. The salience of *jichikai* as the most widely acknowledged, affective geographic unit is augmented by the fact that in Kodaira the 380 neighborhood associations are not even informally incorporated as a federation. Rather, each constitutes an entirely autonomous enclave within the city, just as certain *jichikai* are independent enclaves within the territory of a larger neighborhood association.

In order to assess the degree of residents' commitment to Furusato Kodaira, city hall conducted a questionnaire survey in 1974, hoping to measure the extent of their *jimoto-ishiki*, or local-*person* consciousness. This is not the same as nativeness but, rather, is an approximation of nativeness. Thirty-five of the sixty-six respondents claimed to possess local-person consciousness, while seven indicated that they had "something that approached local-person consciousness." Two persons actually said that they were local persons and that Kodaira was their native place. City analysts concluded that 67 percent (forty-four respondents) therefore possessed *kyōdo-ishiki*, or local-*place* consciousness. What they did was conflate local-person (*jimoto*) and local-place (*kyōdo*) consciousness. For natives both aspects of local consciousness stem from their genealogical and residential history in Kodaira. Among newcomers *jimoto* names their acquired familiarity with Kodaira, and *kyōdo* names their anticipated future (and imagined past) in Kodaira.

In 1962 the former *shinden* territories were reorganized as *chō* (also *machi*), or city divisions (see map 6). Following the opinion of the Diet, Kodaira's administrators regarded *chō* as "more modern and rational" units of sociogeographic organization. In a series of articles published in the local newspaper during the period 1960–61, the administrators attempted to convince residents of the need for boundary changes, which were scheduled for implementation in October 1962. The introductory article stressed that "compared to the West, the Japanese system of address is confusing and irrational: house no. 5 could be flanked by nos. 20 and 300, because they were numbered according to the order in which they were built" (*KCH*, 1 June 1960).

In the 1920s Kodaira had been divided into eight *ōaza*, or major (village) sections: the seven *shinden* villages and Kodaira Gakuen. In the context of imminent cityhood, their awkward shapes were deemed inconvenient and unbefitting a modern city. Moreover, the names "such-and-such *shinden*" were declared bumpkinish and wholly contrary to a city image, although in the context of *furusato-zukuri* there is a movement under way to restore historical place-names, now valued for their nostalgic worth, lest they be completely forgotten. Mail delivery and travel were unnecessarily complicated under the old system, since, for example, five different locations bore the name Nonaka Zenzaemon-*gumi* (*KCH*, 1 July 1960).

Cityhood, then, effectively marked a purposive geohistorical shift from an agrarian past to a present dominated by office workers and high-rise apartment buildings. Complementing the "modern," albeit impersonal and cramped, cement high-rises was a new concern for punctuality and Clock Time, the opposite of which was disparaged as Kodaira Time. A "punctuality campaign" was inaugurated by city hall in 1961, and punctuality itself was lauded as both the key to increased productivity and the very foundation of a "cultured life." The campaign was spearheaded by the newly elected mayor, Ōshima, and supervised by retired army officers. The mayor declared a "Commemoration of Time Day," to be observed annually on 10 June. Four years earlier, when elected chair of the assembly, Ōshima had vowed to eradicate Kodaira Time, epitomized by farm households, which he defined as chronic tardiness and a complete disregard for fixed schedules. The assembly was to serve as an exemplary model of punctuality, to which end the members were required to be seated three minutes before a session began (*KSH*, 5 June 1965).

Clock Time is exalted in the Kodaira citizens' charter, whose third article proclaims, "Let's build a city characterized by punctuality and clockwork orderliness." To concretize the charter's proclamation, a pedestal clock, donated by the Kodaira Lions Club, was installed in front of the old city hall. Although it since has been replaced, photographs show it to have been a cement obelisk. The present clock is incorporated into the marble archway fronting the new (1983) city hall. In a very conspicuous and literal way, then, spatial reorganization has been accompanied by temporal reform. More specifically, the replacement, in the 1960s, of *shinden* divisions and rustic place-names with *chō* and other more modern-sounding toponyms, together with the replacement of Kodaira Time with Clock Time, signaled the ascendance of white-collar style and the concomitant demographic dominance of newcomers.

When Old-timers Are Immigrants

Immigration was a routine feature of *shinden* village—making and characterizes the postwar development of Kodaira. Historically, immigrants or newcomers were not marginal; rather, "immigrant" designated a temporary status category, which changed automatically into that of "old-timer." "Newcomer," in comparison, is a permanent status category; for the postwar tendency, epitomized by the editors of the *Kodaira chōshi*, has been toward freezing the dichotomy of farm household and nonfarm household. This practice, in turn, has reinforced the ascribed statuses of these two basic categories of Kodaira resident. While newcomers eventually may come to feel like local persons, or to express a local-place consciousness, they will never make the transition to *tochikko*, although as *kodairakko* they may approximate that status.

The numerical superiority of the immigrant population over the "host population," and the city's consequent suburbanization, have provoked among natives a redressive reaction of the sort more typically observed, ironically, among newcomers. The reaction in question consists of three interrelated activities, which collectively amount to a valorization of nativeness within Furusato Kodaira. In Kodaira minority natives behaved like immigrants in their efforts to adjust to the influx of newcomers during the 1960s. Newcomers, on the other hand, did not have to adjust to the natives' society, which at that time was regarded as retrogressive. Thus, in the 1960s, local and national programs were inaugurated to rationalize farm household management; and the need for fixed, annual schedules was stressed (*KCH*, 1 December 1959, 1 May 1960). The adjustment process has three salient features, which also describe the forms of redress employed by Kodaira natives.[6]

The first feature or activity, *information gathering*, is evident in the self-conscious collection and compilation of folkloric and local-history materials as a means of conceptually consolidating the native sector. The research and publications of the Kodaira Local History Study Society, a native group, exemplify this movement.[7] So does the new monthly *Komyunitei Kodaira*, which was founded in 1984 by a group of *tochikko* to publicize the achievements of Kodaira natives. The inaugural issue included a cover story on Mayor Senuma's vision of Kodaira twenty years hence and a long article on a wide-scale riot against the Meiji government in 1870. Senuma, the incumbent priest of Enmei-*ji*, is a *tochikko*, and the feature story both sheds light on a shadowy historical episode and martyrizes the leaders of the Kodaira Seven, for several of the men perished in prison (*Komyunitei Kodaira*, 1 May 1984).[8] These publications are available at city libraries and citizens' halls and, potentially at least, serve to impress upon newcomers the colorful and laudable history of native households. Commemorative steles and signboards marking historical landmarks function in the same way. By locating the remembered past in the present landscape, they reclaim and revivify that past.

A second feature of the adjustment process, the *distinctive presentation of self*, is a strategy to increase visibility and thus win special attention and treatment. Two cogent methods of distinctive presentation are stereotyping and mythologizing. Natives contribute to a stereotype of themselves to ensure their special status within Kodaira. The features of this stereotype include the somewhat ribald and self-consciously maintained *tochikko* dialect; daredevil performances in the citizens' and shrine festivals; and a "traditional" religious piety manifested in the form of the consociations discussed in chapter 4. Mythologization includes the multiplication, exaggeration, and dramatization of historical elements and episodes, such as the 1870 rebellion mentioned above; the samurai-origins thesis about the Ogawa household; and the figure of the intrepid *shinden* pioneer and civic ancestor, Ogawa Kurobei. *Shinden* mythopoeia imbues natives collectively with a certain charisma, and the pioneer spirit recently has been appropriated by city hall toward the reclamation of Furusato Kodaira.

The editors of the *Kodaira chōshi* have helped to magnify the natives' distinctive social presence. A section on "traditional" seasonal activities includes the following anecdote, which in effect, illustrates the differences in sensibility between the native and newcomer sectors:

A Kodaira native immigrated to Tokyo and secured employment as a *sararii-man*. It was a long time before he returned to visit his parents. His mother made a favorite local dish for the occasion, called *dojōgayu*, a gruel made of flour and red beans. All those years in Tokyo had spoiled her son; his palate had become too sophisticated to tolerate the local gruel. The moment his parents left the room, he moved to dump the soup outdoors but, in his hurry, fell off the veranda. (*KC* 1959, 1220–21)

On the one hand, the anecdote suggests the vulnerability of native tastes to the bourgeois climate of Tokyo and, by extension, the incompatibility of farmers (natives) and office workers (newcomers). On the other hand, it satirizes the fickleness of recent converts to a Tokyo lifestyle aesthetic, which is cast as the antithesis of a hitherto unproblematic "Kodaira" lifestyle aesthetic.

Finally, the third activity engaged in by Kodaira natives is the *manipulation of interaction*. The scale of manipulation varies from almost exclusive control over maintaining, and in some cases drawing, historical boundaries, and the determination of land use and disposition, to a tenacious influence in local politics. Two of the city's three mayors have been *tochikko*; and in 1962, when natives (farm households) accounted for 4.5 percent of the total number of households, 35 percent (nine of twenty-six) of the assemblypersons were natives. This is nearly the same percentage as in 1984 (32 percent, or eleven of thirty-one), when 9.6 percent (three of thirty-one) of the assemblypersons but only 2 percent of all householders were farmers.[9] Generally speaking, the relative decline in the number of native assemblypersons has been more gradual than the decline in the overall proportion of natives to newcomers.[10]

Conclusion: Community through Nomenclature Revisited

What was the process by which the Kodaira Seven (*shinden*) were transformed into the Kodaira Thirty-three (*chō*)? In 1962 the city's steering committee for boundary reorganization and renaming decided on a general plan of action, which met with the assembly's approval. The plan spelled out several objectives, not all of which were realized. They are presented below, along with the supporting arguments for their implementation.

1. Boundaries are to be clearly delineated by railroad tracks, roads, canals, and other artificial landmarks. The historical boundaries are not precise. The lack of precision has not posed problems for natives—for whom the border between Ogawa-*mura* and Ogawa-*shinden* is still designated as "*X*'s house" or "*Y*'s tea bushes"—but this essentially mnemonic system of demarcation is extremely inconvenient for newcomers. Moreover, words like *shinden* and *X-gumi* are rustic and uncitylike (*KCH*, 1 July, 1 September 1960; 1 February 1961; 20 February 1962).

2. *Chō* size is to be determined by the character—commercial, industrial, or residential—of the area in question. According to guidelines established by the construction ministry, commercial *chō* should measure about six hectares, industrial *chō* about thirteen hectares, and the residential *chō* about ten hectares.

3. *Chō* names must be easy to learn and remember and should be endearing. Redundancies, as exemplified by Bunkyō ward's sixteen toponyms containing the name Komagome, should be avoided. Moreover, place-names should reflect each *chō*'s "peculiar characteristics."

Place-names were solicited from among the resident public at large, and the new city divisions were introduced formally on 1 October 1962, on which date Kodaira became a city. Map 6 shows the former *shinden* sections, together with the newly designated *chō*. The names were selected for the following reasons:

Nakashima-*chō*: Since the area already was called East/West Nakashima, it was most convenient to keep that name.

Jōsui Hon-*chō*, Jōsui Shin-*machi*, and Jōsui Minami-*chō*: *Jōsui*, or canal, was selected to unite, toponymically, three separate *shinden* sections (Ogawa, Suzuki, and Nonaka Zenzaemon-*gumi*) located south of the Tamagawa main canal.

Takanodai: Since the rather complicated character for *taka* (hawk, falcon) was not among the ideographs designated by the government for daily use, it instead was written in cursive syllabary. The name Takanodai alludes to the fact that the area was part of the Tokugawa's falconry reserve. Between the years 1620–1692 and 1717–1866, the southern portion of Ogawa-*mura* was incorporated into the *takajo*, or falconry reserve, of the Owari province branch of the Tokugawa *ie*. The reserve eventually encompassed 170 villages in

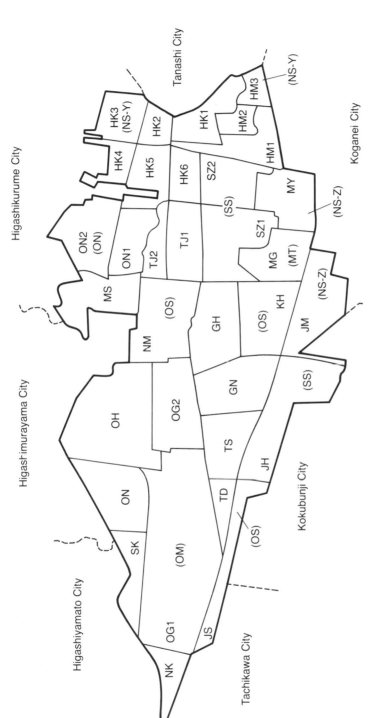

Map 6. Boundaries of new and old divisions. *New divisions*: NK = Nakashima-*chō*; JS = Jōsui Shin-*machi*; TD = Takanodai; OG1 = Ogawa-*chō* 1-*chōme*; OG2 = Ogawa-*chō* 2-*chōme*; SK = Sakae-*chō*; ON = Ogawa Nishi-*machi*; OH = Ogawa Higashi-*chō*; JH = Jōsui Hon-*chō*; JM = Jōsui Minami-*chō*; KH = Kihei-*chō*; TS = Tsuda-*machi*; GN = Gakuen Nishi-*machi*; GH = Gakuen Higashi-*chō*; NM = Naka-*machi*; MS = Misono-*chō*; MG = Megurita-*chō*; MY = Miyuki-*chō*; SZ1–2 = Suzuko-*chō* 1–2-*chōme*; TJ1–2 = Tenjin-*chō* 1–2-*chōme*; ON1–2 = Ōnuma-*chō* 1–2-*chōme*; HM1–3 = Hanakoganei Minami-*chō* 1–3-*chōme*; HK1–6 = Hanakoganei 1–6-*chōme*. (*Old divisions*): (OM) = Ogawa-*mura*; (OS) = Ogawa-*shinden*; (NS-Y) = Nonaka-*shinden* (Yoemon-*gumi*); (NS-Z) = Nonaka-*shinden* (Zenzaemon-*gumi*); (SS) = Suzuki-*shinden*; (MT) = Megurita-*shinden*; (ON) = Ōnumata-*shinden*. (Adapted from *KK* 1983, 244)

the region northwest of Edo. During the period 1731–[1741] and 1759–1793, the reserve was supervised by the Ogawa household, which gained much prestige from this coveted position. Supposedly, only households with a samurai pedigree were selected to supervise the falconry reserve, a point used to validate the samurai-origins thesis of the Ogawa *ie*. The position warranted a modest stipend, but the strict rules under which the reserve was to be administered made it more of a bane than a boon. Hunting, raising poultry, and erecting scarecrows within the precincts were forbidden; and the permission of domain officials was needed in order to stage a festival or to install a water wheel, on account of the potentially disruptive noises generated. Also, villagers were obliged to equip and entertain the falconers, in addition to bearing the cost of maintaining the reserve (*KC* 1959, 82–85).

Ogawa-*chō* (1- and 2-*chōme*), Ogawa Nishi-*machi*, and Ogawa Higashi-*chō*: The name Ogawa was left intact to memorialize both Kurobei and the earliest *shinden* village.

Sakae-*chō*: *Sakae*, which means "flourishing or thriving," was selected for this peripheral *chō* to reflect a desire for prosperous relations between Kodaira and the neighboring town of Yamato (Higashiyamato City since 1970).

Kihei-*chō*: This place-name derives from the bridge of the same name, which in turn was named after a local celebrity of yore.

Tsuda-*machi*: Tsuda Women's College is the namesake of this *chō*.

Gakuen Nishi-*machi* and Gakuen Higashi-*chō*: Kodaira Gakuen, the "academy town" housing tract established in the 1920s in what is now Gakuen Higashi-*chō*, was the inspiration for this place-name.

Naka-*machi*: As I already have noted, the place-name of this centrally located *chō* was selected to signify intracity harmony and neighborliness.

Misono-*chō*: *Misono*, which means "beautiful park," ostensibly was chosen to symbolize Kodaira's "garden citification," although the presence of the municipal cemetery was probably the more influential factor.

Megurita-*chō*: Megurita-*shinden* is the namesake of this division.

Miyuki-*chō*: This place-name memorializes Emperor Meiji's delighted admiration—*miyuki* means "august delight or pleasure"—of the blossoming cherry trees dotting the area. In April 1883, Emperor Meiji and his entourage journeyed to Suzuki-*shinden* to view the cherry blossoms, about which he later composed several haiku. The Suzuki-*shinden* head commissioned and in 1902 gave to Kaigan-*ji* a stele commemorating the imperial visit. Two thousand cherry trees were planted in the 1730s along a six-kilometer stretch of Itsukaichi Road under the orders of the local magistrate (*KK* 1983, 76–78; Kodaira kyōdo kenkyūkai 1983, 41–42; Yamazaki 1983, 23). The precedent set by the local magistrate was followed in 1980, when the Rotary Club donated seventy cherry trees for planting in Hanako-ganei 6-*chōme* as part of the "(re)making of historical Kodaira" campaign inaugurated in 1977 (*KSH*, 5 April 1980).

Suzuki-*chō* (1- and 2-*chōme*): The name is that of the former *shinden*, although both *chō* together constitute a smaller area than their namesake village.

Tenjin-*chō* (1- and 2-*chōme*): Tenjin Hollow is the subject of several folktales and the inspiration for the name of this *chō*. In the folktale "The footprints of Daidara, the Boy Giant," the three hollows in Kodaira (Tenjin, Heian, and San'ō) are said to have been formed when Daidara passed through the area en route to build Mount Fuji. Thus, the hollows (i.e., the giant's footprints) are all the same size and point in the direction of Mount Fuji (Kodaira minwa no kai 1981, 54).

Ōnuma-*chō* (1- and 2-*chōme*): Although this *chō* was named after Ōnumata-*shinden*, the appellation was shortened to the presumably less rustic, and allegedly more easily pronounced, Ōnuma.

Hanakoganei (1–6-*chōme*) and Hanakoganei Minami-*chō* (1–3-*chōme*): As part of a place-name, *hana* (flower) is analogous to the "pearl" in "Hong Kong, Pearl of the Orient." Hanakoganei has up-town overtones and suggests a cultured, residential area. It was a name much preferred to the comparatively boorish Nonaka Yoemon-*gumi*. Although Koganei is a historical place-name, and the name of the city sharing Kodaira's southwest border, the *chō* supposedly was named after Hanakoganei Station (*KCH*, 5 September 1962).

Each municipal mass-housing and high-rise project was provided both with proper names, such as Sakurajōsui, Nobidome, and Hitotsu-bashi, and with impersonal names, such as Nos. 3, 6, and 7 Tōei Jūtaku. Somewhat ironic, in light of the rationale for the renaming campaign, is the presence of several municipal housing tracts bearing such "tabooed" names as Ogawa-*shinden* and Ōnumata-*shinden*. These mass-housing units bear the names of the *shinden* villages originally peopled by new-comers, whose initial status was not unlike that of the residents of the municipal housing tracts. Perhaps the newness of the units was thought enough to offset the backwardness of these historical names.

The proposed boundary and name changes generated both scorn and legitimate worries among natives: scorn because of what they re-garded as the wholly cosmetic rationale for the new *chō* names; worries because of their fear that the territories of neighborhood associations and shrine and temple parishes would be altered drastically, spelling the potential division of hitherto intact neighborhoods. City administrators assuaged such fears by adopting a compromising posture with respect to the geographic correspondence of *jichikai* and *chō*. The partial inclu-sion of Tsuda-*machi* within the territorial scope of the Gakuen Nishi-*chōkai* was one such compromise (*KCH*, 20 February 1962). Shrine and temple parishes retained their native constituency, although their physical boundaries were disrupted by the changes.

Ogawa Eight natives have had altogether less to worry about in either case. First of all, in the area encompassed by the former Ogawa-*mura*, Oume Road was not designated a *chō* boundary (as was Itsu-kaichi Road) but was retained as the organizational nexus of the na-tives' society, thereby contributing to the overall integrity of the Ogawa Eight. Second, as noted in chapter 4, the parishes of both Shinmei-*gū* and Shōsen-*ji* remained as they were prior to the 1962 reorganization, and their constituent divisions continue to be called by their historical names. Although the internal organization of these parishes has grown more complicated since their original twofold division in the seven-teenth century, the former Ogawa-*mura* itself remained a distinct entity until 1962. The newly designated Ogawa-*chō*, on the other hand, cross-cut these historical boundaries, effectively fragmenting the territorially intact *shinden*-village units and creating, virtually overnight, new geo-graphic entities. To circumvent the disruptive influence of *chō*-level identification, the parish boundaries of Shinmei-*gū* and Shōsen-*ji* were retained by those institutions as they were before cityhood. These are the same borders—the parishes and the *bangumi*, as op-posed to the *chō* or school districts—that are maintained collectively by Kodaira natives through religious (e.g., the Yagumo lantern-float procession) and secular (e.g., neighborhood association) activities. The borders also are demarcated symbolically by memorial steles and signboards, just as they were demarcated in the Edo period by small shrines and religious statues.

The fluidity of contact in everyday life—commuting to school or work, shopping—almost ensures that natives and newcomers engage in a broad dialogue on place identity. It is a dialogue that gravitates toward collective representations which have credence to both groups (Suttles 1972, 51–52). Of course, dialogue is not just a modulating activity, for it also constitutes a means by which to highlight and rationalize that which differentiates one interlocutor from others. Thus, it may serve as a process by which diverse groups and individuals arrive at agreements and disagreements about the meaning(s) of a given place, such as Furusato Kodaira (cf. Erickson 1980, 50, 94, 104). This dialogue may assume dramaturgical proportions, as represented by the Yagumo lantern-float procession in April and the citizens' festival in October, or it may assume the more literal form of a mayor-citizens roundtable discussion. The boundary reorganization and renaming campaign of 1962 and the ongoing reformulation of land use constitute yet other modes of dialogue.

Generally speaking, whereas local-person and local-place identity among natives emerged from and continues to be generated by historically structured modes of consociation, this identity among newcomers is a recent by-product of voluntary, obligatory, and/or solicited relationships. Writing in the late 1950s, the editors of the *Kodaira chōshi* claimed that, although newcomers were not incorporated into the historical (native) neighborhood divisions and consociations, such institutions were not necessary for the "urban lifestyle" embodied by the newcomers (*KC* 1959, 761). City hall has since retracted that allegation, for the romanticized notion of an agricultural-like lifestyle as inherently neighborly motivates both the production (and reproduction) and the consumption of *furusato-zukuri* rhetoric.

The entity "newly reclaimed Kodaira" suddenly was acclaimed in the industrializing 1960s. Reclamation does not denote an end state but, rather, involves a continual effort to remedy something and make it fit, and ultimately to contemporize it. In the 1650s and 1720s, barren land was made fit for cultivation, and villages were built; in the early postwar period, farmland was made fit for commercial, industrial, and residential use; and in the 1970s, the reclamation of Furusato Kodaira from urban sprawl was initiated. The version of the "newly reclaimed Kodaira" salient in the 1960s was but one episode in the ongoing contemporization of the city. While "progressive" newcomers were lauded by city hall and in the local press, Kodaira natives were gearing up to redress their threatened place through such reparative strategies as parish exclusivity and the formation of a local-history and conservation society, whose publications commemorate the intrepid *shinden* pioneers and their descendants. These strategies have, in effect, contemporized the "living history" of the native sector, for through them history has become historicism: an appeal to a cultural genealogy that distinguishes even *sarariiman*-ized natives from newcomers. It is a historicism that serves well city hall's recent *furusato-zukuri* campaign and earlier efforts to "reclaim" Kodaira. The names selected for the *chō* created in 1962, for instance, effectively redistributed the local color and historicity formerly locked up within each *shinden* name. Stripping an area— Nonaka Zenzaemon-*gumi*, for example—of its nominal patina exposed a surface dotted with symbolic landmarks (e.g., Tenjin Hollow) and exotic flora (e.g., Hanakoganei, or Flower of Koganei), ripe for nomenclatural exploitation.

Furusato Kodaira may be conceptualized as a relationship of past, present, and future, in which the present is a staging ground for imagining the future by remembering (re-membering) the past. The paradox remains that the promotion of Furusato Kodaira has also had the effect of emphasizing sectoral differences, because the "authentic" community to be reclaimed conceptually and nomenclaturally amounts to a tenuous compromise between the city's natives and newcomers mediated by city hall. Were it not a tenuous compromise, repeated references in the local media to such oppositions as "then" (past and future) and "now" (present), "traditional" and "modern," and "farm household" and "nonfarm household" would not be necessary. Cities, villages, neighborhoods, associations, and consociations are not iso-lable, transcendent entities; they are the mental and material construc-tions of identifiable individuals and groups operating under certain sociohistorical conditions. Like overworked palimpsest, these construc-tions bear the indelible imprint of the beliefs and ideas, whims and cogitations, pettifoggeries and values of those individuals and groups. The making of Kodaira is a perpetual task, and Furusato Kodaira is the latest contemporized version of a "newly reclaimed Kodaira."

CHAPTER SIX

The Making of Kodaira
Revisited

Slogans and Charters

The land, an endless brocade of green,
Ripe and fruitful Musashino, where hopes are sown.
Always progressing, Kodaira,
Carrying out ideals. Proud of
Our pioneer past—the heart's native place.[1]

Six years after the "Kodaira Song" was written to celebrate the "progress" made since the Edo period, the first aerial photograph of Kodaira was published in the August 1960 edition of the local newspaper. "The sight of Kodaira from the air," the caption reads, "apart from being interesting in itself, stimulates all kinds of new thoughts and ideas about the town where we live." The photograph, the first in a short series of aerial pictures of the town, was published to provoke contemplations on Kodaira in the wake of the merger dispute. The caption continues: "That wide swath of trees in the middle of the picture is the verdant Oume Road; to its north is the Bridgestone factory. The municipal housing projects appear, characteristically, as dense clusters. From the air, the fields to the south resemble *tatami* mats on which are scattered private homes" (*KCH*, 1 July 1960).

The aerial photograph was the first public envisagement of Kodaira as a whole greater than the sum of its constituent sectors. An experiment in cognitive mapping engineered by city hall, it, together with the

"Kodaira Song," marked the informal beginning of the making of that yet-unnamed imagined community Furusato Kodaira. The citizens' charter of 1972, along with the first citizens' festival four years later, heralded the formal commencement of the *furusato-zukuri* project. A giant aerial photograph of the city hangs in each citizens' hall and library, as well as in the foyer of city hall. The pictures integrate Kodaira by the seemingly paradoxical device of making visually explicit the configurational differences between native and newcomer settlements. The result, theoretically at least, is a more efficient dialectic of native and newcomer, motivating both the rhetoric of *furusato-zukuri* and the imagination of Furusato Kodaira. The citizens' festival similarly ensures that residents see and remember the city in terms of its constituent social sectors, for the perceived solidarity of each kind of residential group depends on the reactions of its adversaries. City hall has attempted to forge a collective (as opposed to unitary) Kodaira identity by negotiating the interaction between the native and newcomer sectors. The ongoing historical process of the making of Kodaira is not limited to the city's physical terrain but includes the mental terrain of residents as well. And Furusato Kodaira ultimately is a mental terrain—a landscape of nostalgia.

A local historian has noted in the preface to his book on "olden Kodaira" that "nostalgia is not simply sentimentalism but derives from the lifestyle of natives and [their/our] ancestors. Inherent to nostalgia is common sense and practical wisdom [*jōshiki*] as well as a consciousness of nationality [*kokuminteki ishiki*]. Nostalgia is something to respect and revere" (Itō 1961, 5). He posits *furusato* as the landscape of childhood—"an unforgettable childhood dream to which one yearns to return"—and describes his book as a contribution to the realization of that dream; namely, the making of Furusato Kodaira (ibid., 5–6).

In his preface to the above book, the superintendent of schools declares that "the ancestors of Kodaira natives made this place their *furusato*." The "second reclamation of Kodaira is not something that can be accomplished overnight, but calls for [years of] cooperation, sacrifice, and toil." Through nostalgia, he continues, local customs and know-how can be salvaged before they are irretrievably lost (ibid., 3–4). The author himself adds that, over the course of Kodaira's postwar transformation from a "pure agricultural village" to a "hygienic metropolitan bedroom town," local history has been neglected and nostalgia (*kyōshū*) discouraged. His book on historical incidents and local lore, published about fifteen years before the city formally implemented its *furusato-*

zukuri program, represents a type of restorationism: a local patriotism nurtured by a nostalgia for what Kodaira once was and could be again.

Identities in general are often proposed to people rather than being self-produced (Suttles 1972, 53). It was in the 1950s, in the context of the town-merger campaign, that Kodaira natives first began asserting what was later claimed as "nativeness"; twenty years later, local-person and local-place consciousness became a citywide pursuit initiated by city hall. The administration's "soft" or cultural policies counterpoint the revanchism of the city's indigenes, although in other respects the native sector has been appropriated by city hall as living testimony of Kodaira's unique historicity. The "adult" shrine segment of the citizens' festival, for example, amounts to a local cultural show—natives on parade. Likewise, newcomers are encouraged to take local-history tours designed to introduce them to the historical features of their "new *furusato*."

With the declaration in the 1970s and 1980s of the dawning of the "age of localism," development manifestos were published in regional cities. The documents are variously known as city proclamations (*toshi sengen*), citizens' charters (*shimin kenshō*), and city charters (*toshi kenshō*). Generally speaking, the city proclamation is a short, sloganized statement of collective civic purpose. Its equivalent is the preamble of the longer and more explicit citizens' or city charters. The main, somewhat academic, difference between the citizens' and city charters lies in their primary subjects: residents and civil servants, respectively (Isomura 1981, 182–83).

The Kodaira citizens' charter was promulgated in 1972, on the occasion of the tenth anniversary of cityhood. A public competition was staged to solicit ideas for its content and composition. There was never any public debate as to whether a charter was either necessary or desirable; rather, residents simply were informed that "it has been decided to create a citizens' charter." Persons living or working in Kodaira were eligible for the first prize of 50,000 yen. Announcements of the contest were published in the city newspaper and included examples of other city charters for reference, together with sample slogans designed to point contributors in the right direction. One such slogan was "Midori yutaka na kai o kokoro no furusato ni" (Make verdant avenues the *furusato* of the heart) (*KSH*, 20 May 1972, 5 June 1972).

The preamble and five articles of the charter were presented in chapter 2. The first four articles are directed toward the improvement of the environment, and the fifth encourages the development of local-person and local-place consciousness. The council responsible for actualizing the citizens' charter, chaired from the start by former Mayor Ogawa, consists of two vice-chairs, eleven secretaries, one accountant, and two supervisors. During his tenure, Mayor Ōshima served as honorary chair. Over one hundred civic leaders attended the council's inaugural meeting, at which the five "special sections" were created, each named after the article of the charter it was responsible for actualizing. Through their combined activities, the special sections were to facilitate the making of a "community based on collective identity."

Specific activities for each section were drawn up at the second annual council meeting, convened in June 1976. The "beautiful city" section was to promote trash disposal and work to eradicate pollution; recruit children during the summer holidays to clean the Tamagawa main canal; initiate a one-day citywide cleanup campaign; and distribute vinyl trash bags. The "compassionate society" section was to initiate a "one kind word" campaign; instruct residents to give up bus and train seats to the elderly; and help senior citizens in crossing busy intersections. The "orderly civic life" section was to start a campaign to observe Clock Time and practice punctuality; adopt and promote the slogan "Defend [Clock] Time"; distribute rubber stamps featuring that slogan; and urge the regular use of schedules. The "healthy city" section was to sponsor walkathons and walking tours of local historical sites. Lastly, the "affluent city" section was to spearhead the revaluation of "olden Kodaira"; support the citizens' festival; and work to preserve historical objects and landmarks (*KSH*, 20 October 1975, 20 June 1976).

Council officials were quick to emphasize that, in the final analysis, the creation of an "attractive and livable regional society" depended on the "originality" (*sōi*) and "innovativeness" (*kufū*) of each Kodaira resident. To encourage public participation, the council inaugurated an annual awards ceremony to honor individual activists (*KSH*, 20 June 1976). Like the situation in Ogawa-*mura* centuries ago, the local autonomy of the suburban city of Kodaira ultimately is ensured by activities initiated and maintained by each resident householder. Significantly, the overall theme of the council's second annual meeting was "The basis of neighborhood-making [*machi-zukuri*] is person-making [*hito-zukuri*]" (*KSH*, 20 June 1977).

For a while, a new sloganized theme for the council was decided each year. These have included "Toward affective, spiritual city-making fostered by the charter" (1977); "Widening the scope of *furusato* through the charter" (1978); and "Amplifying affective city-making through the charter" (1979). The 1979 theme, eventually declared the permanent slogan for council activities as a whole, was given much attention in the annual newsletter established by the council that same year. As Mayor Senuma noted in the fifth edition of that newsletter (30 May 1984), "Furusato Kodaira [is] a place suffused with compassion nurtured by intertwined hearts." The council represents the "soft" or cultural administrative arm of city hall, where it operates under the auspices of the Civic Life Department. As demonstrated by the language of the charter itself, together with council slogans, much emphasis is placed on the process of *tsukuri* (making), in contrast to *naru* (to become, evolve, be), as I have discussed in chapter 1. Kodaira, the local media explain, "has become" (*narimashita*) a suburban bedroom town lacking integrity and fouled by unrestrained sprawl. It is up to Kodaira residents, however, "to make" (*tsukuru*) the city into an "attractive and livable regional society." *Naru* is used to describe—or, rather, rationalize—the existence of undesirable features such as air and noise pollution, uncontrolled sprawl, juvenile delinquency, and antinomy between natives and newcomers. The use of this intransitive verb symbolically absolves residents and administrators alike from responsibility for the city's demerits and drawbacks. The sociohistorical conditions and circumstances under which such undesirable features emerged are elided. At the same time, the future—Kodaira as it *should* be—is envisaged as a consequence of constructive, intentional actions. Semantic acrobatics like this suggest that the existence of pollution, sprawl, delinquency, and antinomy will continue to be explained away as preexisting, irruptive undesirables. However, unintended consequences are conditions of action, just as intentional actions may have unintended consequences. If no concerted effort is made to understand the historical relations between theories, ideas, beliefs, and aspirations, then both the eradication of these undesirable features and the resolution of social problems will remain elusive.

Hearts and Borders

The revanchist bent of Kodaira natives' interpretation of *furusato* was evident as early as 1959, when the editors of the *Kodaira chōshi* made note of the affective barriers erected by the native sector against newcomers. They explained that the neighborhood divisions (discussed in chapter 3) enclose people who share, and are bounded by, the same *kokoro*, or heart (but also, in this context, mind-set and values) (*KC* 1959, 878). *Kokoro* thus signifies and symbolizes an impermeable, affective boundary that both divides natives from newcomers and encompasses natives within the landscape of nostalgia. The experience of insideness for natives is occasioned by the regular reenactment of historical festivals, membership in shrine and temple parishes, yard shrine oblations, and consociational events, such as mountain pilgrimages. The exclusivity of the parishes and consociations makes membership in them all the more cogent for natives, whose claims on Furusato Kodaira are thereby reinforced. For newcomers, insideness, as defined earlier, is not so much experienced as encouraged, most conspicuously by the rhetoric of *furusato-zukuri*.

Among the qualities especially emphasized in the context of "old village"–making are *fureai* and *uruoi*. *Fureai* implies physical contact (touching, brushing) between people and refers to warm, neighborly relations, which *uruoi* further qualifies as being "wet" (as opposed to "dry"). Since mere propinquity does not in itself guarantee "wet" relations, they must therefore be actively cultivated.

The citizens' festival, the linchpin of the city's *furusato-zukuri* program, may be interpreted as a variation on the theme of *hiroba*, or public place. *Ba* is a "frame" that "sets a boundary and gives a common basis to a set of individuals who are located or involved in it" (Nakane 1973, 1). These boundaries may be physical or affective or both. *Ba* "is not just a spatial parameter, and physical environment, in which interaction 'occurs': it is these elements mobilised as part of the interaction" (Giddens 1979, 207). (*Hiro*) *ba* is used by city hall to refer to the foundation of "an attractive and purposeful civic life." A list of *ba-zukuri* projects drawn up in 1969 included the following *ba*: sewer system, hygienic environment, parks, street signs and lights, and fire-prevention provisions. With the advent of "cultural administration" in the 1970s, *ba-zukuri* has been interpreted more narrowly as the creation of occasions for the cultivation of local-person and local-place consciousness.

One of the major *ba-zukuri*, or place-making, projects sponsored by the citizens' charter council (i.e., the "beautiful city" section) is Green Road. Construction work on the twenty-one-kilometer tree-lined path encircling the city was begun in 1980, in accord with the first article of the charter: "Let's build a verdant city to which small birds will flock." The road is the first of the several projects comprising the Kodaira City

Green Master Plan scheduled for completion in the year 2000. The public relations pamphlet distributed by the Parks Department explains that Green Road was constructed to "enable Kodaira residents to retrace the footsteps of their pioneering ancestors and to become intimately acquainted with nature."

Green Road symbolizes the coevalness of the native and newcomer sectors. It runs parallel to the Tamagawa and Nobidome canals and at the same time incorporates newly paved cement sidewalks and bikeways. The nearly thirty bridges crisscrossing the two canals are referred to (in the above pamphlet) as *fureai no hashi*, or "neighborly-contact bridges." Illustrated maps of Green Road include cartoon renditions of both native shrines, temples, and farmland and such modern structures as the city hall, libraries, day-care centers, parks, and train stations (map 7). Just as the Ogawa branch canal encircles and thereby demarcates the Ogawa Eight, so Green Road encircles Kodaira City, demarcating it from the neighboring cities. In both cases, the affective boundaries of insideness are drawn, those of Green Road being more inclusive. Recognizing that "propinquity without centers and borders is unenduring" (Erickson 1980, 50, 125), city hall has set out to redraw affective boundaries: those who share the boundary are insiders; those who do not are outsiders. *Fureai no hiroba* thus are places where movements in physical space—such as walking or bicycling along Green Road, viewing photographs of Kodaira then and now, attending the citizens' festival, and participating in *furusato* seminars—correspond to a movement in consciousness.

Green Road is one manifestation of city hall's slogan "A charter visible to the eye." Another is the charter-images exhibition first held at the *fureai* gallery in the central citizens' hall. Kodaira residents, young and old alike, are encouraged to interpret artistically, using a variety of media, the articles of the citizens' and senior citizens' charters. The purpose of the annual exhibition is to give artistic expression to Furusato Kodaira. Posters, prints and drawings, photographs, and sculptures are solicited from residents at large. Most of the exhibits in 1984 were based on the first, "verdant city," article of the charter. Consequently, the majority of the art works submitted were alike in featuring trees, bushes, and wide swaths of lawn.

The annual citizens' festival and other festivals, together with the daily, weekly, and monthly events comprising the city's cultural administration policy, distinguish the temporal dimension of Furusato Kodaira. The regularity (predictability) of these new festivals and

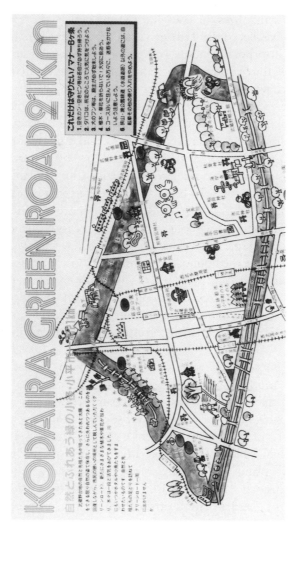

Map 7. Green Road. (From a pamphlet on Green Road issued by the Parks and Greenery Section, Kodaira City Hall, 1982)

events helps to occasion the ontological security (*anshin*) of the residents. After the Meiji period, the types of and dates for shrine and temple festivals were standardized, in order to ensure the dominance of the state at local levels. Similarly, in the Edo period, the *bakufu* had exerted its authority at the local level by strictly monitoring religious activities. The festivals and events sponsored today by Kodaira City Hall are not overtly religious in nature, although city hall and Shinmei-*gū* collaborate to a certain extent in the *furusato-zukuri* project. The New Year's walkathon, for example, is routed past Shinmei-*gū*, where —in the words of the city newspaper advertisement—"free worship" (*jiyū sanpai*) and sweet *sake* are made available to participating walkers (*KSH*, 20 January 1981).

The collaboration of city and shrine is also evident in local newspaper articles focusing on ceremonial etiquette. One article dealing with the New Year's pilgrimage begins by noting that "The *kokoro* of the Japanese people resides in the inseparable connection between New Year's Day and the New Year's pilgrimage" (*KSH*, 20 December 1970). The article introduces nine local shrines, "established three hundred years ago during the reclamation period," where Kodaira residents may pay their New Year's respects. Then follows a lengthy discussion, excerpted below, on the proper etiquette for New Year's visits.

On New Year's Day itself, visits to neighbors and acquaintances should be made after 10 o'clock in the morning and limited to the foyer [*genkan*]. Longer visits to relatives and close friends should be made on the second day. When one is visiting on New Year's Day, the foyer door should be closed behind one and one's overcoat removed; it is rude otherwise and, moreover, will bring on foul weather. Even women must drink the first cup of *sake* offered by the host, and, since it is rude to leave *sake* standing in the cup, teetotalers should request only a small amount to begin with. Children may be taken along, but should not be allowed to scamper about like mice. Since the local people are very critical and reproachful, one's children must be trained to behave in public. (*KSH*, 20 December 1970)

The article ends with a selection of New Year's games for families, described as "traditional games revived in a different form."

The apparent motive of the article, written two years before the citizens' charter was promulgated, was to promote and reproduce "traditional" social etiquette and propriety. Natives were portrayed as embodying normative sanctions, by which newcomers must abide if they were to assimilate successfully, even though it was the natives who had assimilated to the extent that the majority had become *sarariiman*-ized.

Two Traditions Are Better Than One

The attribution of traditionality to city hall–sponsored events, such as the annual citizens' festival, bespeaks the emergence of a second "tradition" intersecting with the one signified by the native sector. As I discussed in chapter 1, "traditional" does not signify the past but, rather, is an attribution of pastness. An event such as the citizens' festival becomes a "tradition" when its performance is authorized and validated by the knowledge or assumption of previous performances (cf. Giddens 1979, 200).

Kadomatsu, the New Year's pine branch decoration placed outside the main entrance of a house or shop, illustrates well the dialectic of native and newcomer "traditions" in Kodaira. In 1771 the rank-and-file villagers of Ogawa-*mura* conspired to boycott the New Year's custom of *kadomatsu*. Their decision signaled the hardening of an anti-village-head stance assumed earlier that year, when the autocratic leader had imposed certain austerity measures in the wake of a poor harvest. The village head initially had agreed to suspend indefinitely the practice of having each villager present him with a New Year's gift. However, he later reneged and declared that this time-honored custom—which symbolized village integrity and harmony, requiring as it did a collective effort—should be continued by all means. (Apparently, however, the practice had been discontinued during the inauspicious year in question.) The head also insisted that the custom of *kadomatsu*, "symbolic of support for *bakufu* law and order," be continued despite other austerity measures. With the exception of several farm households located next to the village head's spacious homestead, the majority of Ogawa villagers boycotted the custom of *kadomatsu* and demolished the decorations of their more timorous neighbors. The disgruntled farmers instead celebrated by pounding glutinous rice (*mochi*), a New Year's ritual that had been proscribed by the village head (Itō 1966, 101; 1981, 348–49). Festive customs and ceremonial rituals, in short, not only were enforced as symbols of central and local authority but also were exploited by the exploited as symbolic expressions of dissent.

Even today Ogawa-*chō* natives—undoubtedly following the "tradition" created in 1771—do not erect *kadomatsu* to celebrate the New Year and, instead, pound *mochi* on New Year's Day. Natives also stage *mochi*-pounding demonstrations at the citizens' festival. The editors of the *Kodaira chōshi*, ever keen to downplay rebellious actions in

Kodaira's ancestral village, attributed the discontinuation of *kadomatsu* to dwindling pine groves and tree conservation measures (1959, 1206). The 1978 New Year's edition of the city newspaper featured an article on *kadomatsu* without any mention of the boycott of the practice by Ogawa villagers and their descendants. The article's implicit message was that historical customs, regardless of their social context, are good in themselves. Residents, therefore, were encouraged to erect a *kadomatsu* as an outward expression of their local-person and local-place consciousness. Six years later, in 1984, the city newspaper carried an advertisement for a *kadomatsu* sticker—a small paper rectangle imprinted at the top with a red orb (symbolizing the Japanese nation) and at the bottom with a *kadomatsu* arrangement. Printed in between was the word *geishun*, or "welcoming the New Year." The stickers, billed as "representing frugality, forest conservation, and roadway beautification," were sold for twelve yen by the Social Education Department on behalf of the Tokyo Metropolitan New Life Movement Association, an organization dedicated to improving the quality of urban life (*KSH*, 5 December 1984).

The promotion of *kadomatsu* among newcomers as a "traditional" custom representative of the aspirations and objectives of the Kodaira citizens' charter is ironic from a historical perspective. The New Year's decoration was not a salient feature of ceremonial life in Ogawa-*mura*, the *shinden* village whose history Kodaira acquired by nomenclatural fiat. *Kodairakko* have been encouraged to adopt, as an expression of their consciousness of place, a custom rejected two centuries earlier by ancestors of the *tochikko*. The rhetoric of *furusato-zukuri*, in short, has overshadowed the historical symbolism of *kadomatsu*.

The "present-past" (*imamukashi*) photography show, held annually since 1979, also exemplifies the city's coeval, dialectical "traditions." Photographs of local sites (and sights) dating to the early 1960s or earlier are paired with their modern-day counterparts. According to the catalogue, the purpose of the exhibition is to "foster an awareness of the unknown"—the "unknown" being both the unacknowledged processes of sociohistorical change and the future, namely, Furusato Kodaira. And while materialistic progress is extolled—sometimes anachronistically, as in "Kurobei probably never thought this area would develop into such a prosperous Kodaira!" (*Kodaira yomiuri nyūzu*, 4 October 1981)—the very existence of a "Kurobei" to claim as Kodaira's pioneering ancestor is equally eulogized.

Among the twenty-six cities, five towns, and one village making up the Santama district of Tokyo metropolitan prefecture, Kodaira City Hall alone has drawn parallels and posed metaphorical links between the *shinden* village–making of the past and "new *furusato*"–making of today. The very construction of the Kodaira citizens' festival epitomizes the past-present-future relationship at the crux of the city's *furusato-zukuri* project. In general, the form and content of citizens' festivals are informed by the historical conditions and present exigencies peculiar to a given city. A citizens' festival thus may be thought of as a "key signature" indicating the style and modality of a city's *furusato-zukuri* program: the "intertwinement of 150,000 hearts" in Kodaira, a metaphysical return to a "new *furusato*" in Tokyo (for other examples, see Sakada 1984c).

Furusato-zukuri itself is used by the state (but not the state alone) and in the Japanese media as a synonym for "cultural administration" (*bunka gyōsei*), or the administration (also reinvention) of culture and "tradition" toward the signification of a new "value consciousness" (*kachi ishiki*) (see Tamura and Mori 1985). Japanese city planners, bureaucrats, advertisers, and the general public seem to recognize implicitly that "traditional" aspects of culture and social life do not constitute an objectively definable inheritance—although they may appraise them as such—but are symbolic constructs continuously reinvented and reproduced in the present. The new value consciousness amounts to both an appreciation of the "modishness" of "the Japanese tradition," as Kurita has suggested (1983, 131), and a recognition that in the representation of the past is the imagination of the future. According to the logic of *furusato-zukuri*, the past itself is a mnemotechnic aid transformed into topoi of discourses on the past-present-future relationship.

Furusato may be a dominant trope, but it is a representation of "the Japanese" past and future that is collective without being unitary in its meaning. Thus, LDP politicians, localists, environmentalists, advertisement agencies, Kodaira administrators and residents, and the post office, among others, have all appropriated the rhetoric of *furusato-zukuri* toward realizing their respective interests, whether altruistically social, unabashedly political, or overtly commercial. However, *furusato* also has been reified to some extent by all of the above agents as *the* image of the past, constituting a more sociable, spiritually richer, and more wholesome way of life. The historicist aspects of *furusato-zukuri*, in short, are evident in the general reluctance of some of these interest groups to acknowledge the various sociohistorical conditions and agents responsible for making the "future" a vexing problem. At its best, *furusato-zukuri* can encourage among Japanese an appreciation for natural resources and regional differences, but at its worst, it can foster an ahistorical culturism that glosses over problematic asocial practices, such as sexist and racist discrimination, industrial pollution, rural depopulation, urban sprawl, and bureaucratic centralization.

The chief priest of Hanazono Shrine in Tokyo has declared that, without shrines as the focus of civic life, "mass panic will ensue, and cities fall into ruin." He chides city planners today for failing to provide space in their blueprints for such institutions (Katayama 1981, 26–27). The priest promotes, however dramatically, the effectiveness of shrine festivals in both fostering and affirming a sense of community (*komyunitei*) among relative strangers. Although they are in basic agreement with the priest, municipal authorities, ever mindful of the separation of Shinto rites and government, have instead inaugurated shrinelike festivals toward this end. *Matsuri* are both a symbol of "new *furusato*" in general and a chronicle—a narrative emplotment—of the past and present social texture of a particular city. The principle at work here is the dialectical relationship of past significance and present discourse, for the making of Furusato Kodaira, and Furusato Japan, is as much a retroactive as a proactive process.

Appendix

Shinden Typologies

One of the most pervasive of the *shinden* myths is the image of a parent-village head leading a group of villagers in a campaign to reclaim and domesticate the hostile Musashino wilderness (cf. Kata-yama 1959, 167). Miyazaki, the Shinmei-*gū* priest, effectively upholds this myth with his "clan settlement" proposition. Certain types of *shinden*, moreover, lend themselves to a pioneer mythology—particularly, *nōmin ukeoi*, or farmer-contracted, *shinden*; *hyakushō yoriai*, or farmer-initiated, *shinden*; and *mura uke*, or village-initiated, *shinden*. Village-initiated *shinden* are discussed in chapter 3 (in the section headed "Making Ogawa-*shinden*"). Other types of *shinden* are reviewed below.

Farmer-Contracted/Initiated *Shinden*

Yajima (1955, 101) classifies Ogawa-*mura* as a *shinden* contracted by a farmer, namely, Ogawa Kurobei. Other *shinden* scholars, however, prefer to type Ogawa-*mura* as a *dogō kaihatsu shinden*, or *shinden* established by a wealthy, landed household (*dogō*) (Kimura 1964, 108–30). Generally speaking, these households represent former samurai whose leaders were vanquished by the Tokugawa, for whom the headship of a *shinden* village offered security and a semblance of prestige.

It is not entirely clear whether the Ogawas were actually of the samurai class, despite the household's apparently illustrious genealogy.

Therefore, it perhaps is more accurate to regard Ogawa-*mura* as a farmer-contracted/initiated *shinden*. Whatever the case, the basic strategy required an individual with the wherewithal to undertake a reclamation program. The background and character of such an individual, in turn, provide ready material for the making of a pioneer myth, Ogawa Kurobei being an exemplary case in point.

Merchant-Initiated (*chōnin ukeoi*) *Shinden*

In 1722, when the *bakufu* advertised for *shinden* investors, many influential merchants stepped forward to finance land reclamation projects. They paid the *bakufu* "key money" for the right to reclaim *shinden*, capitalized reclamation projects, and recruited settlers from whom they collected rent, thereby recouping their initial investment. Such *shinden* villages did not have a parent village; rather, the merchants served as *shinden* landlords. Merchants also underwrote reclamation projects undertaken by farmers, villages, and domains (*han*).

Merchant-initiated *shinden* have been the subject of a protracted debate among Japanese social and economic historians. The crux of the controversy is whether or not *shinden* financed and overseen by merchants signaled the emergence of a "capitalistic agricultural administration." Matsuyoshi ([1933] 1955) promotes the view that merchant-initiated *shinden* spurred the emergence of large-scale landlords and tenant farmers, in addition to occasioning the "capitalism-ization" of agricultural land management. Nakai (1951) and Ōishi ([1961] 1976), on the other hand, assert that *shinden* reclamation hindered capitalist development insofar as it bolstered the *bakuhan* (*bakufu* + *han*) system. These politicoeconomic works in turn contrast sharply with such historical geographic studies as those by Yajima (1955) and Nō (1935), the latter being especially concerned with distinguishing Japanese linearly developed villages (such as Ogawa-*mura*) from the German *Strassendorf*.

Government-Initiated *Shinden*

The types of *shinden* discussed thus far generally are referred to as *min'ei shinden*, or *shinden* reclaimed and administered by civilians. *Kan'ei shin-*

den, on the other hand, were *shinden* reclaimed and administered by the government (central and local) directly. They included *shinden* established by the local magistrature (*daikan mitate shinden*); *shinden* supervised by the treasury (*kanjōjō shudō shinden*); and *shinden* administered by a domain (*han'ei shinden*). There was considerable overlap between civilian- and government-administered *shinden*, since the *bakufu* and local magistrates were closely involved in the reclamation of the former.

Notes

Introduction

1. As Bourdieu notes, practical knowledge "has nothing to do with phenomenological reconstitution of live experience" but, rather, integrates the reality of practical experience and "the practical mode of knowledge which this learned knowledge had to be constructed against" (1986, 4).

2. Similarly, in his article on "places" as the "objects of anthropological study as well as the critical links between description and analysis in anthropological theory," Appadurai remarks that "place is not just a trivial contingency associated with data gathering, but a vital dimension of the subject matter of the disciplines" (1986, 357, 360).

3. See especially Fabian (1983) for an extensive treatment of this issue.

4. Following Scott, I use "discourse" to mean "not a language or a text but a historically, socially, and institutionally specific structure of statements, terms, categories, and beliefs. . . . Discourse is thus contained or expressed in organizations and institutions as well as in words" (1988, 35).

5. I became aware of the ubiquitous use of *furusato* during a three-year stay in Japan (1978–1981), which was funded in part by a grant from the Monbushō. Chapter 1 is a reworked version of my article "*Furusato* Japan: The culture and politics of nostalgia," *Politics, Culture, and Society* 1 (4) (1988): 494–518, which was a reworked version of the first chapter of my dissertation.

6. I use the term *state* to mean not simply an "organ of coercion" or a "national government" or a "bureaucratic lineage" but, rather, a "repertoire of activities and institutions" that reproduce the status quo and shape, and are shaped by, sociohistorical factors (Corrigan and Sayer 1985, 2–3). The repertoire of state formation includes "laws, judicial decisions, registers, census returns, licenses, charters, tax forms," and so forth (ibid., 197) .

7. An abridged version of chapter 2 was published under the title "A dialectic of native and newcomer: The Kodaira citizens' festival in suburban Tokyo," *Anthropological Quarterly* 60 (3) (1987): 124–36.

Chapter One

1. "Mirai shakai wa furusato no aji" (*Nostalgia of Kobe* 1983, 12).
2. Other character compounds for *furusato* include 故里 and 古里.
3. Professor Robert J. Smith mentioned to me that, during his period of fieldwork in Shikoko in the 1950s, most of his Japanese acquaintances referred to their "native place" as *kokyō*. By the "miracle 1960s," the relentless pace of industrialization, urbanization, and urban migration had significantly reduced the number of viable "old villages." Thus, when localism emerged as a movement in the mid-1970s along with the revaluation of indigenous customs and ceremonies, it was not the physical "village" that was resuscitated but, rather, the affective potential of "old villages."

Kyōdo is an often-encountered word signifying local or native place, and, in fact, its dictionary definition is *furusato* (*Kōjien* 1978, 575). It appears that *kyōdo* is used primarily when location is the primary aspect emphasized. Thus, *kyōdoshi* is the word for local history, while local patriotism is referred to as *kyōdoai*. Unlike *kokyō* (i.e., *furusato*), *kyōdo* has no alternative syllabic reading.

4. During my periods of fieldwork in 1983–1985 and part of the summers of 1986 and 1987, there were many articles in the *Asahi shinbun* and other newspapers, weeklies, magazines, newsletters, posters, and the like, extolling the virtues of *furusato*. Similarly, the film *Furusato*, released in 1983, juxtaposed the death of an elderly man and the loss of his village, which was flooded in a dam construction project.

5. Regarding the symbolic association of "mother" and rice, and agriculture in general, see Robertson (1984b). In the booklet accompanying the 1983 movie *Furusato*, the director links "mother" to Furusato Japan: "*Furusato* is the ancestral land (*sokoku*). My ancestral land is Japan, it is Gifu prefecture, it is Saigō-*mura*, it is the village section (*aza*) of Hachioji, it is [my] household, it is mother."

6. In a 1987 municipal poll conducted of 3,500 Kyoto residents over twenty years of age (2,000 women and 1,500 men, an average 55 percent of whom responded), about 10 percent of the women and 44.7 percent of the men felt that only men should work for wages and that women should look after household matters ("otoko wa shigoto, onna wa katei") (*Asahi shinbun*, Osaka ed., 25 August 1987). Although, as Atsumi (1988) notes, many women employed full-time outside their households are made to feel that they are not performing their roles as mothers properly, Japanese companies nevertheless blatantly exploit married women as part-time workers. See also the twelve-part series titled "Tsuma tachi wa uttaeru" (The wives protest), *Asahi shinbun* (23 May–5 June 1984).

7. Gender (and gender role) pertains to sociohistorical conventions of deportment attributed to either females or males and is not related to, although often premised upon, the various capabilities of female and male sex (i.e., genitalia and reproductive organs). Female sex and "female" gender may be popularly perceived as naturally joined, but this is a situational, and not a permanently fixed, condition. For further insights and elaborations on sex, gender, and sexuality, see Kessler and McKenna (1985); De Lauretis (1987); and Vance (1985).

8. Regarding local autonomy, see Gluck (1985, chap. 6) and Samuels (1983) for a cogent summary and a case history, respectively.

9. The director is Kurozawa Takeo, mayor of Ueno-*mura*, Gunma prefecture; and among the consultants are elderly and established businessmen, politicians, former cabinet officials, and actors.

10. The center is located within the National Town and Village Institute (Zenkoku chōson kaikan) in Chiyoda-*ku*, Tokyo.

11. In September 1989, Kaifu announced that Suzuki Eiji, director of Nikkeiren (Japan Federation of Employers), would head the association, whose twenty-two members include university professors, local and national politicians, and business executives. Only two of the members are female (*Asahi shinbun*, International ed., 14 and 15 September 1989). I thank Professor Masao Miyoshi for providing me with these articles.

12. The term *localists* refers to subscribers to the Yanagita Kunio (1875–1962) school of Japanese folklore studies. Localism is premised on the assumption that the restoration of local political autonomy, together with the preservation and enhancement of a "unique local culture," will transcend the myriad social problems associated with postwar "Western-type" modernization. Moreover, the urge toward autonomy and local patriotism is regarded as stemming from "local residents' sense of belonging to their own local community due to a shared ethnic consciousness and historical experience" (Miwa 1976, 44).

13. See, for example, the magazine *Furusato-mura jōhō* (Tokyo: Sōei Shuppan).

14. Similarities can be drawn with MacCannell's theory of tourism as a pursuit of authentic social experience in "post-industrial or modern society," a society which has "turned in on itself" (1976, 182).

15. Maruyama Masao's discourse on reality and the process of creation (in the context of the thought and behavior patterns of Japan's wartime leaders) offers valuable insights into the distinction between *tsukuri* and *naru*. Maruyama shows that for Japan's wartime leaders reality was "not something in the process of creation or about to be created; rather it [was] that which has already been created or, to be more specific, that which has arisen from somewhere in the past. Therefore to act realistically [meant] to be tied to the past. Similarly, reality [was] not something to be grasped by the individual in order to build a new future; it [was] a blind inevitability flowing from a determined past" (1969, 196).

16. "Administration of culture" and "culturization of administration" bring to mind Pyle's notion of "the technology of nationalism" of the 1920s and 1930s; that is, the techniques devised by bureaucrats "to mobilize the material

and spiritual resources of the population in order to cope with social problems and to provide support for Japanese imperialism" (Pyle 1973, 53). While Furusato Japan probably is not an imperialist design, the characterization of *furusato-zukuri* as a type of "technology of nationalism" emphasizes not the "what" but the "how"—how public consciousness and popular memory are made.

17. For perspective on Nakasone's political and ideological project against the background of the international dilemmas facing Japanese society, see Pyle (1987) and Muramatsu (1987).

18. The same can be said about the several television quiz shows created in the mid-1980s, in which celebrity contestants (based in Tokyo) try to guess the logic behind certain historical local and regional practices, usually of an agricultural nature.

19. The Meiji government inaugurated the shrine-merger program in 1906. The plan was to have a single, central shrine as the exclusive focus of both communal solidarity and national consciousness (see Fridell 1973) .

20. *Furusato-zukuri* contains the seeds of Japanese chauvinism; whether they take root and grow is cause for concern. Nevertheless, at the risk of oversimplification, a major difference between the jingoism of the 1930s and 1940s and the *furusato* rhetoric of today is that, whereas the former fueled an imperial war machine, the latter sustains, and often is sustained by, at different times and in different contexts, pompous culturism and reflexive retrospection.

Chapter Two

1. "Child" shrines are now a virtually standard feature of even such historically "traditional" festivals as Kyoto's Gion *matsuri* in July (*Asahi shinbun*, Osaka ed., 12 and 16 July 1987).

2. For other ethnographic accounts of the centrality of festivals in community life, see Doi (1981), Kenji (1981), Nakagawa (1981), Takada (1981), and Tanigawa (1978).

3. This information is from interviews in July 1986 with several Asakusa (Tokyo's "low town") natives, and also from the article "Iki de inasena matsuri no kikonashi" (1985).

4. Japanese cities compete with each other for mass media coverage of their respective festivals. During the fall, when most of these events take place, many television news programs feature highlights of regional festivals, particularly those with novel attractions. Higashiyamato City, northwest of Kodaira, made a media splash with a "treasure boat" (*takarabune*) parade sponsored by local farmers. In each boat was mounted a giant sculpture created entirely of vegetables arranged ingeniously to resemble Uncle Sam, an Australian frilled lizard, and Konishiki, the mammoth sumo wrestler from Hawaii (*Asahi shinbun*, 3 November 1984).

5. The DSP assemblyperson subscribed to a romantic notion of festivals as

spontaneous celebrations of communality, which he felt was incommensurable with commercial motives. There is ample evidence for the prevalence, since at least the seventeenth century, of a commercial motive for festivals, from fund raising to marketing.

6. The "Kodaira Citizens' Festival Song" contest was held in March 1982. Lyrics were solicited from both residents and individuals employed in Kodaira, who were advised to create uplifting, festive verses on the theme of *furusatozukuri*. A female resident won the cash prize and a certificate of merit. Her lyrics were set to marching music composed by a (female) musician commissioned by city hall. A dial-the-festival-song service was inaugurated shortly afterward (*KSH*, 5 March, 20 June, 20 August 1982).

7. Except where noted otherwise, data are from the committee's blueprint for, and final report of, the 1983 festival.

8. *Ondo* refers to a type of folksong especially suited for en masse folkdancing featuring an uncomplicated, repetitive, syncopated rhythm.

9. See, in this connection, the articles in MacCormack and Strathern (1982), especially MacCormack (1982).

10. Although he does not problematize "community," some of Smith's observations about competing ethnic myths are relevant here: "[E]thnic myths . . . provide frameworks of developmental meaning which underpin the sense of community among all strata, and answer to the problems of insecurity shared by members. In the longer term, the rival definitions . . . coalesce to form a community which, while still riven by social conflicts, has become more unified at the level of history and culture" (1984, 122).

11. The specialty products included salmon and rice from Niigata; wine and ornamental garden boulders from Yamanashi; salted bracken, rice crackers, fermented soybeans (*nattō*), and buckwheat noodles (*soba*) from Fukushima; and boiled potatoes from Yamagata. Kodaira's current specialty products are *udo*, a type of asparagus, and *nashi*, or pear-apples. The production of local specialty products under the rubric "one village, one specialty" dates to the eighteenth century, as a response to the growing market economy, and recently has been revived as an expression of local autonomy.

12. The Kōsei Group is affiliated with Risshō kōseikai, a Nichiren Buddhist organization created in 1938 as an independent branch of Reiyūkai, which was founded in 1925.

13. The year 1981 was an especially noisy one in Kodaira. Neighborhoods were terrorized by a 300-member gang headquartered in Kodaira that included high school boys from the surrounding cities. The gang had been founded a year earlier as the dreadful Shikōkai, or Death Emperors, which later was changed to the homonym Willful Emperors. The reason for switching the character *kō*, explained one member, was to keep people from assuming that the gang wished death upon the frail Hirohito, who died in January 1989. Since the arrest of ten Willful Emperors that summer for possession of firearms, the gang has maintained a low profile (*Tōkyō shinbun*, 20 September 1981).

14. The search for a logotypic emblem that epitomized Kodaira's "unique character and future ideals" got under way in the fall of 1959. Unlike the festival song competition, the emblem-design competition was nationwide. Of the

one thousand entries, 30 percent were submitted by Kodaira residents. The first-place award of 10,000 yen was pocketed by a Sendai man; the runner-up was a Kodaira resident. The winning design was praised as being simple and readable, yet conveying stability and strength (*KCH*, 1 August 1959, 1 December 1959).

15. All but the palanquin shrine owned by the coterie Keyaki-*mutsumi* were in the charge of local shrine patrons. The Keyaki-*mutsumi* is a Shinto association of men in their thirties—natives of the region—whose hobby is shrine bearing.

16. This and other information attributed to the festival's public relations director was obtained from interviews with Ichikawa K. over the period 1984–1986.

Chapter Three

1. This chapter constitutes the most extensive treatment in English, to my knowledge, of the process of *shinden kaihatsu*, or the reclamation of arable land in conjunction with village-making. For example, in his important book on the agrarian origins of modern Japan, T. C. Smith (1980) does not mention *shinden* reclamation as a motive and context for the formation of branch households, and the term *shinden* itself is mentioned only in passing in a footnote on land-tax categories.

2. The preamble to the senior citizens' charter—promulgated in 1976, when the "graying" of Japan was first recognized as a pressing social problem—also commemorates the *shinden* legacy: "We, the citizens of Kodaira, in keeping with the spirit of humanitarianism and mutual aid cultivated continuously since the reclamation period, have promulgated this charter to ensure that all senior citizens are provided with the opportunity to lead productive lives."

3. Unlike Kodaira, Higashiyamato is neither a place-name redolent of an intrepid pioneering spirit nor a forward projection of that city's sociohistorical origins. Yamato—the prefix *higashi*, or east, was added after cityhood in 1970—was coined in 1919 to name an amalgamation of six villages. This word, which means "great peace," was selected in an attempt to symbolically unite these villages, which earlier had waged bitter antimerger campaigns (Higashi-yamato-*shi* keikaku zaiseibu kōhō kōchōka 1982). Although such a purpose is not mentioned explicitly in the literature, Yamato, the mythopoeic name for ancient Japan, may also have been selected to give a transcendent and grandiose aura to the new administrative village.

4. My conclusion is based on an examination of the citizens' charters of these cities, towns, and villages, included in the *benrichō*, or residents' handbooks. The preamble to the Tachikawa charter, promulgated in 1982, mentions the word *kaitaku* (reclamation) in reference to the city's having been "reclaimed from the Musashino plateau as a social-life setting." Unlike Kodaira's charter, however, this charter makes no mention of pioneers or a pioneer spirit.

5. Conventionally translated as "household," *ie* means both a dwelling and a continuing entity that includes a household's actual residential members (whether or not they are members of the immediate family) as well as its dead members (i.e., the ancestors, active as guardian spirits). The concept of *Ie* also incorporates the unborn future generations, for the continuity of the household over time and through space is of primary importance. *Ie* encompasses both a main household and those branch households established through fission as either economically dependent or nondependent branches.

6. *Shinden* is a generic term; several of the dialect versions are *hiraki* (Kanazawa), *kaisaku* (Hagi), and *komori* and *karame* (Saga) (Kimura 1964, 1). The large number of place-names containing the compound *shinden*, or its dialect variants, attests to the extensive scale of land reclamation and village-making undertaken during the Edo period in particular. In the Japanese-language literature, *shinden* is used to refer to a specifically demarcated area of land of varying size earmarked for reclamation and, usually, village-making.

7. There is some discrepancy as to the actual number of Musashino *shinden* villages founded. I have cited the figure given in the 1739 document *Nanboku Musashino debyakushō kusawakesho jōchō* (Record of land reclamation in north and south Musashino, vol. 1) (*KC* 1959, 101). The *Shinpen Musashino fūdoki* (New geography of Musashino) (1818–1829), on the other hand, records eighty-two *shinden* villages; perhaps the four additional villages were established between 1739 and 1829 (Ashida 1977).

8. Of the *shinden* reclaimed in the Musashino area after 1716, approximately 68 percent were dry fields and 32 percent paddy. Whereas earlier land reclamation schemes had concentrated largely on paddy expansion in the Kansai region, the majority of *shinden* projects carried out after 1716 involved the reclamation of dry fields in the Kanto region. Consequently, in or around the 1720s, an estimated 63 percent of the total registered arable land in the entire Kanto region was dry field, as opposed to only 19 percent in the Kansai region. However, of the total arable land registered in the Kanto and Kansai regions collectively, in or around the 1720s, about 44 percent (1,320,000 hectares) was dry field and about 56 percent (1,650,000 hectares) paddy (Kimura and Itō 1972, 14).

9. Portuguese Catholics arrived in Japan in the 1540s. Although their presence initially was accepted by the military authorities, it was under the Tokugawa *bakufu* that Christianity was outlawed in 1638 and non-Japanese Christians expelled from Japan. Japanese Christians were forced to apostatize under the threat of crucifixion. The criterion in the *shinden* petition refers to the *bakufu*'s policies against Christians and foreigners.

10. Shingaku was founded in 1729 by the farmer turned merchant Ishida Baigan (1685–1744), who promoted a syncretistic (Buddhist, Confucian, Shinto, and Taoist) merchant ethic as a "national" ethos. Of the 104 colleges, 63 were founded in farm villages and staffed by local disciples (Bellah 1957; Ishikawa 1931, 210–11; Robertson 1979, 1984b, 1991).

11. There were forty-nine individuals directly involved with the project, including Mayor Ogawa, university professors, amateur local historians, Kodaira elementary school principals, and local administrators and civic lead-

ers. Brown's (1979) translation of a village chronicle provides an important and useful look at this literary genre for readers of English.

12. While the depth of both the homestead and low-grade field was more or less fixed at 45 and 90.5 meters, respectively, that of the low-low-grade fields varied from 127 to 362 meters.

13. See Nakane for a concise description of paddy irrigation in the Edo period (1967, 73–81).

14. Until the 1720s, when the position of elder (*toshiyori*) was created, Ogawa-*mura* was administered by the village head and division leader. The post of farmer representative (*hyakushōdai*) was created sometime during the 1820s (*KC* 1959, 76).

15. Although a document dating to the 1750s refers to a *mukō sangen* unit in conjunction with a *ryōdonari mukō* unit, these units probably were temporary, composite entities formed at a time when the *goningumi* and *ryōdonari mukō* were being reorganized and consolidated (*KC* 1959, 855–56). Reference to a *ryōdonari goningumi* appears in a document dating to the 1750s, further suggesting that the five-household division was superimposed on the more fundamental neighborhood division.

16. In the *Kodaira chōshi*, the *kumiai* is referred to inaccurately as *goningumi*.

17. In this connection, one of the ideas offered by the native sector in response to city hall's call for *furusato-zukuri* strategies (*YC* 1983, 67–70) was that the "atmosphere of olden Musashino" (*Musashino no omokage*) should be preserved.

18. There is a significant discrepancy between the number of farm householders accounted for in local (Kodaira City) statistics and the number given in the Tokyo metropolitan government's 1980 census report. The former lists a total of 512 farm households for 1980 and the latter 577, a difference of 65 households. The discrepancy is related to the fact that the Tokyo census includes farm householders working less than five ares of land, while Kodaira surveys tend to draw the line at five ares or more of land. However, where Kodaira surveys include farm householders who earn over 70,000 yen annually from the sale of agricultural produce, the Tokyo census covers those who earn 100,000 yen or more.

More pertinent, as the section chief of the Economics Department (Kodaira City Hall) explained to me, is the fact that most Kodaira surveys are based on the number of farm householders owning ten ares or more listed in the agricultural committee election registry—ten ares being the minimum amount of farmland necessary to qualify a farm householder for candidacy and/or voting privileges in committee elections. The section chief also mentioned that in city surveys many farm households underreport the extent of their actual holdings in order to avoid certain taxes, particularly the inheritance tax. The Tokyo census, however, is much more exacting and therefore statistically more reliable, and has been cited when feasible.

Full-time farm households are those in which the head of the household spends less than twenty days a year on nonagricultural work. Part-time farm households are further divided into those that are mostly occupied with agricultural productions and those that mainly pursue nonagricultural activities. In 1959 full-time farm households were still in the majority (55 percent); from 1960 onward, part-time farm households predominated (54 percent in 1960, increasing to 93 percent by 1980) (*KCH*, 20 July 1951; *KK* 1983, 224; *Sekai nōringyō sensasu: Kodaira* 1980, 1).

Chapter Four

1. The first issue of this newsletter was printed in October 1983. In the first-anniversary edition, Miyazaki invited shrine patrons and readers to submit questions for him to answer in a new question-and-answer column intended to personalize shrine affairs.

2. The *bakufu* was particularly wary of such impromptu festivities as *mushi-okuri*, a torchlight procession staged to ward off noxious insects (to which repressive officials were sometimes equated), and *amagoi*, or rainmaking ceremonies, often of a boisterous nature (Itō 1981, 350).

3. The usual extrapolations on the symbolic meaning of Inari/*inari* involve stages in the cultivation and preparation of paddy, which, generally speaking, was not cultivated in the Musashino *shinden* (see, for example, Uegaki [1803] 1981, 97).

4. Since the postwar period, the date of *hatsuuma* has been fixed at 11 February, although at Shinmei-*gū* it continues to be celebrated on 6 February.

5. *Shōichi-i*, or "top rank," refers to a prestigious title or grade for yard shrines. In the Edo period, titles were purchased from the magistrate in charge of temple and shrine affairs. There were also *mui*, or ungraded shrines, as well (Miyamoto 1981, 282). *Daimyōjin* simply means "august *kami*."

6. There are several local folktales lauding the wart-removing, scar-effacing, and overall complexion-clearing prowess of this Inari.

7. Although a native, Ogawa is not related to Kurobei; rather, as he explained to me, his ancestors adopted the name from the name of the village in the early Meiji period. (During the preceding Edo period, farmers, with the exception of the wealthy landowners among them, were not allowed to have last names.) However, it is possible that his ancestors were servants of the Ogawa household, from which they then "borrowed" the name. Still, as a native, Ogawa S. harbored an attitude of superiority toward newcomers. Nativeness, in other words, picks up where "blood" and fictive kinship leave off. Ogawa Z., chair of the Gakuen Nishi-*chōkai* and a descendant of Kurobei, adamantly stated that his namesake, Ogawa S., was "not related by 'blood' [*ketsu*]." The purity of their lineage is a matter of continuing importance for the Ogawas, who are alone in maintaining close ties with their Kishi-*mura* line (*KC* 1959, 899).

8. Also *mantō*. The most basic construction is a bamboo umbrella frame pushed through a rectangular paper box in which a candle or light bulb is placed. The sides of the box are inscribed with *X ujiko*, *kazoku anzen* (family security), or *X bangumi*. Fancier versions sport a multifaceted box papered in

colorful hues or sometimes decorated with elaborate *ukiyoe*-style drawings in addition to cartoon characters. These more elaborate lantern-floats may have two or three tiers.

Mandō are gendered objects. The bamboo spokes of the "male" umbrella are alternately bound in gold and silver foil, while those of the "female" are affixed with bright hibiscuslike paper flowers. At the apex of the "male" umbrella is a pentagonal plaque, a giant replica of a Japanese chess (*shōgi*) piece—the king. The top of the "female" umbrella is crowned with a plume of paper flowers (Musashino bijutsu daigaku seikatsu bunka kenkyūkai 1983, 416). The *mandō* assembled by the Ogawa Eight, however, were a most eclectic, gender-bending lot!

9. There are some exceptions to this rule. Oda T.'s family lived in central Tokyo prior to the 1940s, when they were evacuated to Oda's hometown in Niigata prefecture. After the war, he "somehow acquired," as he put it, a substantial amount of land in Ogawa Higashi-*chō*, part of which was eventually sold to the Bridgestone Company. The land in question had been expropriated from local farmers by the military and was later sold on favorable terms to persons such as Oda who agreed to farm it temporarily in order to alleviate the postwar food shortage (*KC* 1959, 585; *KK* 1983, 211).

Oda's claim to nativeness, and the basis for his honorary native status, lies in his apprenticeship to the late Ogawa A., the eleventh-generation head of the Ogawa main household. Ogawa, a Waseda University professor and dedicated local historian, founded the Kodaira Local History Study Society in 1960. Oda declared that Ogawa had ordered him to devote himself to researching Kodaira's history and that he had succeeded Ogawa as the city's preeminent local historian.

If Oda is proud of his honorary native status, his daughter still regards herself, after thirty years in Kodaira, as a "Tokyo person." The fact that she was born in Kundanshita, in central Tokyo, is a matter of undisguised pride for her.

10. Dore notes that *sūkeikai* were formed in place of the *ujiko* system of shrine administration, which SCAP (Supreme Commander of Allied Powers) ordered abolished (1958, 297). In Kodaira, however, the *ujiko* was not dismantled; and the *sūkeikai*, instead of replacing the parish, comprises a broader-based group of worshipers.

11. These conditions for membership are demonstrated by Meiji-*jingū*'s *sūkeikai*. According to the application form/PR flier distributed at the shrine, prospective *sūkeikai* members need only promise to worship the *kami* and ancestors, revere the emperor (Meiji in particular), and love the nation. Unlike its Kodaira counterpart, the Meiji-*jingū* worshipers' association does not limit membership to persons from a given territory. The association is divided into three classes according to the amount of annual dues paid, which in 1984 ranged from 2,000 yen to 50,000 yen. (Members of the Shinmei-*gū* worshipers' association pay 1,500 yen annually.) The tens of thousands of individuals in the Meiji-*jingū sūkeikai* enjoy such fringe benefits as a tour of the National Diet, *sumō* and baseball passes, and discounts on wedding ceremonies performed at the shrine.

12. Shintoists stress that, although the ancestors' festival conventionally is regarded as a Buddhist event, ancestor worship predates the introduction of Buddhism to Japan. Therefore, *obon*-related events are staged at shrines as well as at temples. Shinmei-*gū* holds a piecemeal *obon* throughout July.

13. To be sure, Hikawa-*jinja* is small and lacking a resident priest—it is hardly the same caliber of shrine as Shinmei-*gū*. However, like the Ogawa Eight *jichikai*, the Megurita-*chōkai* is an association into which the *ujiko* is incorporated, as is made explicit in its handbook. Herein also lies the basis for comparison.

14. The Rinzai sect, named after its Chinese founder, was introduced to Japan in 1191 by the priest Eisai. Enkaku-*ji*, founded in 1282, represents one of the ten branches of the sect, which teaches that enlightenment is a sudden revelation unrelated to scholarly study. Local historians proudly note that Shōsen-*ji* is "highly ranked," since its main temple, Gekkei-*ji*, is one of the three "special" temples within the 208 affiliated with Enkaku-*ji* (Harada 1964, 42). Temple ranks, however, were far from systematized and varied over time and between sects.

15. The sect was introduced to Japan from China in 1228 by the priest Dōgen. In contrast to Rinzai Zen, Sōtō teaches that enlightenment is contingent upon assiduous moral training and is occasioned by an ethical lifestyle.

16. In addition to tax-exempt land (*jochi*), "red-seal land" (*shuinchi*) was granted by the *bakufu*, and "black-seal land" (*kokuinchi*) was donated by *daimyō* and high-ranking retainers. Andō provides evidence that until 1622 the *bakufu* also granted black-seal land as a means of encouraging arable-land reclamation and that this designation often preceded red-seal status. Although black-seal land and tax-exempt land were similar in content, the latter lacked the official documentation and seal accompanying the former (Andō 1977, 28, 32, 36–38, 43, 68).

17. Sometimes, however, the reasons for choosing one temple or sect over another were fortuitous, as in the case of Kaigan-*ji*, a Rinzai temple in Suzuki-*shinden*. According to a Suzuki household document, a statue of Kannon, a Bodhisattva of mercy, purchased by the village head at an antique sale, turned out to be the former main image of a temple in the Chichibu region (west of Tokyo). Construing the find as an omen, the head elected to commission a temple from that area and enshrine the statue as its main image (*KC* 1959, 164).

18. Ōbaku Zen was introduced to Japan by the Chinese priest Ingen, who build the sect's temple on land granted by the *bakufu*. The first thirteen priests were Chinese, and the Chinese character of the sect probably was a major reason for the favor shown it by the Confucian-oriented *bakufu*.

19. Tendai, introduced to Japan from China in the ninth century by Saichō (Dengyō Daishi), worships Shaka Nyorai. Less mystical than its contemporary, Shingon, Tendai recognizes the quintessential truth of the apocalyptic Lotus Sutra. The Chinese Shingon sect was introduced to Japan in the ninth century by Kūkai (Kōbō Daishi). Its main tenets are that the world is a manifestation of Dainichi Nyorai, the sun Buddha, and that the key to illumination lies in orally

communicated doctrines, which further assist in decoding the sect's twofold mandala. Shingi Shingon, or "reformed" Shingon, refers to a division of the sect created in 1130 by Kakuhan. Kakuhan adapted the *nenbutsu*, a prayer formula hugely popular at the time, in promulgating a doctrine that sought to awaken people to the fact that they already were in paradise.

20. Founded in the 1170s by Genkū, formerly a devotee of Tendai, the Jōdō sect advocates the repetition of prayer formulas (*nenbutsu*) as a special ritual for salvation. One of his six leading disciples, Shinran, established the Jōdō Shin sect in the 1220s. Shinran broke with the practice of celibacy, and his use of a vernacular script reflects his interest in promulgating Shin sect doctrines among the rank and file. The "reformed" sect, unlike its precursor, recognizes Amida Nyorai, the present Buddha, who alone bestows salvation upon the faithful.

21. Nichiren Buddhism is named after its zealous founder, who, in the thirteenth century, sought to make it a state sect.

22. According to Miyamoto Akeko, a feminist who is best known for her investigative research on "baby hotels," Japanese women average from six to ten induced abortions during their fertile years. Some women have as many as twenty. Japanese feminist groups have been working to raise women's consciousness about their bodies and sexuality, especially in the wake of the 1982–83 debate over the prospective restriction of legal abortion in Japan. This information is from Amemiya (1989) and a film and panel discussion I attended on abortion and its patriarchal context in Japan at the Toshima-kumin sentā (Tokyo, 10 April 1985). See also Coleman (1983).

23. The Obaku Zen sect is also referred to as "*nenbutsu* Zen," because invocations for this-worldly success were early incorporated into its liturgy.

24. The territoriality of the Kannon and *nenbutsu* consociations contrasts with Jōdō Shin sect consociations, which congregate at private homes in keeping with the sect's principle of "independent proselytizing" (Kodama 1976, 235–38). The millenarian sect did not emphasize the achievement of a village identity, for which reason perhaps virtually no Jōdō Shin temples were established in *shinden* villages, including the Kodaira Seven.

25. The chief priest of Gekkei-*ji*, Shōsen-*ji*'s main temple, died several years ago; until another is appointed by Enkaku-*ji* in Kamakura, Miura is responsible for the temple's administration. Herein, Miura pointed out, is revealed the tenacity of historical ties between a main temple and its branch (i.e., commissioned temple).

26. It is estimated that there will be a nationwide shortage of cemetery space within a decade. Already at city temples, cinerary urns are temporarily stored in banks of lockers until proper burial sites are located (*Asahi shinbun*, 2 May 1984). The shortage has been exploited by cemetery corporations now developing the mountainous region west of Tokyo as a mammoth "memorial park."

27. Miura disapproved of Miyazaki's strict criteria for parish and worshipers' association membership, chiding him for putting the shrine's needs above the people's, although, in actuality, Miura applies equally strict membership criteria.

Chapter Five

1. Construction of a citywide sewer system began in 1962, when Kodaira attained city status, and as of June 1984 was 54 percent complete. The corresponding national percentage for 1983 was 32 percent (Kodaira kyōdo kenkyūkai 1984, 136.) The Gakuen area was the first to receive modern sewerage; the eastern and western ends will be the last. In a 1983 survey, inadequate sewerage was the main reason given by residents of the eastern and western sectors for their desire to leave Kodaira (*YC* 1983, 45). Nearly 26 percent of the 1984 budget was earmarked for sewer construction and maintenance. In addition, a number of *jichikai* have assumed the responsibility of improving neighborhood sewage disposal and drainage facilities.

2. *Kai Kodaira* (Avenue Kodaira) was introduced in 1984. It is a public relations magazine that seeks to present the city's shopping districts in a novel and glamorous light. It also contains information on seasonal events and sports meets, interviews with celebrities and residents, and local gossip.

3. *Katakana* is the syllabary especially reserved for foreign and foreign-derived words or Japanese slang and/or for imbuing Japanese words with special emphasis.

4. *Rusuban* is the term for both caretaker and the practice of having someone look after a house in the owners' absence. In the past, the task of caretaking was most typically assumed by the owners' live-in parents; but today, with the predominance of the nuclear family, neighbors are asked to perform this service. Given the general reluctance of many Japanese to invite guests into their homes, the matter of asking a neighbor to look after the house bespeaks a fairly high degree of familiarity between the two parties.

5. The number of privately owned tractors and plows (averaging 15–20 horsepower) has increased fivefold since the late 1950s, although the number of jointly owned heavy equipment (20–30 horsepower) also has increased, albeit minimally (Kodaira-*chō* nōgyō iinkai 1958, [7]; Kodaira-*shi* sōmubu shomuka 1975, 13; *Sekai nōringyō sensasu: Kodaira* 1980, 48–52).

6. I have adapted and modified the useful typology developed by Bar-Yosef in her study of the adjustment process of immigrants in Israeli society (1968, 37–40).

7. An anecdote based on my personal experience illustrates the native bias of the Kodaira Local History Study Society. In the spring of 1984, the society placed an advertisement in the city newspaper soliciting new members. Interested persons were asked to contact the Social Education Department at city hall. I decided to register, since membership in the society offered an ideal opportunity to gain access to local-history materials and meet those individuals responsible for salvaging the *shinden* past. At the department, however, I was told that the society's core study group was limited to a select number of natives (and "honorary natives") and that the purpose of the advertisement was to recruit "docents" from among interested residents, including newcomers, to lead groups on local-history tours throughout the city—the native sector being

a "museum without walls."

8. The incident in question is known both as the *shakura sōdō* and as the *gomonsō*. The Meiji Restoration brought an end to the *bakuhan* system, which was replaced by prefectures. Ogawa-*mura* and Ogawa-, Megurita-, and Nonaka- (Zenzaemon-*gumi*) *shinden* were incorporated into Nirayama prefecture, and Nonaka- (Yoemon-*gumi*), Ōnumata-, and Suzuki-*shinden* were incorporated into Shinagawa prefecture.

The incident was triggered by the crop failure of 1870. Each of the new prefectures implemented its own famine relief measures. Those deployed by Shinagawa were modeled after the Edo-period granaries, except that the prefecture rather than the village supervised the system. Farmers were required to contribute the cash value (determined by the annual yield) of a portion of their (dry-field) rice crop to the prefectural government, which then used the cash to purchase and distribute rice to needy farmers.

Farmers from twelve *shinden* within the jurisdiction of Shinagawa protested that in an unproductive year these contributions were tantamount to a tax increase. The head of Nonaka-*shinden* was arrested and eventually died in prison, as did six other protestors from the four Kodaira *shinden*. Other village officials were relieved of their offices for the "crime" of supporting destitute farmers in their protest for a tax reprieve. Kanagawa prefecture, into which the Kodaira Seven were reincorporated in 1983, continued the granary (*shakura*) policy of its predecessor, Shinagawa prefecture, although the Mitsui-*gumi*—forerunner of today's Mitsui Bank—was entrusted with the management of granary operations. In 1943 Kodaira was incorporated into newly designated Tokyo metropolitan prefecture, an entity that signified the consolidation of the central government's authority.

The account in *Komyunitei Kodaira* was adapted in large part from a compendium of source materials related to the incident (e.g., Kodaira-*shi* kenkyūkai 1980). A brief account also appears in Yamamoto (1984, 174–88).

9. Criteria for distinguishing native from nonnative assemblypersons were based on the correspondence of last names, home addresses, occupations, and verbal or textual evidence. Since only the most prevalent native names are accounted for, the actual number of *tochikko* politicians is probably slightly higher than my estimated percentages.

Between 1889 and 1955, an average of 80.5 percent of the assemblypersons were farmers (90 percent from 1889 to 1945, 80 percent from 1947 to 1955, and 67 percent in 1955). Thirty-five percent (122) of the total number (348) of assemblypersons serving during the period 1889–1955 hailed from the Ogawa Eight. These latter figures were 19 percent (5 of 26) in 1962 and nearly 10 percent (3 of 31) in 1984 (*KC* 1959, 767–75; *KK* 1983, 224; Kodaira-*shi* gikai jimukyoku 1982, 35; 1984).

10. Differences between farm households and nonfarm households also are evident in their respective voting behavior. Statistics for 1958–59 show that in city assembly elections 91 percent of the farm household voters and 80 percent of the nonfarm household voters favored the person over the party. The editors of the *Kodaira chōshi* suggest that longtime residence and close interpersonal contacts in Kodaira account for the personal bias of native voters.

At the prefectural and national levels, however, these differences grow less distinct, inasmuch as the impersonality factor increases with the size of a constituency. (Television was not exploited then, nor is it now, to present prefectural and national candidates in a more engaging and personal, albeit artificial, light.) Thus, 67 percent of the farm householders and 63 percent of the nonfarm householders favored the person over the party in prefectural assembly elections, and 52 percent and 58 percent, respectively, in Diet elections (*KC* 1959, 744–49).

There is a striking correspondence between native assemblypersons and the lack of party affiliation, or *mushokuzoku* (MSZ) status, particularly in the 1980s. Generally speaking, nonnative MSZ assemblypersons have tended to switch to LDP affiliation, whereas most native MSZ assemblypersons (75 percent in 1984) have maintained that status. Thus, the 1962 assembly comprised twenty-three (88 percent) MSZ, two (8 percent) JSP, and one (4 percent) JCP members. Nine (39 percent) of the MSZ members were natives according to the criteria in note 9. In 1984 the breakdown was eight (26 percent) MSZ, six (19 percent) LDP, six (19 percent) CGP, five (16 percent) JCP, four (13 percent) JSP, and two (6.5 percent) DSP (Kodaira-*shi* gikai jimukyoku 1982, 35; 1984).

As for affiliation with a political study group or faction within a given party, all but one of the MSZ assemblypersons in 1984 belonged to the Seiwakai, a local faction to which all of the assembly's LDP members also belong, indicating the close alignment of MSZ and LDP members. The Seiwakai, which bills itself as a "conservative organization," is dedicated to pursuing a policy based on the principle of "harmonizing tradition and modernity and honoring and promoting the citizens' and senior citizens' charters" (*Seiwakai nyūzu*, January 1984).

Chapter Six

1. The term *native place* in the last line of this verse is written with the characters 故郷, which are pronounced *kokyō*, and not *furusato*, as indicated in the lyrics (written in both Chinese characters and *hiragana*) appearing in the frontispiece of the *Kodaira chōshi*.

Bibliography

English Sources

Agar, M. 1986. Foreword. In *Self, sex, and gender in cross-cultural fieldwork*, ed. T. L. Whitehead and M. E. Conaway. Urbana and Chicago: University of Illinois Press.

Aguilera, E. E. 1978. *Santa Eulalia's people: Ritual structure and process in an Andalucian multicommunity*. American Ethnological Society Monograph, no. 63. New York: West.

Allinson, G. D. 1979. *Suburban Tokyo: A comparative study in politics and social change*. Center for Japanese Studies, no. 15. Berkeley and Los Angeles: University of California Press.

————. 1984. Japanese urban society and its cultural context. In *The city in cultural context*, ed. J. Agnew, J. Mercer, and D. Sopher. Boston: Allen & Unwin.

Amemiya, K. 1989. Japanese pro-choicers: A woman's right to make her own decision. Department of Sociology, University of California, San Diego. Photocopy.

Anderson, B. 1983. *Imagined communities: Reflections on the origin and spread of nationalism*. New York: Schocken Books.

Appadurai, A. 1981. The past as a scarce resource. *Man*, n.s. 16:201–19.

————. 1986. Theory in anthropology: Center and periphery. *Contemporary Studies in Society and History* 28:356–61.

Atsumi, R. 1988. Dilemmas and accommodations of married Japanese women in white-collar employment. *Bulletin of Concerned Asian Scholars* 20 (3): 54–62.

Barthes, R. 1983. *Barthes: Selected writings*. Ed. S. Sontag. New York: Fontana/Collins.

Bar-Yosef, R. W. 1968. Desocialization and resocialization: The adjustment process of immigrants. *International Migration Review* 2 (3): 27–43.

Befu, H. 1968. Village autonomy and articulation within the state. In *Studies in the institutional history of early modern Japan*, ed. J. W. Hall and M. B. Jansen. Princeton, N.J.: Princeton University Press.

———. 1983. Internationalization of Japan and Nihon bunkaron. In *The challenge of Japan's internationalization*, ed. H. Mannari and H. Befu. Tokyo: Kodansha International.

Bellah, R. 1957. *Tokugawa religion: The values of pre-industrial Japan*. Glencoe, Ill.: Free Press.

Bestor, T. 1985. Tradition and Japanese social organization: Institutional development in a Tokyo neighborhood. *Ethnology* 24:121–33.

Bommes, M., and P. Wright. 1982. "Charms of residence": The public and the past. In *Making histories: Studies in history-writing and politics*, ed. R. Johnson, G. McLennan, B. Schwarz, and D. Sutton. London: Hutchinson.

Bourdieu, P. 1986. *Outline of a theory of practice*. Trans. R. Nice. Cambridge: Cambridge University Press.

Brittan, A., and M. Maynard. 1984. *Sexism, racism and oppression*. New York: Blackwell.

Brown, K. 1979. *Shinjō: The chronicle of a Japanese village*. Ethnology Monographs, no. 2. Pittsburgh: University Center for International Studies in cooperation with the Department of Anthropology, University of Pittsburgh.

Coleman, S. 1983. *Family planning in Japanese society: Traditional birth control in a modern urban culture*. Princeton, N.J.: Princeton University Press.

Comaroff, J. 1985. *Body of power, spirit of resistance*. Chicago: University of Chicago Press.

Corrigan, P., and D. Sayer. 1985. *The great arch: English state formation as cultural revolution*. London: Blackwell.

Davis, F. 1979. *Yearning for yesterday: A sociology of nostalgia*. New York: Free Press.

De Lauretis, T. 1987. *Technologies of gender: Essays on theory, film and fiction*. Bloomington: Indiana University Press.

Doane, J., and D. Hodges. 1987. *Nostalgia and sexual difference: The resistance to contemporary feminism*. New York: Methuen.

Doi, T. 1986. *The anatomy of dependence*. Trans. J. Bester. New York: Kodansha International.

Dore, R. 1958. *City life in Japan: A study of a Tokyo ward*. Berkeley and Los Angeles: University of California Press.

Dubrick, R. 1984. *The structure of obscurity: Gertrude Stein, language, and cubism*. Urbana and Chicago: University of Illinois Press.

Erickson, E. G. 1980. *The territorial experience: Human ecology as symbolic interaction*. Austin: University of Texas Press.

Fabian, J. 1983. *Time and the other: How anthropology makes its object*. New York: Columbia University Press.

Fridell, W. M. 1973. *Japanese shrine mergers, 1906–12*. Tokyo: Sophia University.

Giddens, A. 1979. *Central problems in social theory: Action, structure, and contradiction in social analysis.* Berkeley and Los Angeles: University of California Press.

————. 1983. *A contemporary critique of historical materialism.* Vol. 1: *Power, property, and the state.* Reprint of 1981 ed. London: Macmillan.

Gluck, C. 1985. *Japan's modern myths.* Princeton, N.J.: Princeton University Press.

Handler, R. 1987. Heritage and hegemony: Recent works on historic preservation and interpretation. *Anthropological Quarterly* 60 (3): 137–41.

Handler, R., and J. Linnekin. 1984. Tradition, genuine or spurious. *Journal of American Folklore* 97 (385): 273–90.

Handler, R., and W. Saxton. 1988. Dyssimulation: Reflexivity, narrative, and the quest for authenticity in "living history." *Cultural Anthropology* 3 (3): 242–60.

Hane, M. 1986. *Modern Japan: A historical survey.* Boulder, Colo.: Westview Press.

Havens, T. R. H. 1974. *Farm and nation in modern Japan: Agrarian nationalism, 1870–1914.* Princeton, N.J.: Princeton University Press.

Hayward, D. G. 1975. Home as an environmental concept and psychological concept. *Landscape* 20 (1): 2–9.

Higuchi, T. 1981. *The visual and spatial structure of landscapes.* Trans. C. S. Terry. Cambridge, Mass.: MIT Press.

Inoue, N., et al. 1979. A festival with anonymous *kami*: The Kobe *matsuri*. *Japanese Journal of Religious Studies* 6 (1–2): 163–85.

Irokawa, D. 1973. Japan's grass-roots tradition: Current issues in the mirror of history. *Japan Quarterly* (20) 1: 78–86.

————. 1978. The survival struggle of the Japanese community. In *Authority and the individual in Japan: Citizen protest in historical perspective*, ed. J. V. Koschmann. Tokyo: University of Tokyo Press.

Jameson, F. 1972. Walter Benjamin, or nostalgia. In *The legacy of the German refugee intellectuals*, ed. R. Boyers. New York: Schocken Books.

Kelly, W. W. 1982. *Water control in Tokugawa Japan: Irrigation organization in a Japanese river basin, 1600–1870.* Cornell University East Asia Papers, no. 31. Ithaca, N.Y.: Cornell China-Japan Program.

————. 1986. Rationalization and nostalgia: Cultural dynamics of new middle-class Japan. *American Ethnologist* 13 (4): 603–18.

Kessler, S., and W. McKenna. 1985. *Gender: An ethnomethodological approach.* Chicago: University of Chicago Press.

Kihara, K. 1986. Nature and history at stake—the emerging national trust movements. *Japan Quarterly* 33 (2): 190–95.

Kurita, I. 1983. Revival of the Japanese tradition. *Journal of Popular Culture* 17 (1): 130–34.

Littleton, S. 1986. The organization and management of a Tokyo shrine festival. *Ethnology* 25:195–202.

MacCannell, D. 1976. *The tourist.* New York: Macmillan.

MacCormack, C. 1982. Nature, culture and gender: A critique. In *Nature, culture and gender*, ed. C. MacCormack and M. Strathern. Cambridge: Cambridge University Press.

MacCormack, C., and M. Strathern, eds. 1982. *Nature, culture and gender.* Cambridge: Cambridge University Press.

Maruyama, M. 1969. *Thought and behavior in modern Japanese politics.* Trans. M. Hane. Reprint of 1963 ed. London: Oxford University Press.

Mattelart, M. 1986. *Women, media, crisis: Femininity and disorder.* London: Comedia.

Mitchell, D. D. 1977. *Amaeru: The expression of reciprocal dependency needs in Japanese politics and law.* Boulder, Colo.: Westview Press.

Miwa, K. 1976. Toward a rediscovery of localism. *Japan Quarterly* 23 (1): 44–52.

Muramatsu, M. 1987. In search of national identity: The politics and policies of the Nakasone administration. *Journal of Japanese Studies* 13 (2): 307–42.

My Town Concept Consultative Council, ed. 1982. *Tokyo tomorrow.* Tokyo: Tokyo Metropolitan Government.

Nakane, C. 1967. *Kinship and economic organization in rural Japan.* London School of Economics Monographs on Social Anthropology, no. 32. London: Athlone Press.

————. 1973. *Japanese society.* Reprint of 1968 ed. Middlesex: Pelican Books.

Nisbet, R. 1977. *Sociology as an art form.* London: Oxford University Press.

Nolte, S., and S. Hastings. 1991. The Meiji state's policy toward women, 1890–1910. In *Recreating Japanese women, 1600–1945,* ed. G. L. Bernstein. Berkeley and Los Angeles: University of California Press.

Popular Memory Group. 1982. Popular memory: Theory, politics, method. In *Making histories: Studies in history-writing and politics,* ed. R. Johnson, G. McLennan, B. Schwarz, and D. Sutton. London: Hutchinson.

Pyle, K. B. 1969. *The new generation in Meiji Japan: Problems of cultural identity, 1885–1895.* Stanford, Calif.: Stanford University Press.

————. 1973. The technology of Japanese nationalism: The local improvement movement, 1900–1918. *Journal of Asian Studies* 33 (1): 51–65.

————. 1987. In pursuit of a grand design: Nakasone betwixt the past and the future. *Journal of Japanese Studies* 13 (2): 243–70.

Robertson, J. 1979. Rooting the pine: Shingaku methods of organization. *Monumenta Nipponica* 34 (3): 311–32.

————. 1984a. Japanese farm manuals: A literature of discovery. *Peasant Studies* 11 (2): 169–94.

————. 1984b. Sexy rice: Plant gender, farm manuals, and grass-roots nativism. *Monumenta Nipponica* 39 (3): 233–60.

————. 1985. The making of Kodaira; Being an ethnography of a Japanese city's progress. Ph.D. diss., Cornell University.

————. 1987. A dialectic of native and newcomer: The Kodaira citizens' festival in suburban Tokyo. *Anthropological Quarterly* 60 (3): 124–36.

————. 1988. *Furusato* Japan: The culture and politics of nostalgia. *Politics, Culture, and Society* 1 (4): 494–518.

————. 1989. Doing Japan: Sketching the landscape of Japan anthropology since the seventies. Typescript.

————. 1991. The Shingaku Woman: Straight from the heart. In *Recreating Japanese women, 1600–1945*, ed. G. L. Bernstein. Berkeley and Los Angeles: University of California Press.

Sadler, A. 1972. Carrying the *mikoshi*: Further field notes on the shrine festival in modern Tokyo. *Asian Folklore Studies* 31:89–114.

Samuels, R. J. 1983. *The politics of regional policy in Japan: Localities incorporated?* Princeton, N.J.: Princeton University Press.

Scott, J. 1988. Deconstructing equality-versus-difference: Or, the uses of post-structuralist theory for feminism. *Feminist Studies* 14 (1): 33–50.

Searle, J. 1984. A changing reality. *The Listener*, 6 July, 15–18.

Smith, A. 1984. National identity and myths of ethnic descent. *Research in Social Movements, Conflict and Change* 7:95–130.

Smith, Robert Jerome. 1975. *The art of the festival as exemplified by the fiesta to the patroness of Tuzco: La Virgen de la Puerta*. University of Kansas Publications in Anthropology, no. 6. Lawrence: University of Kansas Press.

Smith, Robert John. 1961. The Japanese rural community: Norms, sanctions, and ostracism. *American Anthropologist* 63:522–33.

————. 1974. *Ancestor worship in contemporary Japan*. Stanford, Calif.: Stanford University Press.

Smith, Robert John, and E. Wiswell. 1982. *The women of Suye Mura*. Chicago: University of Chicago Press.

Smith, T. C. 1980. *The agrarian origins of modern Japan*. Stanford, Calif.: Stanford University Press.

Stein, G. 1959. *Picasso*. Boston: Beacon Press.

Stewart, K. 1988. Nostalgia—a polemic. *Cultural Anthropology* 3 (3): 227–41.

Strawbridge, S. 1982. Althusser's theory of ideology and Durkheim's account of religion: An examination of some striking parallels. *Sociological Review*, n.s. 30:125–40.

Suttles, G. D. 1972. *The social construction of communities*. Chicago: University of Chicago Press.

Turner, V. 1982. *From ritual to theatre: The human seriousness of play*. New York: PAJ Publications.

Vance, C., ed. 1985. *Pleasure and danger: Exploring female sexuality*. Boston: Routledge & Kegan Paul.

Wagatsuma, H. 1975. Problems of cultural identity in modern Japan. In *Ethnic identity: Cultural continuities and change*, ed. G. DeVos and L. Romanucci-Ross. Palo Alto, Calif.: Mayfield.

Yano-Tsuneta Kinenkai, ed. 1985. *Nippon: A survey of Japan*. Tokyo: Kokuseisha.

Yoshida, T. 1964. Social conflict and cohesion in a Japanese rural community. *Ethnology* 3:219–31.

————. 1984. Spirit possession and village conflict. In *Conflict in Japan*, ed. E. S. Krauss, T. P. Rohlen, and P. G. Steinhoff. Honolulu: University of Hawaii Press.

Zwingmann, C. A. A. 1959. "Heimweh" or "nostalgic reaction": A conceptual analysis and interpretation of a medico-psychological phenomenon. Ph.D. diss., School of Education, Stanford University.

Japanese Sources

Aiba M. et al. 1985. Ronten: Shitsugi ōtō (Problematic issues: Questions and answers). In *Bunka gyōsei to machi- zukuri* (Cultural administration and city/ place-making), ed. Tamura A. and Mori K. Tokyo: Jiji Tsūshinsha.

Andō N. 1977. *Jisha ryōshikō—Meiji ishin o chūshin ni shite* (Reflections on temple and shrine territories and the impact of the Meiji Restoration). Nagoya: Aichi-ken kyōdō shiryō kankōkai.

Andō S. 1984. "Gyōsei no bunkaka" o megutte (Examining the "culturization of cultural administration"). In *Hirogaru bunka gyōsei* (The spread of cultural administration), ed. Sakada T. Chihō no jidai / jissen shiriizu (Age of localism: Empirical example series), vol. 6. Tokyo: Gyōsei.

Ashida I., ed. [1818–1829] 1977. *Shinpen Musashino fūdokikō* (New geography of Musashino), vol. 6. Tokyo: Yūzankaku.

Chiba M. 1970. *Matsuri no hōshakaigaku* (The legal sociology of festivals). Tokyo: Kōbundō.

Doi I. 1981. Kenkō to kurashi o mamoru "mura-zukuri" ("Village-making" for the maintenance of health and livelihood). *Shakai Kyōiku* 1 (285): 27–34.

Furusato jōhō sentā, ed. 1985. *Furusato gaido, ibento, gyōji* (Furusato guide, events, seasonal activities). Tokyo: Furusato jōhō sentā.

———. 1986. *Toshi seikatsusha no furusato jōhō ni kansuru niizu chōsa kekka hōkokusho* (Report on the survey of the *furusato* information needs of city dwellers). Tokyo: Furusato jōhō sentā.

Furusato Tōkyō matsuri jikkō iinkai, ed. 1986. *Dai yon kai Furusato Tōkyō matsuri* (The fourth Furusato Tokyo Festival). Tokyo: Tōkyō-to seikatsu bunkakyoku.

Furushima T. 1975. *Kinsei Nihon nōgyō no kōzō* (The structure of premodern agriculture in Japan). Vol. 3 of *Furushima Toshio chōsakushū* (The collected works of Furushima Toshio). Tokyo: Tōkyō Daigaku.

Futagawa Y. 1980. *Kinsei no tochi shiyūsei* (The private landownership system in premodern Japan). Tokyo: Shinchi.

Harada S. 1964. Shōsen-ji. *Kodaira Kyōdo Kenkyūkai Kaihō* 2:42–43.

Higashikurume-*shi* hensan iinkai, ed. 1979. *Higashikurume-shi shi* (A history of Higashikurume City). Tokyo: Higashikurume-*shi*.

Higashimurayama-*shi* hensan iinkai, ed. 1971. *Higashimurayama-shi shi* (A history of Higashimurayama City). Tokyo: Higashimurayama-*shi*.

Higashiyamato-*shi* jishū gurūpu, ed. 1984. *Yashikigami chōsa hōkokusho* (Report on a survey of yard shrines), vol. 1. Tokyo: Higashiyamato-*shi*.

Higashiyamato-*shi* keikaku zaiseibu kōhō kōchōka, ed. 1982. *Watashi no benrichō* (My handbook). Tokyo: Higashiyamato-*shi*.

Iki de inasena matsuri no kikonashi (The proper way to wear the chic and stylish festival costume). 1985. *Taiyō*, 15 August.

Ishihara K. 1964. Ogawa-*shinden* no minka (The farmhouses of Ogawa-*shinden*). *Kodaira Kyōdo Kenkyūkai Kaihō* 2:4–9.

Ishikawa K. 1931. *Shingaku kyōka no honshitsu narabi ni hattatsu* (Fundamental

Shingaku teachings and their development). Tokyo: Shōkasha.

———. 1964. *Shingaku: Edo shōmin no tetsugaku* (Shingaku: Edo commoners' philosophy). Nikkei shinsho, no. 7. Tokyo: Nihon Keizai Shinbunsha.

Isomura E. 1981. *Chihō no jidai—sōzō to sentaku no shihyō* (Age of localism—indicators for creation and selection). Tokyo: Tōkai Daigaku.

Isoya S. 1984. "Nō" bunkaron/josetsu: Gendai shakai ni okeru "nō" shisō no fukken (An introduction and cultural discourse on "agriculture": The revival of "agricultural" thought in modern society). In *Hirogaru bunka gyōsei* (The spread of cultural administration), ed. Sakada T. Chihō no jidai/jissen shiriizu (Age of localism: Empirical example series), vol. 6. Tokyo: Gyōsei.

Itō K. 1961. *Kyōdo yawa* (A local history miscellany). Fuchū-*shi*, Tokyo: Kamioka.

Itō Y. 1966. *Edo chi mawari keizai no tenkai* (The expansion of commerce in the Edo area). Tokyo: Kashiwa.

———. 1981. Nōmin shakai (Farmers' society). In *Nenjūgyōji no rekishigaku* (History of annual event calendars), ed. Endō M. and Yamanaka Y. Tokyo: Kōbundō.

———. 1984. *Musashino to suishaya—Edo-kō seifun jijō* (Musashino and millers—milling conditions on the outskirts of Edo). Tokyo: Kuori.

Iwama Y. 1984. Toshi de atarashiki ikiru (Revitalized in the cities). *Yurika-mome* 9:4–9.

Kamishima J. 1978. Furusato sōshitsu no genzai kara (From the beginning of the loss of *furusato*). *Dentō to Gendai* 11 (55): 8–14.

Katayama F. 1981. Toshi ni okeru jinja bukkaku no yakuwari (The role of Shinto shrines and Buddhist temples in cities). *Den'en Toshi* 5:26–29.

Katayama M. 1959. *Tokura-shinden to sono debyakushō* (Tokura-*shinden* and its settlers). Tokyo: Tama Bunkasha.

Kawashima M. 1984. "Furusato-mura" o yugamemai (Do not demean "*furusato* villages"). In *Atarashii chiiki shakai-zukuri* (Making a new regional society), ed. Sakada T. Chihō no jidai/jissen shiriizu (Age of localism: Empirical example series), vol. 5. Tokyo: Gyōsei.

Kenji K. 1981. Matsuri no sōzō to chiiki-zukuri (The creation of festivals and place-making). *Shakai Kyōiku* 1 (285): 10–18.

Kimura M. 1964. *Kinsei no shinden-mura* (Newly reclaimed farm villages in premodern Japan). Tokyo: Yoshikawa Kōbunkan.

Kimura M. and Itō Y. 1972. *Shinden sonraku—Musashino to sono shūhen* (Newly reclaimed villages—Musashino and its environs). Tokyo: Bungadō Ginkō Kenkyūsha.

Kobayashi H. [1933]. 1975. Kokyō o ushinatta bungaku (Homeless literature). In *Kobayashi Hideo shū* (The collected works of Kobayashi Hideo). Chikuma gendai bunkaku taikei (Chikuma anthology of modern literature), vol. 43. Tokyo: Chikuma Shobō.

Kodama S. 1976. *Kinsei shinshū no tenkai katei—nishi Nihon o chūshin to shite* (The process of expansion of the Shin sect in premodern Japan). Tokyo: Yoshikawa Kōbunkan.

Kōjien. 1978. S.v. *furusato, kyōdo*. Tokyo: Iwanami Shoten.

Koyama S. 1982. Kindaiteki joseikan to shite no ryōsai kenbo shisō (Good wife, wise mother as a modern view of females). *Joseigaku Nenpō* 3:1–7.

Maruyama Y. 1975. *Kinsei shukuba no kisoteki kenkyū* (Fundamental study of post stations in premodern Japan). Vol. 2. Tokyo: Yoshikawa Kōbunkan.

Matsudaira M. 1980. *Matsuri no shakaigaku* (Sociology of festivals). Tokyo: Kōdansha.

———. 1983. *Matsuri no bunka—toshi ga tsukuru seikatsu bunka no katachi* (Festival culture: The making of a civic-life culture). Yūhikaku senshō, no. 883. Tokyo: Yūhikaku.

Matsumoto K. 1980. Sengo sono seishin fūkei: Kotoba (The affective landscape of the postwar period: Words). *Asahi shinbun*, 19 August, 5.

Matsuyoshi S. [1933] 1955. *Shinden no kenkyū* (*Shinden* studies). Enl. ed. Tokyo: Yūhikaku.

Minami H. 1980. Nihon no ryūkōka (Japanese pop songs). In *Ryūkōka no himitsu* (The mystery of pop songs). Enl. ed., ed. Kata K. and Tsukuda S. Tokyo: Bunwa.

Mita M. 1980. Kindai Nihon no shinjō no shinboru no jiten (A dictionary of symbols of modern Japanese sentiments). In *Ryūkōka no himitsu* (The mystery of pop songs). Enl. ed., ed. Kata K. and Tsukuda S. Tokyo: Bunwa.

Mitsuda K. 1985. Kindaiteki boseikan no juyō to henkei (Acceptance and transformations of the modern view of motherhood). In *Bosei o tou: Rekishiteki hensen* (Exploring motherhood: Historical transformations), ed. Wakita H. Tokyo: Jinbun Shoin.

Miyamoto M. 1981. Chōnin shakai: Shōnin (Townspeople's society: The merchants). In *Nenjūgyōji no rekishigaku* (History of annual event calendars), ed. Endō M. and Yamanaka Y. Tokyo: Kōbundō.

Miyata N. 1972. *Kinsei no ryūkōshin* (Popular deities in premodern Japan). Nihonjin no kōdō to shisō (Action and thought of the Japanese), no. 17. Tokyo: Hyōronsha.

———. 1976. Minkan shinkō to seijiteki kisei (Popular creeds and political control). In *Nihon shūkyō shironshū* (Historical essays on Japanese religion), vol. 2, ed. Kasahara I. Tokyo: Yoshikawa Kōbunkan.

Mori K. 1985. Gyōsei no bunkaka (The culturization of administration). In *Bunka gyōsei to machi-zukuri* (Cultural administration and city/place-making), ed. Tamura A. and Mori K. Tokyo: Jiji Tsūshinsha.

Munamiya S., Kimura M., and Itō Y., eds. 1954. *Ogawa-ke bunsho mokuroku* (Index of Ogawa household documents). Tokyo: Meiji Daigaku Toshokan.

Musashino bijutsu daigaku seikatsu bunka kenkyūkai, ed. 1983. *Higashiyamato no seikatsu to bunka* (Life and culture in Higashiyamato [City]). Tokyo: Higashiyamato-shi kyōiku iinkai.

Nakagawa H. 1981. Chiiki-zukuri seisaku to shakai kyōiku jissen no kadai (Practical issues regarding strategies and social education for place-making). *Shakai Kyōiku* 1 (285): 35–43.

Nakai N. 1951. Chōnin ukeoi shinden no seiritsu jijō (Circumstances of the establishment of farm villages reclaimed by merchant investors). *Shigaku* 24 (4): 54–107.

Nakajima M. 1986. Furusato jōhō sentā no genkyō (The present status of the Furusato Information Center). *Rinsō Tenbō* 1:102–9.

Nakasone Y. 1984. Kokumin to susumu 21-seki e no kōro (A path to the 21st century in accord with the people). *Jiyūminshu* 4:173–80.

Namiki S. and Tachikawa K. 1964. Ogawa no shūzoku to nenjūgyōji ni tsuite (Customs and annual events in Ogawa). *Kodaira Kyōdo Kenkyūkai Kaihō* 2:29–37.

Nō T. 1935. Musashino daichi no gaison ni kansuru kenkyū (Research on linear settlements on the Musashino plateau). *Chirigaku Hyōron* 11 (1): 48–65.

Nōrinsuisan daijin kankyoku chōsaka, ed. 1989. *Nōgyō hakusho fuzoku tōkeihyō: 1988* (Agricultural white paper and statistics). Tokyo: Nōrin tōkei kyōkai.

Nostalgia of Kobe 1983. No. 95. Kobe: Kobe-*shi* kezaikyoku bōekikankyoka.

Ogawa N. 1983. Bu-shū Tama-gun Megurita-shinden no kazoku kōsei (The composition of households in Megurita-*shinden*, Tama district, Musashi province). *Gakushuin Daigaku Shiryōkan Kiyō* 1:109–200.

Oishi S. [1961] 1976. *Kyōhō kaikaku no keizai seisaku* (The economic policy of the Kyōhō reforms). Enl. ed. Tokyo: Ochanomizu Shobō.

Okuno T. 1975. *Bungaku ni okeru genfūkei* (Original landscapes in literature). Tokyo: Shūeisha.

Onuki H. and Ōtani Y. 1964. Ogawa-ke no kakei ni tsuite (On the Ogawa household genealogy). *Kodaira Kyōdo Kenkyūkai Kaihō* 2:50–52.

Sakada T. 1984a. Atarashii chiiki keizai no fukkō (The revival of the new regional economy). In *Atarashii chiiki shakai-zukuri* (Making a new regional society), ed. Sakada T. Chihō no jidai/jissen shiriizu (Age of localism: Empirical example series), vol. 5. Tokyo: Gyōsei.

———., ed. 1984b. *Atarashii chiiki shakai-zukuri* (Making a new regional society). Chihō no jidai/jissen shiriizu (Age of localism: Empirical example series), vol. 5. Tokyo: Gyōsei.

———. 1984c. Bunka gyōsei—kaku jichitai no jissenrei (Cultural administration: Empirical examples from each municipality). In *Hirogaru bunka gyōsei* (The spread of cultural administration), ed. Sakada T. Chihō no jidai/jissen shiriizu (Age of localism: Empirical example series), vol. 6. Tokyo: Gyōsei.

———., ed. 1984d. *Hirogaru bunka gyōsei* (The spread of cultural administration). Chihō no jidai/jissen shiriizu (Age of localism: Empirical example series), vol. 6. Tokyo: Gyōsei.

Sakai T. 1971. *Shi to kokyō [furusato]* (Poetry and native place). Tokyo: Ōfūsha.

Sakamoto K. 1966. Bakuhansei "jiin to nōson" to no seidoteki seiritsu to sono tenkai katei ni tsuite (The systematic development and process of expansion of "temples and farm villages" under the *bakuhan* system). *Risshō Shigaku* 32:79–104.

Sekai nōringyō sensasu: Kodaira (World census on agriculture and forestry: Kodaira). 1980. Tokyo: Kodaira-*shi* seikatsuka.

Sekiguchi S. 1972. Nōson ni okeru sairei to ikke ketsugō (The relation between *ikke* [a unit comprising the head and its branch households] and festivals in farm villages). *Nihon Minzokugaku* 83:23–25.

Shōwa 59-nen tō undō hōshin (1984 [Liberal Democratic] Party platform). 1984. *Jiyūminshu* 3:164–240.

Sunagawa no rekishi (History of Sunagawa). 1963. Tokyo: Sunagawa-*chō*.

Tachikawa-*shi* shi hensan iinkai, ed. 1969. *Tachikawa-shi shi* (A history of Tachikawa City). Vol. 2. Tokyo: Tachikawa-*shi*.

Takada N. 1981. Minshū bunka o ikasu chiiki-zukuri (Place-making that invigorates the people's culture). *Shakai Kyōiku* 1 (285): 19–26.

Takeshita N. and Kusayanagi D. 1986. "Nippon rettō furusato ron" no zentaizō (Outline for the "Proposal for Furusato Japan"). *Biggu Ee* 12.

Tamura A. 1985. Bunka gyōsei to machi-zukuri (Cultural administration and city/place-making). In *Bunka gyōsei to machi-zukuri*, ed. Tamura A. and Mori K. Tokyo: Jiji Tsūshinsha.

Tamura A. and Mori. K., eds. 1985. *Bunka gyōsei to machi-zukuri* (Cultural administration and city/place-making). Tokyo: Jiji Tsūshinsha.

Tanaka K. 1973. *Nippon rettō kaizō ron* (Proposal for remodeling Japan). Tokyo: Nikkan Kōgyō Shinbunsha.

Tanigawa K. 1978. "Furusato" to iu yōkai (The apparition called *furusato*). *Dentō to Gendai* 11 (55): 15–24.

Tarumi M. 1983. Nihon no sonkyō no keikan to gyōji (Spectacles and events enacted at Japanese village borders). Paper presented at the 65th Minpaku Seminar, 17 September, National Museum of Ethnography, Osaka.

Tōkyō-*to* Kitatama chūgaku kōchō, ed. 1962. *Kyōdo Kitatama* (Local Kitatama). Tokyo: Tōkyō-*to* Kitatama-*gun* Hoya chūgaku kōchō.

Tōkyō-*to* seikatsu bunkakyoku bunka jigyōka, ed. 1984. *Furusato Tōkyō matsuri* (Furusato Tokyo Festival). Festival program.

Tōkyō-*to* sōmukyoku tōkeibu kanrika, ed. 1985. *Kurashi to tōkei* (Livelihood and statistics), no. 2. Tokyo: Tōkyō- *to*.

Tsujimura A. 1981. *Sengo Nihon no taishū shinri* (Popular psychology in postwar Japan). Tokyo: Tōkyō Daigaku.

Uegaki M. [1803] 1981. Yōsan hitsuroku (Sericultural memorandum). In *Nihon nōshō zenshū* (Complete collection of Japanese farm manuals), vol. 35. Tokyo: Nōsangyōson Bunka Kyōkai.

Uruoi no aru machi-zukuri kenkyūkai, ed. 1984. *Uruoi no aru machi-zukuri* (Place-building with a neighborly charm). Tokyo: Taisei.

Yajima H. 1955. *Musashino no shūraku* (Musashino villages). Tokyo: Furuima Shoin.

Yamaguchi A. 1981. "Chihō no jidai" no onimotsu—chihō gikai (The impedimenta of the "age of localism": Regional assemblies). *Chūō Kōron* 2 (February): 208–23.

Yamamoto C. 1984. *Oumekaidō—Edo no han'ei o sasaeta michi* (Oume Road—the key to Edo's prosperity). Tokyo: Shūkai Shorin.

Yamazaki Y. 1983. *Ojōsui sakura to Kodaira* (The Tamagawa canal cherry trees and Kodaira). Kodaira-*shi*, Tokyo: Yamazaki Yūji.

Yanagita K. 1985. *Nihon no matsuri* (Japanese festivals). Kadokawa bunko, no. 1448. Tokyo: Kadokawa.

Yoshida S. [1795] 1979. *Kaikō shuchi* (Necessary knowledge for land reclamation, 1795). In *Nihon nōsho zenshū* (Complete collection of Japanese farm manuals), vol. 3. Tokyo: Nōsangyōson Bunka Kyōkai.

Yoshino Y. 1981. *Kitsune* (Foxes). Mono to ningen no bunka shi (Cultural history of people and things), no. 39. Tokyo: Hōsei Daigaku.

Zenkoku shichōson yōran (A nationwide survey of cities, towns, and villages). 1989. Tokyo: Jijisho Kōseikyoku Shinkōka.

Kodaira City Hall Publications

Kodaira-*chō* nōgyō iinkai, ed. 1958. *Kodaira-chō nōgyō gaikyō* (An overview of Kodaira agriculture).

Kodaira chōshi henshū iinkai, ed. 1959. *Kodaira chōshi* (Local history of Kodaira).

Kodaira kyōdo kenkyūkai, ed. 1980. *Kodaira ni nokoru gomonsō jiken kankei shiryōshū* (Extant documents in Kodaira pertaining to the petition incident). Kodaira-*shi* bunkazai shiriizu (Kodaira cultural properties series), no. 1.

————. 1983. *Kodaira no bunkazai mite-aruki* (A walking tour of Kodaira's cultural properties). Reprint of 1979 ed.

————. 1984. *Komonjo ni miru Kodaira no mizu: Tamagawa jōsui to bunsui* (Water in Kodaira as reported in historical manuscripts: The Tamagawa main and branch canals). Kodaira-*shi* bunkazai shiriizu (Kodaira cultural properties series), no. 3.

Kodaira minwa no kai, ed. 1981. *Kodaira mukashimukashi* (Kodaira long, long ago).

Kodaira-*shi* fukushibu, ed. 1983. *Jigyō gaiyō* (Summary of operations).

Kodaira-*shi* gikai jimukyoku, ed. 1975–1983. *Kodaira-shi gikai kaigiroku* (Proceedings of the Kodaira City Assembly).

————. 1982. *Kodaira-shi giin meikan* (Directory of city assemblypersons).

————. 1983. *Shōwa 57-nenpan shisei yōran* (Survey of city administration, 1982).

————. 1984. *Kodaira-shi gikai giin meibo* (Registry of city assemblypersons).

Kodaira-*shi* keikaku zaiseibu keikakuka, ed. 1980. *Kodaira-shi dai-niji chōki sōgō keikaku kihon keikaku* (Second comprehensive long-term plan for Kodaira City).

Kodaira-*shi* keikaku zaiseibu kōhō kōchōka, ed. 1979, 1981, 1983a. *Kodaira shisei ni tsuite yoron chōsa* (Public opinion survey on the administration of Kodaira City), nos. 4, 5, 6.

————. 1983b. *Watashitachi no machi Kodaira—shimin benrichō* (Our town Kodaira: Citizens' handbook).

Kodaira-*shi* kyōiku iinkai, ed. 1979, 1980. *Kodaira-shi fujin no tsudoi* (Kodaira Women's Association).

————. 1981. *Miyazaki-ke (Kumanomiya) monjo mokuroku* (Index of Miyazaki household [Kumanomiya branch] documents).

Kodaira-*shi* seikatsuka, ed. 1973. *Jichikai nado keijiban setchi hojokin kōfu yōkō* (Directive regarding subsidies for the erection of neighborhood association bulletin boards).

————. 1983. *Katei saien yōhō* (Directive on home vegetable gardens).

————. 1983–1984. *Jichikai meibo* (Neighborhood association registry).

Kodaira-*shi* shiminbu shiminka, ed. 1983a. *Kodaira-shi no idō jinkō chōsa hōkoku* (Report of a survey on the transient population of Kodaira City [January–December 1982]).

————. 1983b. *Kodaira-shi no jinkō* (The population of Kodaira City).

Kodaira-*shi* sōmubu shomuka, ed. 1975. *Kodaira-shi no nōgyō* (Agriculture in Kodaira City).
————. 1983. *Kodaira-shi tōkeisho* (Statistical handbook for Kodaira City).
Kyōdo Kodaira henshū iinkai, ed. [1967] 1983. *Kyōdo Kodaira* (Local Kodaira).

Documents Published by Kodaira-Based Organizations

Gakuen Nishi-chōkai, ed. 1982. *Kai'in meibo* (Members' register).
————. 1983. *Chōkai sainyū saishutsu kessan hōkokusho* (Report of revenues and expenditures).
————. 1984a. *Hosei yosan an* (Revised budget).
————. 1984b. *Jōkanki kaikei hōkoku* (Report of expenditures, January–June).
————. 1984c. *Shūkaijo narabi ni fūzoku hiroba kensetsu shūshi kaikei hōkokusho* (Report of expenditures for the meeting house and attached field).
Ogawa Higashigaoka-jichikai, ed. 1978. *Ogawa Higashigaoka-jichikai kiyaku* (Bylaws of the Ogawa Higashigaoka neighborhood association).

Newspapers and Newsletters

Newspapers and newsletters published in Kodaira include the following: *Kai Kodaira*, *Kodaira bōhan nyūzu*, *Kodaira chōhō*, *Kodaira kensho nyūzu*, *Kodaira-shi fujin no tsudoi nyūzu*, *Kodaira shihō*, *Kodaira shōkōkai-dayori*, *Kodaira yomiuri nyūzu*, *Komyunitei Kodaira*, *Seiwakai nyūzu*, and *Shin-meisama*.

Obira is published by sister-city Obira.

Minna no Tōkyō is a Tokyo municipal newsletter, and *Furusato jōhō sentā-dayori* is published by the Furusato Information Center.

The national newpapers cited are *Asahi shinbun* (Tokyo ed. unless otherwise noted in text), *Japan Times* (English), and *Tōkyō shinbun*.

Index

Abortion, and soul of fetus, 141, 210n22
Administrative village (*gyōsei mura*), 8
"Adult" shrines (*otona mikoshi*), 48, 62–64, 65
Advertisements, reflecting Furusato Japan, 33–37
Agar, M., 2
Agricultural servants (*genin*), 88
Agriculture: and Inari, 120; jointly owned equipment for, 168, 211n5; in Kodaira, 105; present status of, 18, 106; "tourist," 105, 109
Amae (dyadic relationship of mutual dependency), 20–21
Amemiya, K., 210n22
American Occupation, xiv, 33
Anderson, B., 73
Andō, N., 209n16
Appadurai, A., 199n2
Asahi shinbun, 19; essays on *furusato* in, 19–23; festivals listed in, 38; on shrines, 65
Assemblypersons, predominance of natives among, 173, 212n9

Ba (public place), 44–45, 186
Ba-zukuri: Green Road, 186–87
Bakufu (military government), xiii; control of festivals by, 114–15, 207n2; and *kinjogumi*, 100; and merchant-initiated *shinden*, 196; on Ogawa-*shinden*, 103; temple policy of, 136–37

Bangumi, 124, 128, 132; and consociations, 142; and *jichikai*, 168; and membership in the parish, 134, 135; and nativeness, 165
Banquets, paraphernalia for, 143
Bar-Yosef, R. W., 211n6
Bodai-ji (type of Buddhist temple), in Kodaira Seven, 139–40
Bodhidharma, 140
Bourdieu, P., 2–3
Buddhism: *bodai-ji*, 139; in Edo period, 136; *kitō-ji*, 139; and *obon* events, 209n12; paraphernalia shops for, 146–47; sects of, 139, 209nn14,15,18,19; 210nn20,21,23; temples of, 115
Bungaku ni okeru genfūkei (Original landscapes in literature; Okuno), 25
Bunka kokka (cultural state), 37
Bunrei (also *wakemitama*; a *kami*-share), 112, 113
Burial sites, 144, 145, 210n26

Capitalism, in merchant-initiated *shinden*, 196
Caretaker (*rusuban*), 167, 211n4
Caretakers (*yamori*), 102
"Cemetery temples," 146–47
Charter-images exhibition, and Furusato Kodaira, 187
Chihō no jidai ("age of localism"), 23, 24
"Child" shrines (*kodomo mikoshi*), 38, 48–51